J. J. Dickison

Swamp Fox of the Confederacy

J. J. Dickison

Swamp Fox of the Confederacy

by

John J. Koblas

North Star Press of St. Cloud, Inc.

Library of Congress Cataloging-in-Publication Data

Koblas, John J., 1942-
J.J. Dickison : swamp fox of the Confederacy / by John J. Koblas.—1st. ed.
p. cm.
Includes bibliographical references (p.) and index.
ISBN 0-87839-149-5 (pbk.) — ISBN 0-87839-150-9 (cloth)
1. Dickison, John Jackson, 1816-1902. 2. Confederate States of America. Army. Florida Cavalry Regiment, 2nd. 3. Guerrillas—Confederate States of America—Biography. 4. Confederate States of America. Army—Biography. 5. Florida—History—Civil War, 1861-1865—Cavalry operations. 6. Florida—History—Civil War, 1861-1865—Underground movements. 7. United States—History—Civil War, 1861-1865—Cavalry operations. 8. United States—History—Civil War, 1861-1865—Underground movements. I. Title.

E558.6 2nd .K63 2000
973.7'459'092--dc21 00-058246

Frontis: J. J. Dickison, Courtesy Florida State Archives

First Edition July 2000

ISBN: 0-87839-149-5 (paper)
ISBN: 0-87839-150-9 (hardcover)

Cover art: John Stevens

Printed in the United States by Versa Press, Inc., East Peoria, Illinois.

Published by
North Star Press of St. Cloud, Inc.
P.O. Box 451
St. Cloud, Minnesota 56302

For my daughter Sarah

When on my lonely march at night
And naught to comfort me but the stars of light
And weariness has lulled to rest
All other thoughts within my breast
Then I'll think of thee.

Albert S. Chalker,
Confederate Florida Soldier
Myron C. Prevatt, Jr., Collection

Table of Contents

Acknowledgments

The author wishes to thank the following individuals and organizations for their support during preparation of this manuscript: Elizabeth Baker of the Halifax Area Historical Society, Daytona Beach, Florida; Harold D. Cardwell, Sr., of the Volusia Anthropological Society, Daytona Beach, Florida; David J. Coles, Leslie Lawhon, and Joan L. Morris of the Florida State Archives, Tallahassee, Florida; Thomas R. Fasulo of the University of Florida, Gainesville, Florida; Jane George of the Dakota County Library, Burnsville, Minnesota; Charles Jackson, editor at The Daytona Beach News-Journal, Daytona Beach, Florida; Janice S. Mahaffey, archivist at the Putnam County Archives, Palatka, Florida; Joanne Smalley of the Georgia Department of Archives and History in Atlanta, Georgia; Shayera Tangri, Southern Historical Collection, Wilson Library, University of North Carolina at Chapel Hill, North Carolina; and Karen Thomas of the Baker County Historical Society, Macclenny, Florida.

Several individuals donated their time, memories, family documents, and expertise over the seven years I struggled researching and writing about J. J. Dickison. This is not my story—much of it belongs to them: Robert Lionel Baldwin-SCV #1282, Georgia Atkinson Bradfield, A. M. Decker, Armand DeGregoris, George Diezel, II, Richard Ferry, J. Walker Fischer, Gerard Flynn, Jan Godown, Robert Bruce Graetz, Gary Hibbing, Don Hillhouse, Susan Jacobson, John S. Koblas, Sarah Koblas, Gary Luther, Paul Meredith, Scott Nelson, Marie North, Dave Page, Audrey Parente, David Parente, Raymond B. Patterson, James Patton, Diana Pierce, Jen Pierce, Keith Pierce, Zach Pierce, Barbara Long Pliter, Myron C. Prevatt, Jr., Darren and Stacy Radcliff, Chris and Stephanie Rugg, John Stevens, Alice Strickland, Ed Wilks, and Joseph Wise.

A special thank you to Thomas Hayes for allowing this author the privilege of quoting from his own project, "Letters from Olustee." Also, a very special thank you to Zack C. Waters who sent this author ten pounds of material via the United States Mails and provided additional data over the telephone. Mr. Waters could easily have written this book himself.

The author also wishes to express his gratitude to staffs of the Daytona Beach,

City Island, and Ormond Beach Libraries (Florida), Minneapolis, St. Paul, Savage, and Prior Lake Public Libraries (Minnesota), Jacksonville Maritime Museum (Florida), Jefferson Davis Museum (Irwinville, Georgia), New Smyrna Beach (Florida) Information Center, and Olustee Battlefield (Florida).

Prologue

He was called the "Swamp Fox of the Confederacy" by grateful Floridians, and "Knight of the Silver Spurs" by admiring Southern belles. Others labeled him "Gray Fox" or "War Eagle," but to anyone Confederate or Union, John Jackson Dickison was a hero to Florida as John Mosby was to Virginia, John Hunt Morgan to Kentucky, and Nathan Bedford Forrest to Tennessee and Mississippi.

Florida, the third state to secede from the Union, following South Carolina and Mississippi, provided over 15,000 troops to the Confederate army during the four years of the war.[1] Unfortunately for the defense of the state, few of these soldiers were ever to fight on Florida soil.[2] Jefferson Davis had originally pledged to defend all territory in the Confederate states, but, by April 1862, defeats in Tennessee forced him to take drastic measures.

With a population of 140,000, nearly half of whom were slaves, Florida had about 1,200 miles of largely unpopulated coastline. President Davis saw no need to defend a virtual swampland, and with troops badly needed in other theaters, he decided Florida was expendable. By the summer of 1862, nearly all Confederate forces had left the state, despite protest from Governor John Milton.

Palmetto scrub typical of northeast Florida terrain. (Photo by J. Walker Fischer)

Home of Confederate General E. Kirby Smith, St. Augustine. (Photo by J. Walker Fischer)

Union forces were quick to capitalize on the virtual abandonment. On March 3, a combined land and naval force sailed into Fernandina harbor just as the last of the Confederate evacuees were leaving aboard a railroad train. Troops soon marched into Jacksonville, which they found abandoned and in flames set by irregular Confederate forces as they withdrew. St. Augustine was also taken with no resistance as the army was met by a peaceful delegation led by the mayor. Union gunboats patrolled the St. Johns River, and with little of a defending army to hamper their operations, maintained a firm grip on northern Florida.

The St. Johns River provided a natural boundary that could be patrolled by naval ships and a limited land force.[3] Federal control of the region ended near the town of Palatka, which boasted a Union garrison for much of 1864 and 1865. The area along the St. Johns River above Palatka was more difficult to patrol and became a hotbed of Confederate guerilla activity.

These guerilla forces were led by Captain John J. Dickison, whose name struck fear into the hearts of wary Federals who searched in vain for his elusive little army. . . .

Notes

[1]David J. Coles, "Volusia County: The Land Warfare 1861-1865," *Civil War in Volusia County: A Symposium,* Daytona Beach, Halifax Historical Society, Inc., 1987, pp. 39-52; Gary W. Gallagher, editor, *Fighting for the Confederacy: The personal Recollections of General Edward Porter Alexander,* Chapel Hill/London, The University of North Carolina Press, 1989, p. 560; John MacDonald, *Great Battles of the Civil War,* New York, Collier Books—Macmillan Publishing Company, 1988, pp. 8-10.

[2]Jerrell H. Shofner, "Florida in the Civil War," *Civil War in Volusia County: A Symposium,* pp. 4-5.

[3]David J. Coles, "Volusia County: The Land Warfare 1861-1865," *Civil War in Volusia County A Symposium,* pp. 45-46.

J. J. Dickison

Swamp Fox of the Confederacy

J. J. Dickison. (Courtesy Richard J. Ferry)

Chapter 1

The Despot's Heel

John Jackson Dickison was born in Virginia, but there is some discrepancy as to what year. This enigma becomes even more puzzling since Dickison and his immediate family members furnished all the dates. The marker at Dickison's grave gives the birth date as March 27, 1816, the census records indicate 1822, and his obituaries cite 1815.[1]

Dickison's father had fought in the American Revolution and the young man worshipped him. Moving to Charleston, South Carolina, at a young age, Dickison married Mary Elizabeth Ling, although he may have had an earlier marriage, however brief. Dickison's heart was set upon a military career, and he served proudly in the South Carolina State Militia as a cavalry officer.[2] He also worked as a clerk in a shoe store in Georgetown, South Carolina.[3]

In 1856, he, his wife, and their four children—Charles, born in 1845; R.L., born in 1849; John J., born in 1851; and Mary Elizabeth 1853—moved to Florida. Settling on a vast tract of land near Orange Lake, a small community north of Ocala, in Marion County, the Dickisons lived amongst several other South Carolina transplants, and the plantations were among the largest and finest in the entire South. Dickison's plantation was called Sunnyside.[4]

This plush community organized the East Florida Independent Institute five years before the arrival of the Dickisons, and it had become the East Florida State Seminary when they joined the community. As Florida's first state-supported institution of higher learning, it became a parent of the University of Florida.

Marion County boasted one of the most significant agricultural producing areas of Florida, and J. J. Dickison owned one of the largest plantations in the Orange Lake section of the county. The federal census of 1860 reveals his real estate value at $14,000, his personal property at $12,000, and records indicate he owned eight slaves.

This great prosperity was short-lived, however, as the Republican Party replaced the dying Whig platform, and the great American compromise came to an end. The presidential election of November 7, 1860, resulted in a victory for Abraham Lincoln, although not a single vote was cast for him in the state of Florida. Men like Dickison who owned land and slaves became his bitterest critics.

Dickison referred to the President-elect as "the Republican sectional candidate" who supported "an avowed sectional policy."[5]

Florida had lived under four flags—Spanish, French, British, and American. With Abraham Lincoln's victory in the presidential election, Floridians gathered to protest the Republican attack on slavery. *The Fernandina East Floridian* declared, "We say Resist," a slogan echoed by the majority of the state's white population.[6]

On November 14, 1860, the *Fernandina East Floridian* printed boldly on its masthead: "The Secession of the State of Florida, The Dissolution of the Union, The Formation of a Southern Confederacy." On November 26, the state legislature was called into special session, and four days later a bill was signed for a convention to meet in Tallahassee on January 3, 1861, with the sole purpose of secession from the Union.[7]

Most Floridians subscribed to the policy of secession, but none were more vocal and more adamant in his convictions than Dickison, who insisted "the ablest jurists and statesmen of the country, having firmly asserted, clearly educated and bravely vindicated the legal right of a State to secede from the general government, and intelligent, chivalrous people, proudly assured of the justice of their convictions, could not forswear the great principles of a lifetime."[8]

Marion was one of the first Florida counties to call for secession from the Union. A white banner with a lone blue star embroidered with the slogan "leave us alone" flew from a staff on the square in Ocala in November 1860. Each day the courthouse was filled with prominent Marion County citizens discussing secession.[9]

Three weeks before South Carolina voted to leave the Union, the Marion County leaders drafted a program for a convention to leave the Union. A large number of South Carolinians, including J. J. Dickison, had moved to Marion County during Florida's first fifteen years of statehood. Thus, Marion was among the first Florida counties wanting to leave the Union. On November 26, the Marion County leaders passed the following resolution:

"We, the citizens of Marion County, ignoring all party names and past issues, do earnestly recommend to the General Assembly of Florida, now in session, immediately do enact a law providing for a meeting at an early date of a Convention of Delegates from the several Counties of the State, to take into consideration the expediency of dissolving our connection with the Federal Union."[10]

On January 10, 1861, following a week of stormy anti-Union speeches, the convention members voted sixty-two to seven in favor of secession, and Florida severed all legal ties with the United States. On February 28, the newly independent nation of Florida joined the Confederacy and ratified its provisional constitution.[11]

While Florida was steam-rolling toward an armed conflict with the Union, along with her Southern sister states, the editor of the *St. Augustine Examiner* pessimistically warned of such action: "The advices from Washington are by no means encouraging, on the contrary they announce preparations for a coming conflict. All the indications now are that the Republican party are resolved not only against compromise guarantees, but upon a war for coercion and subjection of the South."[12] Few paid heed to the warning.

In January 1861, three months before the war officially erupted at Fort Sumter, Florida troops already occupied Forts

Barrancas and McRee on the mainland, seizing the Pensacola Navy Yard and all the cannon and ammunition that went with it. Fort Pickens, only two miles offshore on a narrow island, remained in Federal hands, however. Four days after the bombing of Fort Sumter, a large United States Naval squadron arrived to reinforce Fort Pickens.[13]

When the Southern Confederacy was divided into departments by the Secretary of War, the Department of South Carolina, Georgia, and Florida was established. General James H. Trapier of South Carolina was assigned as its first commander, and he made Tallahassee his headquarters. No general, however, remained long as head of this department.[14]

Fort Barrancas, Pensacola, Florida, attacked by Seccessionists January 8, 1861, is considered by some to be the site of the first shots of the Civil War. (Photo by Dave Page)

Advance Redoubt at Pensacola. (Photo by Dave Page)

On March 9, Florida's first requisition for 500 troops was received by Governor Edward Perry. L. Pope Walker, Confederate Secretary of the Army, cautioned: "If you can supply this requisition immediately without publication of your order it would be better to do so, as it is advisable as far as practical to keep our movements concealed from the Government of the United States."[15]

On the same day, General Braxton Bragg arrived in Pensacola to take over command of all Confederate forces from Major-General William H. Chase. Bragg immediately ordered the completion of land batteries in the area.

When the war erupted in April, Florida was rich in cotton, oranges, sweet potatoes, corn, sugar cane, cattle, hogs, turpentine, and lumber. Very little manufacturing was done with most of the labor done by slaves. Newport and Jacksonville boasted small iron factories, Monticello a shoe factory, a cloth mill, a wool card factory, and Madison a tannery. Grist mills and sugar mills were in abundance throughout portions of the state.[16]

Florida had few roads in 1861 and most of those were merely rough trails. Unlike some other Southern states, Florida had only one cross-state railroad, and telegraph lines were few. But thousands, from wealthy cotton planters to poor farmers and fishermen, answered the call to duty.

There were never sufficient arms and ammunition for the soldiers, as infantry drilled without rifles or bullets; cavalry drilled without horses. While money was raised privately to outfit a few, many companies without equipment were refused admission into the Confederate army.

Robert E. Lee, based on two visits to Fernandina, insisted that the Confederates must hold the interior of Florida and protect the food-producing farmlands and cattle ranches. Cattle were being driven north from the ranches at about 600 head per week. Some unethical South Florida cattlemen sold to the highest bidder—whether it was the Confederacy, the Union troops at Fort Myers and Key West, or the Cubans in Havana.[17]

Salt was another precious item because it was used for the preservation of meat. Salt was also utilized in the prepararation of hides for tanning leather. Florida's main saltworks, where men boiled seawater in large kettles and sheet-iron boilers, were situated at St. Andrews Bay and Apalachee Bay. At one time during the war, the Confederacy employed 5,000 men in the salt industry and all were exempt from military service. As long as each saltmaker produced twenty bushels per day, he received exemption from conscription into the Confederacy.[18] Union blockade squadrons destroyed the saltworks whenever possible, but they were quickly rebuilt.

The price of salt varied from thirty to sixty dollars per sack, and it was contracted and paid for before it was received. Citizens of St. Johns County (later Flagler County) removed iron kettles from the old St. Joseph Plantation, which the Seminoles had destroyed in 1836. These hearty Floridians used sugar kettles at Mala Compra to boil condensed ocean brine to produce the salt. The operation was eventually moved closer to the beach due to Union raids, and the finished salt was taken overland to the St. Johns River. Loyal Floridians not engaged in salt or cattle production joined the military.[19] Not all Floridians, of course, were loyal to the Confederacy. Halcomb Stephens, of the Panama City area, led one of several Federal expeditions up East Bay in search of a barge carrying 1,500 bushels of salt down Wetappo Creek and helped destroy numerous salt works along the bay.[20]

The Marion Rifle Guards became one of the first military units to be organized in the state of Florida. County Treasurer W. L. Fletcher became its captain. The unit's battle flag, made by the women of Ocala, was presented to the unit on May 2, 1861, by Jefferson Crutchfield. The Marion Rifle Guards joined the Fourth Florida Infantry under Colonel Edward Hopkins. Another Hopkins, J. S., then organized the Hammock Guards.[21]

Local companies were organized from the more heavily populated areas of Florida: the Duval County Cowboys, the Pensacola Rifle Rangers, the Crystal River Coast Guards, the Milton Confederates, the Jacksonville Light Infantry, the Taylor County Eagles, and a group consisting of refugees calling itself the Key West Avengers.[22]

One member of the Key West Avengers left a diary revealing how his fortunes had changed in only a single year from one Christmas to another. Writing on Christmas Day 1861, he stated enthusiastically from Pinellas Point (later St. Petersburg) that he "took dinner with Mr. George Rickards and a splendid dinner it was. We spent a very agreeable day at his house and at night he had some of the best eggnog I ever drank."[23]

The following Christmas this same soldier had been paroled after his capture three months earlier: "Christmas day and I was in bed all day from chills and fever," he wrote from Tampa. "I ate nothing as there is no liquor in the place of course I drank nothing. I have been since ever since last date [Dec 14] and I see no prospect of getting any better for I am in worse health than when I arrived here."[24]

Near Tampa, prominent cattleman, John T. Lesley, organized the Sunny South Guards, whose members came from the best families in the area. These troops had to wait almost two months to be sworn into Confederate service. Lesley refused to obey the orders of the post commander, Colonel William Iredell Turner, whom he referred to as a "mere Florida militia colonel."[25]

In Marion County, William A. Owens organized a totally independent company of cavalry known as the Marion Dragoons. Dickison, as one of its officers, was proud of his men and described the organization as "so superb, their horsemanship so splendid, and their equipments of such superior quality," that Robert E. Lee, in visiting Fernandina in November, compared them favorably with the Black Horse Cavalry of Virginia.[26]

One writer wrote of Dickison: "At the head of the column rode a tall man garbed in the faded gray uniform of the Confederacy. Beneath the wide brim of his hat, dark hair tinged with silver, crowned a bronzed, weathered face. His eyes, deep set and piercing, scanned the country ahead for signs of an ambush."[26]

Considering Lee had very little positive to say about the defenses of Fernandina and Amelia Island when he returned to Savannah on November 21, this was quite a compliment. He termed the defenses "poor indeed" and expressed "the hope that the enemy will be polite enough to wait for us." He quickly ordered the Twenty-fourth Mississippi Infantry and the Fourth Florida Regiment to Fernandina to back those faltering defenses.[28]

Declaring a genuine scarcity of ammunition in East Florida, Lee impressed upon his officers "the absolute necessity of economizing the supplies they have on hand." Guards were forbidden to load their rifles unless in the actual presence of the enemy or in danger of surprise, and hunting parties could no longer use public ammunition. Lee also asked his Floridian troops to respect the rights of private citizens and reminded them "as they take up arms to repel the enemy from our soil, they still be more careful to preserve it sacred from their own depredations."

New Florida State Governor John Milton also found the defenses at Fernandina leaving much to be desired. He discovered the gun batteries "very injudiciously" arranged and a serious shortage of ammunition on the island. In town, his adjutant, General Dancy, found "men and officers . . . staggering through the town on the Sabbath day. They are sadly in want of an efficient commander and a good drill-master for both artillery and infantry."[29]

In a letter to President Jefferson Davis, Milton conveyed that he felt it was a mistake on the part of the Federals in not attacking and capturing Florida at the beginning of the war. Such action would have "had a powerful influence upon foreign nations . . . would have checked Virginia and other states that have not seceded, and dispirited many in the seceded states." Other than troops at Pensacola, he felt there were only insufficient forces to defend the state. The Third Regiment, scattered from Fernandina to St. Augustine, was "in a deplorable condition" and the Fourth Regiment consisted only of eight "imperfect companies."[30]

Governor Milton, however, came under fire from some of the South's military officers who resented his "meddling" in military matters. General William Scott

Fort Clinch on Amelia Island, commanding Cumberland Sound. (Reproduced from *New York Illustrated News*, April 15, 1862)

Dilworth of the Third Florida Infantry, temporarily in command of Confederate forces at Amelia Island, wrote Secretary of War Judah P. Benjamin of this meddling:

"When raised by the State the whole military body has been . . . painted with the political hues of the poor politicians, and our citizens are very averse to going through the chrysalis condition of State service, and after being pulled, hauled, and packed as a gambler would his cards, for three or four months, then turned over to the Confederacy, unarmed, undisciplined, and undrilled, their time wasted and their country unbenefited. There has been in Florida East too much politics mixed with the military in organizing the regiments."[31]

When Brigadier-General John B. Grayson arrived in Florida to assume command of the Confederate Military Department of Middle and East Florida, he too reported to Richmond the "deploring conditions" in Fernandina. "As sure as the sun rises," he predicted, "unless cannon, powder, etc., be sent to Florida in the next thirty days, she will fall into the hands of the North. Nothing human can prevent it. . . . Florida will become a Yankee province unless measures for her relief are promptly made."[32]

Grayson, a West Pointer who had served in Florida during the Indian Wars and on the staff of Winfield Scott in the Mexican War, found "guns and chassis lying on the beach" at Fernandina and had to order the sand battery and its magazine torn down and rebuilt correctly. He pleaded for more heavy ordnance and experienced officers to direct gun mounting.[33]

When Fernandina fell into Federal hands, the Marion Dragoons were ordered to other parts of the state. Captain Owens retired due to illness, and the Dragoons were split into two units under the leadership of Captain Samuel F. Rou and Captain William E. Chambers.[34]

Florida, initially overlooked as a virtual swampland, began to draw some attention from the Confederate War Department in Richmond. Confederate lines were spread thinly across the Confederacy, and these areas that had hitherto fed the army were becoming devastated by occupancy of first one army and then the other.[35]

Eyes were suddenly turning toward Florida as the Federals sought ways to occupy the state, and the Confederates looked for a means of pushing them back. Only a few troops had been kept in Florida, but the government sent some regiments from Georgia to Lake City, and troops from Alabama waited near the Florida line.

The population of Marion County by the time the war began was 8,609, and 1,200 of those lived in Ocala. Less than half the population, 3,295, was white. Ninety percent of the men eligible to fight, however, fought in some capacity.[35]

Over the summer and early fall of 1861, J. J. Dickison decided to organize a second cavalry company in Marion County. Before he had all the men he needed, however, Captain John M. Martin, a local celebrity and former fellow South Carolinian, persuaded him to change the company to an artillery unit. In October 1861, the Marion Light Artillery was organized with Martin as captain and Dickison as lieutenant. It would soon become one of Florida's most renowned Civil War fighting units.[36]

Dickison's wife, Mary, made a flag from a crimson silk shawl, and it became the official flag of the Marion Light Artillery. The colorful flag was attached to its staff by silver rings made from jewelry from the ladies of Orange Springs, and its silver ferrule was made of Mrs. Dickison's wedding comb.[37]

The Marion Light Artillery became part of the command of General Edmund Kirby Smith and was the first Florida unit to see action in the war. The Marion

Light was the only Florida unit to fight in the Battle of Richmond, Kentucky, on August 14, 1862. Captain Martin was severely wounded in that battle and was forced to resign his commission. While recuperating from his wounds, he served a term in the Confederate Congress. Colonel S. St. John Rogers of Ocala succeeded him as head of the Marion Light Artillery.[38]

Three other companies left Marion County that year: a cavalry company under Captain Dickison, the Marion Hornets under Captain Wade Eichelberger, and an infantry unit under Captain S.M.G. Gary.

At Orange Lake, Mrs. Dickison formed a soldiers' relief association called the "Thimble Brigade," to provide comforts for the Marion County soldiers. Also

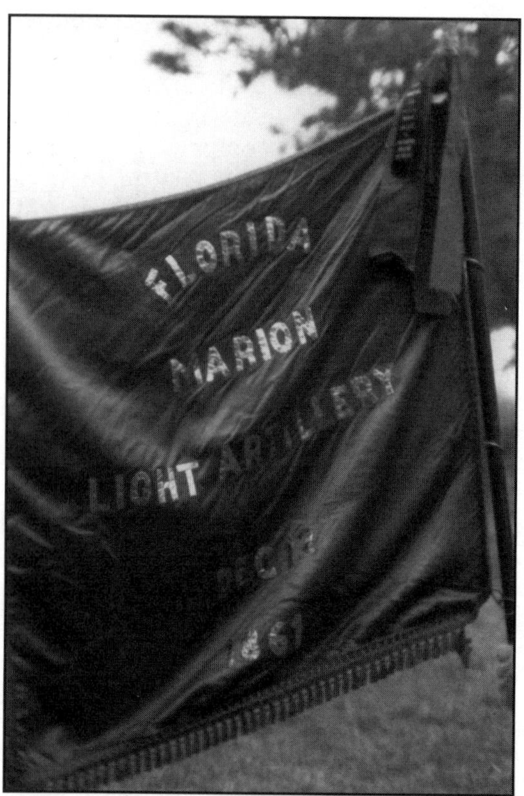

Battle flag of Dickison's Florida Marion Light Artillery. (Photo by J. Walker Fischer)

referred to as the "Soldiers' Friends' Association," they did all they could to make the soldiers comfortable. As one of their first projects, the ladies made thirty pairs of pants for the soldiers at Fernandina, besides knitting socks and other garments.

Daily life for the plantation wives of Marion County became suddenly harsh during the war. The ritual of visiting neighbors, entertaining guests, and changing outfits as often as fifteen times a day, came to an abrupt halt. These women found themselves instead cutting trees, rolling logs, clearing fields, growing crops, weaving, sewing, cooking, and caring for livestock. They made coffee from dried peas and parched corn and produced everything from soap to shoes.[40]

Two-thirds of the Marion County crops went to Florida's Confederate soldiers and many of the Marion County plantations provided sugar and wheat flour for the army.

Maria Baker Taylor, wife of Marion County's John Taylor, ran her Osceola Plantation, southwest of Ocala, after her husband went to war. "I rode to the stores and purchased some black pins, a toothbrush and some Castor Oil," she penned in her diary on May 9, 1864. "One quart of oil cost $50 and four rows of pins $100."[41]

There were now seven companies of cavalry existing in Florida. Local gray-clad troops and homespun Yankee-haters with squirrel rifles crowded into Pensacola spoiling for a fight. Raw troops drilled all day long and dug breastworks, and discipline became a lasting ritual.

When the First Florida Special Battalion was mustered into Confederate service under Lieutenant Colonel Daniel Pope Holland, they retained four guns that belonged to the state of Florida. Dickison requested that Holland turn over the four six-pounders to the Marion

Light Artillery under Governor Milton's order of October 4. Initially, Holland refused the order, but soon the guns were turned over to Dickison.[42]

On November 4, Dickison's unit was ordered to Fernandina and remained there another four months until the Federals invaded Amelia Island. After departing from Fernandina, the company made camp near the St. Mary's River, moved to Sanderson, and journeyed to Camp Langford and Three Mile Branch near Jacksonville. With every intention of organizing his own cavalry unit, Dickison resigned and returned to Ocala in late May 1862, when the company reorganized.[43]

During this period of reorganization, the war erupted throughout Florida, and it was painfully evident to those at home that the Federals had come to stay. On October 9, 1861, General Richard H. Anderson, commanding a thousand Confederates, landed on Santa Rosa Island about four miles east of Fort Pickens. The Federals had been constructing batteries for several weeks, and while their sentries did not discover the presence of the Confederates for nearly an hour and one-half, they responded quickly to the burning of the New York Zouaves' camp. Regulars from Fort Pickens attacked the invaders and a bloody battle ensued. The Battle of Santa Rosa Island terminated with the Confederates retreating.[44]

On November 22, Federal batteries at Fort Pickens opened fire on two Confederate steamers near the Navy yard wharf. Confederate batteries returned the fire, and an eight-hour duel ensued. Confederate-held Fort McRee was heavily damaged by Federal shelling, and early next morning the battle resumed.[45]

The new year brought no let up of battle in the Pensacola area, as Confederate and Federal artillery spit murderous insults at each other daily.[46] On January 8, 1862, General Robert E. Lee penned a letter to government officials in Rich-

Fort Clinch, strongest defensive position on the main shipping channel. (Photo by Dave Page)

Fort Pickens (top) and Pensacola (bottom), San Carlos Battery. (Photos by Dave Page)

mond complaining of Confederate weaknesses along the coasts of Florida, Georgia, and South Carolina. "Our works are not yet finished," he wrote, "and their progress is slow. . . . The forces of the enemy are accumulating, and apparently increase faster than ours. . . . Wherever his fleet can be brought no opposition to his landing can be made except within range of our fixed batteries. We have nothing to oppose its heavy guns, which sweep over the low banks of this country with irresistible force."[47]

That same month the Federals overran Cedar Key and the Confederates offered no resistance. Defending this lack of resistance, General Trapier reported that any attempt would have been "hopeless, and could only result by drawing the fire of the war vessel, in a useless destruction of property and shedding of blood—perhaps the blood of women and children."[48]

Trapier also said he had few troops for any kind of defensive action at Cedar Key, the terminus of the important cross-state railroad. Prior to the attack, he had complied with orders and sent two companies of troops to bolster the forces of Amelia Island, where Dickison and the Marion Light were defending.

With the exception of small fighting forces like those of Dickison's, Florida was nearly defenseless. Acknowledging Governor Milton's request for outside troops to be used for the defense of Florida, Robert E. Lee answered, "Unless troops can be organized in Florida for its defense, I know not whose they can obtain."[49]

In a similar letter to General Trapier, Lee recognized the inability of his forces to cope with the guns of the Union fleet patrolling Florida and informed the general it had to be ascertained which points could realistically be held and which points relinquished. Lee advised the Floridians to withdraw from the islands and draw the enemy into the interior. This type of warfare had been employed by Dickison since the beginning of the war.

Lee imparted pretty much the same message he had offered Governor Milton: "Little aid can be offered . . . from without the state of Florida. You must therefore use every exertion to make available the resources in it, and apply the means at your disposal to the best advantage. Whatever can be given from the means under my control will be cheerfully accorded. You must, however, prepare to concentrate your forces at the point liable to be attacked, and make every arrangement to secure the troops, guns and munitions of war . . ."[50]

In anticipation of an impending Federal invasion, Confederate defenders at Fort Clinch established batteries in and around the fort and the town and in the sand dunes on both Amelia and Cumberland Islands. Following Federal capture of several South Carolina and Georgia coastal islands, Fernandina was completely isolated, and General Robert E. Lee ordered an evacuation.[51]

On March 2, the Federal invasion flotilla had reached Cumberland Sound while Dickison and other Confederate defenders prepared to leave Amelia Island. The following day, Dickison and all Confederate troops, with the exception of three companies from the Fourth Florida, evacuated to the mainland, leaving Fernandina defenseless.[52]

On March 4, the Federal invasion force took sole possession of Fernandina only to find that the Confederates had burned the trestle-work of the bridge to the mainland. This action was taken to slow the Federal advance into the mainland and give resistance fighters such as Dickison time to organize a defense.

Mayor Hoeg of Jacksonville, three days later issued a proclamation announcing the city would offer no resistance to the invasion force. The following day a Federal squadron of four gunboats, two armed launches, and a transport sailed from Fernandina for the St. Johns River, and St. Augustine was quickly evacuated by the two companies of Confederate troops stationed there.

General Lee again wrote General Trapier: "My own opinion and desire is to hold the interior of the state, if your force will be adequate, the St. Johns River, as well as the Apalachicola. I do not think you will be able to hold Tampa Bay, and the small force posted at St. Augustine serves only as an invitation to attack."[53]

Following the Federal takeover of Fort Clinch, workmen began completing construction of the facility. A new development in cannon design—the rifle barrel—changed the feasibility of using brick and stone construction. Rifle

pieces could shoot heavier shot with more accuracy and higher velocity than smooth-bore guns of the same caliber. Masonry fortification became obsolete following devastation by rifle cannon in the bombardment of Fort Pulaski, Savannah, Georgia, on April 10, 1862.[54]

On March 12, six companies of the Fourth New Hampshire occupied a deserted Jacksonville. Smoke hung over the city as the invasion ships entered the port, but there was no resistance.[55]

By the 19th, the Federals occupied not only the coast but the St. Johns River as well. General Trapier and his Confederate forces withdrew to the interior as Federal gunboats cruised the river at will.

Left: Portrait of Robert E. Lee, Julian Vannerson, 1863. (National Archives) Below: Federal picket boat near Fernandina attacked by Confederate sharpshooters stationed in the trees on the banks. (Courtesy Florida State Archives. Reproduced from Joseph T. Wilson's "The Black Phalanx.")

Dickison, involved in organizing a resistance, was aware of their approach.

The Federal offensive became tougher on the Florida east coast; they had swallowed up Fernandina, Jacksonville, and St. Augustine with next to no resistance and moved southward blockading Mosquito Inlet and New Smyrna.[56] New Smyrna was one of the busiest blockade-running ports in the South, as goods carried from Europe to Nassau, landed there and were transported overland to the St. Johns River and Dickison country.[57]

In a letter to Gideon Welles, United States Secretary of the Navy, Flag Officer Samuel F. Dupont, on the flagship *Wabash*, off Mosquito Inlet, stated:

> The department was informed after the capture of Fernandina that so soon as I should take possession of Jacksonville and St. Augustine I would give my attention to Mosquito Inlet, fifty miles south of the latter, which, according to my information, was resorted to for the introduction of arms transhipped from English ships and steamers at the British colony of Nassau into small vessels of light drought.[58]

Early on Saturday morning, March 22, 1862 (Confederate records give the date as March 23), nine small boats with approximately forty-three Federal troops headed south along the Intracoastal Waterway in the vicinity of Mosquito Lagoon. This squadron had received information regarding a small Confederate sailing craft, the *Katie*, which was attempting to run the blockade. Finding the *Katie* abandoned, the Fed-

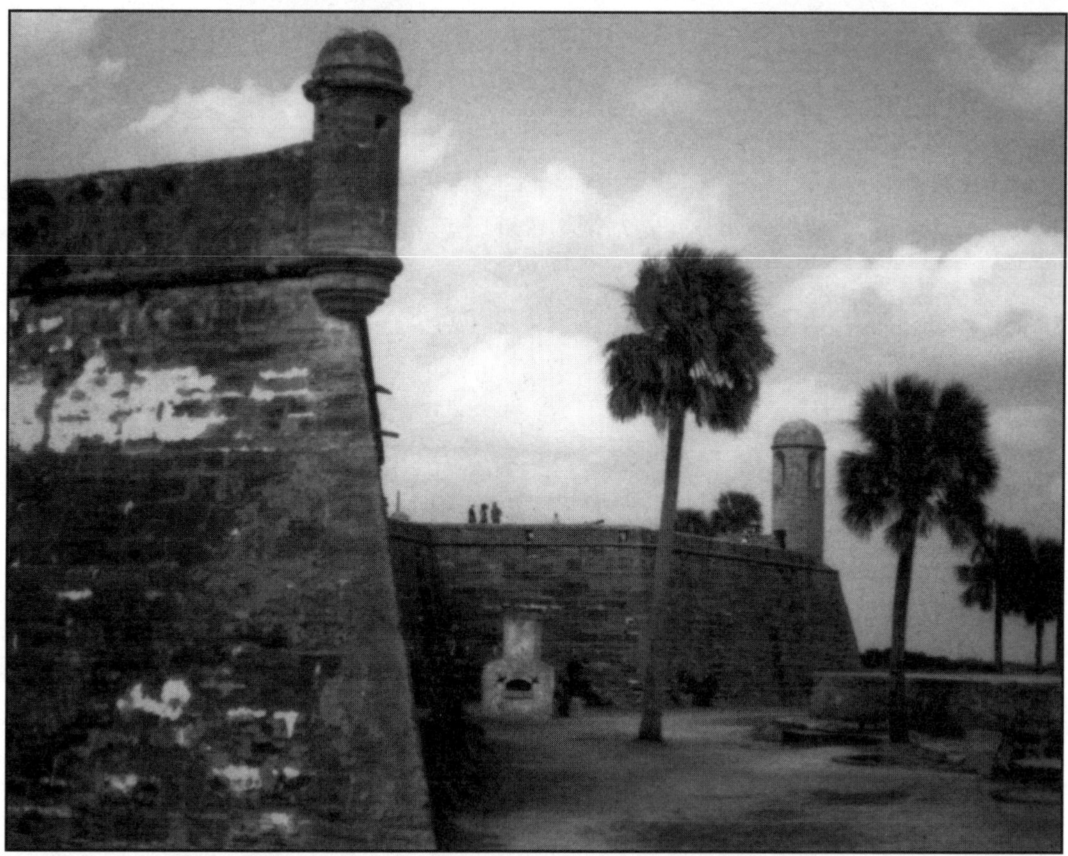

Looking north, Fort Marion, St. Augustine. (Photo by J. Walker Fischer)

St. Augustine entrance gate (above) with street and houses beyond. (National Archives) At right, United States Secretary of Navy Gideon Welles. (National Archives)

erals placed twelve men aboard, and within sight of their sister ship, the *Henry Andrew*, relaxed their vigilance in the afternoon.[59]

Meanwhile, Captain D. B. Bird, Third Florida Volunteers, C.S.A., was accompanying a convoy of arms and ammunition inland while Captain Strain and a detachment of fellow Confederates were on watch in New Smyrna. They had witnessed the boats going south and were watching near the old stone wharf, well-hidden from the passing Federals.[60]

The Coquina Wharf had been constructed by Dr. Andrew Turnbull's colony of Greeks, Italians, and Minorcans in the core area of New Smyrna in 1768. Between 1771 and 1777, 43,283 pounds of indigo were shipped from the colony. In 1777, 5,000 bushels of corn were sold to St. Augustine. During the early 1800s several plantations were established in the area.[61]

The Federal Navy, aware of the heavy Rebel exportation, was keenly interested in the wharf area of New Smyrna. The Confederates under Captain Strain hoped the Federals would merely pass by, but should they come ashore to endanger the stores, he would fire a single shot to signal attack. As the Federal boats returned, two of the craft headed for shore, and the lead boat landed. They were about to examine the abandoned earthworks when Strain stepped out from the underbrush and demanded their surrender. Acting Master, Captain Sam W. Mather of the Henry Andrew, grasped a sailor's musket and aimed it at the Confederates.[62] He was killed.

Acting Lieutenant T. A. Budd of the gunboat *Penguin* was also killed as were six crewmen. Six others were wounded and two taken prisoner. The other boats were fired at as well, but they managed to reach safety under cover of the mangrove-bordered shore where they took shelter. Most of the survivors made their way back to the *Henry Andrew* by wading marshes and swimming creeks.[63]

According to Samuel F. Dupont, Blockade Squadron Leader, recorded in Federal Navy Records:

> As the other boats came up, they were also fired into, and suffered more or less; the rear boat of all had a howitzer, which, however, could not be properly secured or worked, the boat not being fitted for the purpose, and could therefore be of little use. The men had to seek cover on shore, but as soon as it was dark, Acting Master's Mate McIntosh returned to the boats, brought away the body of one of the crew who had been killed, all the arms and ammunition and flags, threw the howitzer into the river, passed close to the Rebel pickets, who hailed but elicited no reply, and arrived safely aboard the *Henry Andrew*.[64]

Dupont referred to this blunder as an error in judgment, since there were not more than two or three houses in sight and no sizeable town between St. Augustine and New Smyrna, it never occurred to Federal officers that a Confederate force could be in the vicinity.

Confederate Records, in the report of Colonel W. S. Dilsworth, vary only in the numbers of casualties:

> I have to report a most successful skirmish which took place at Smyrna on the 23rd ult., Captain D. B. Bird, Third Florida Volunteers C. S. (Army) commanding post, the skirmishers commanded by Captain Strain, Third Regiment and Lieutenant Chambers of Captain Owens' independent troop of cavalry.
>
> The enemy landed, or attempted to land, from gunboats *Penguin* and *Henry Andrews*, in launches when our men fired into them. The enemy retreated to the opposite side of the river and abandoned their launches, five in number.
>
> Captain Bird reports seven killed, three prisoners and about [sic] wounded. Among the killed were Captain Mather of the *Henry Andrew* and Lieutenant Budd of the *Penguin*. A runaway Negro also was captured, who had piloted the enemy into the Inlet to Smyrna, and who was hanged.[65]

Confederate victories such as the skirmish at New Smyrna, were, however, few and far between, and for Dickison and other would-be defenders of the region, there was no time to intervene, even had a courier reached them.

New Smyrna was only one of many targets as the Federal Government tightened its stranglehold on nearly defenseless Florida. In a letter to Richmond dated April 7, 1862, Governor Milton again described the hopelessness of the situation: "The retiring of forces from

Marker at Old Stone Wharf, New Smyrna Beach. (Photo by J. Walker Fischer)

Fernandina and the St. Johns River was attended with the loss of nearly all our guns, etc. The transportation of the arms and munitions of war from Smyrna has also been mismanaged as to cause heavy losses. Moreover, the troops have become demoralized, and the faith of many citizens in the integrity and ability of the government impaired."[66]

During this same period, Confederate forces evacuated Pensacola but were hindered in their movement due to the damaged condition of the railroad. The remaining soldiers were left with antique weaponry, including Spanish muskets.

Inspector General of the Confederate States Army, General Sam Jones, warned that unless they were reinforced with 5,000 infantry, the city would fall. Of course, there were no troops to be sent.

Although General Robert E. Lee called for "every available man in Florida into the field," Governor Milton was unable to comply. Subsistence of a great number of soldiers would have been difficult because of food shortages. Milton did indicate, however, the state militia could be assembled with a day's notice.

Brigadier-General Joseph Finegan, newly-appointed commander of the Department of Eastern and Middle Florida, was quick to remind Richmond that the First Florida Cavalry was under orders for the West, and the Third Florida Infantry enroute to Mississippi. He requested no more armed troops be transferred from Florida and added that new regiments then being formed were still without arms.[67]

"The Federals," he went on, "are in full possession of the St. Johns and their gunboats are able to proceed as far as Palatka."

The lack of Confederate resistance had some Union soldiers believing they were on a mission of rest and relaxation. One Federal officer, who had come to Florida in October 1862 to capture St. Johns Cluff Fort-8 guns, sounded as if he were writing a travel brochure:

> We ascended St. Johns River as far as Jacksonville, twenty miles from the mouth. The river is broad, swelling out at times into almost a succession of lakes. It runs up toward the South. This is a very productive country; rich in all the tropical fruits. It is navigable by steamers for about two hundred miles, and for smaller craft much further. Along its shores are a number of hotels, where persons from the North, especially those with pulmonary complaints, have resorted. Jacksonville was very important at the point was whence all the products of this country were shipped for the north of Europe. It was a very important lumber mart. Eleven steam saw mills were in operation, till they were burned, since the war broke out. The town looks more like a thriving New England town than any place I ever saw south. The chief obstacle

Bastions of Fort Marion, st. Augustine. (National Archives)

to the prosperity of the town is the bar at the mouth of the St. Johns. Vessels drawing over ten feet have sometimes a difficulty in getting in and out. I think, however, with a good system of pilotage, buoys, [et]c., this might be to a great extent obviated. From Jacksonville a railroad runs west reaching to Tallahassee. It was to reach Pensacola in time. I may remark that Jacksonville owes its prosperity to northern men and capital. The railroad was built by northern capital.[68]

According to the officer who had written this account, the capture of Jacksonville in February 1862 had been carried out with little difficulty. He stated that the people of the city came out for the Union and pledged themselves to the cause. But this was not the case as Dickison soon found out.

The heartland, crowded with refugees and under siege, had not given up, despite sudden attacks and occupation of towns along the coasts. All the pride, defiance, and hope were focused on one man, J. J. Dickison, who would become for all Florida an almost legendary figure.[69]

Notes

[1]Samuel Proctor Introduction to Mary Elizabeth Dickison, *Dickison and His Men*, Gainesville, University of Florida Press, Facsimile of 1890 Edition, 1962, pp. VII-X.

[2]Ibid.

Jacksonville signal tower. (National Archives)

[3]Vince Murray, "Captain J. J. Dickison Marion County's Civil War Hero," *Ocala Star-Banner*, 1997, Internet.

[4]Mary Elizabeth Dickison, *Dickison and His Men*, pp. VII-IX (Proctor intro.).

[5]Ibid.

[6]Michael Gannon, *Florida A Short History*, Gainesville, University Press of Florida, 1993, pp. 40-41.

[7]*Fernandina East Floridian*, November 14, 1860.

[8]J. J. Dickison, *Military History of Florida Volume X* of Clement A. Evans, *Confederate Military History*, Atlanta, Confederate Publishing Company, 1899, p. 5.

[9]Darrell G. Riley, "The Civil War Years," *Ocala Star Banner*, 1997, Internet.

[10]Ibid.

[11]Samuel Proctor Introduction to Mary Elizabeth Dickison, *Dickison and His Men*, pp. X-XI.

[12]Samuel Proctor, "Florida a Hundred Years Ago," Coral Gables, published monthly by the Florida Library and Historical Commission and the Florida Civil War Centennial Commission during the One Hundredth Anniversary of the Civil War and Reconstruction era, 1960-1965. Excerpt March 2, 1861.

Artillery inside St. Augustine's Fort Marion. Note the tents on the rampart. (National Archives)

[13]Peter M. Chaitin, *The Coastal War Chesapeake Bay to the Rio Grande,* Alexandria, Virginia, Time-Life Books, 1984, pp. 8-10.

[14]Susan Bradford Eppes, *Through Some Eventful Years*, Gainesville, University of Florida Press, 1968, Facsimile Reprint of the 1926 Edition.

[15]Samuel Proctor, "Florida a Hundred Years Ago," March 9, 1861.

[16]Marjory Stoneman Douglas, *Florida The Long Frontier*, New York, Evanston & London, Harper & Row Publishers, 1967, pp. 172-173.

[17]Michael Gannon, *Florida a Short History*, pp. 42-43.

[18]The Panama City *News-Herald*, Sunday, June 2, 1996. "Alabamian Joined Hundreds in Saltmaking at Time of Civil War."

[19]Harold D. Cardwell, Sr., "Salt Making at Flagler," The Civil War in Volusia County, p. 14; Marion R. Lucas, "Civil War Career of Colonel George Washington Scott," *Florida Historical Quarterly*, Volume 58, 1979, pp. 131-132.

[20]Panama City *News-Herald*, Sunday, March 8, 1987, Marlene Womack, "Civil War Loyalties Unclear."

[21]Darrell G. Riley, "The Civil War Years," *Ocala Star-Banner*, 1997, Internet.

[22]Marjory Stoneman Douglas, *Florida The Long Frontier*, pp. 172-173.

[23]Diary of Richard Watson of Key West, Battle of Olustee Home Page.

[24]Ibid.

[25]Zack C. Waters, "Tampa's Forgotten Defenders The Confederate Commanders of Fort Brooke," *Sunland Tribune: Journal of the Tampa Historical Society*, Vol. XVII, November 1991.

[26]Samuel Proctor Introduction to Mary Elizabeth Dickison, *Dickison and His Men*, p. XI.

[27]Gene Gallant, "The Gray Fox of the Confederacy," Putnam County Archives and History, Palatka, Florida.

[28]Samuel Proctor, "Florida a Hundred Years Ago," November 21, 1861.

[29]Ibid., October 30, 1861.

[30]Ibid.

[31]Don Hillhouse, *Heavy Artillery & Light Infantry, A History of the 1st Florida Special Battalion & 10th Infantry Regiment, C.S.A.*, Jacksonville, privately printed, 1992, p. 13.

[32]Samuel Proctor, "Florida a Hundred Years Ago," September 13, 1861.

[33]Don Hillhouse, *Heavy Artillery & Light Infantry*, p. 7.

[34]Darrell G. Riley, "The Civil War Years," *Ocala Star-Banner*, 1997, Internet.

[35]Susan Bradford Eppes, *Through Some Eventful Years*, pp. 221-222.

[36]Darrell G. Riley, "The Civil War Years," *Ocala Star-Banner*, 1997, Internet.

[37]Marjory Stoneman Douglas, *Florida The Long Frontier*, p. 173; Proctor Introduction to *Dickison and His Men* pp. XI-XII; Mary Elizabeth Dickison, *Dickison and His Men*, pp. 160-163.

[38]Ibid.; Laura Mohammad, "Women Left at Home Forced to Fend for Themselves," *Ocala Star-Banner*, April 22, 1999.

[39]Darrell G. Riley, "The Civil War Years," *Ocala Star-Banner*, 1997, Internet.

[40]Mary Elizabeth Dickison, *Dickison and His Men*, pp. 160-163; Laura Mohammad, "Women Left at Home Forced to Fend for Themselves," April 22, 1999.

[41]Ibid.

[42]Don Hillhouse, *Heavy Artillery & Light Infantry*, pp. 13-14.

[43]Mary Elizabeth Dickison, *Dickison and His Men*, pp. 160-163.

[44]Samuel Proctor, "Florida a Hundred Years Ago," October 9, 1861.

[45]Ibid., November 22-23, 1861.

[46]Ibid., January 2-3, 1862.

[47]Ibid., January 8, 1862.

[48]Ibid., January 31, 1862.

[49]Ibid., February 19, 1862.

[50]Ibid.

[51]"Fort Clinch," Fort Clinch State Park Home Page, Internet.

[52]Samuel Proctor, "Florida a Hundred Years Ago," March 1862.

[53]Ibid.

[54]"Fort Clinch," Fort Clinch Home Page.

[55]Samuel Proctor, "Florida a Hundred Years Ago," March 1862.

[56]Zelia Wilson Sweett, *New Smyrna, Florida in the Civil War,* New Smyrna, A Volusia County Historical Commission Publication, 1962, no page numbers.

[57]Gary Luther, *History of New Smyrna East Florida,* New Smyrna, Privately printed, 1976, pp. 15-16.

[58]*Federal Navy Records,* a Letter from S. Dupont, Flag Officer Commanding South Atlantic Blockade Squadron to Hon. Godeon Welles, Secretary of the Navy, dated March 24, 1862.

[59]Gary Luther, *History of New Smyrna East Florida,* pp. 15-16.

[60]Zelia Wilson Sweett, *New Smyrna, Florida in the Civil War,* no page numbers.

[61]Philip D. Rasico, *The Minorcans of Florida Their History, Language and Culture,* New Smyrna Beach, Luthers, 1990, p. 41; E.P. Panagopoulos, *New Smyrna, An Eighteenth Century Greek Odyssey,* Brookline, Massachusetts, Holy Cross Orthodox Press, 1978, p. 73; Dorothy L. Moore, "Old Stone Wharf," *Musqueto (Mosquitoes) Newsletter,* Southeast Volusia Historical Society, Inc., April 11, 1991.

[62]Charles Bockelman, *Six Columns and Fort New Smyrna,* DeLeon Springs, E.O. Painter Printing Company for the Halifax Historical Society, 1985, pp. 97-98.

[63]*Federal Navy Records*; Zelia Wilson Sweett, *New Smyrna, Florida in the Civil War.*

[64]Ibid.; Dorothy L. Moore, "Old Stone Wharf," *Musqueto (Mosquitoes) Newsletter,* Southeast Volusia Historical Society, Inc., April 11, 1991.

[65]*Confederate Army and Navy Records,* Report of Col. W. S. Dilsworth, Commanding forces of the Department of East and Middle Florida, April 4, 1862.

[66]Samuel Proctor, "Florida a Hundred Years Ago," April 7, 1862.

[67]Ibid., April 29, 1862.

[68]*Chelsea Telegraph and Pioneer,* March 26, 1864.

[69]Marjory Stoneman Douglas, Florida The Long Frontier, p. 181.

Chapter 2

"Dixieland"

The course of the St. Johns River proceeds through eight lakes and for three hundred miles runs northward, unlike most rivers of the world. Only the Oklawaha, one of its tributaries, in all the Floridian peninsula, does likewise. In the middle of the peninsula, the mysterious St. Johns suddenly turns east toward the Atlantic Ocean, while other rivers run west. With this unexpected swing, the St. Johns amputates almost half of Florida from the mainland.[1]

The invading Federal army, as well as the Confederates, referred to this area of the St. Johns River outside Union control as "Dixieland," after the colorful guerilla leader, J. J. Dickison.

Union General Robert Sanford Foster claimed Dickison was such a nuisance that, "Our spies will report that he is at such and such a place with only so many men[;] then, when whole regiments are sent in pursuit the only result in each case has been mortifying defeat but with few returning to tell the tale. Dixie has tricked them again and slain or captured their comrades."[2]

Cypress trees, St. Johns River at Picolata. (Photo by J. Walker Fischer)

One Dickison man recalled what it was like riding with the Swamp Fox following many of their battles:

> A company of Confederate raiders quietly sat upon their horses in the edge of Twelve Mile Swamp while Union cavalry scoured the country roundabout in search of them. They had been [thirty-six] hours on the run. Many were so tired they had fallen asleep. Their leader had to send a rider along the line to awaken them when the command was given to move forward.
>
> To his own men the leader was Cap'n Dickison but the Union soldiers called him Dixie. With a poker hand of none knew how many well mounted backwoods marksmen armed with Enfield guns he had hung upon the flanks of the enemy, driving in their pickets and capturing stragglers, often bluffing isolated garrisons into surrender sometimes without even firing a shot.[3]

Since most of the Floridian troops had been ordered to theaters of war beyond the state's borders, Dickison found little support on which to draw. His army never consisted of more than four hundred men. Despite a lack of manpower, Dickison and his loyal band controlled an area encompassing Orange Springs, Gainesville, Waldo, Starke, and Palatka.[4]

Since his resignation in May from the Marion Light Artillery, Dickison had been busy organizing a new cavalry company of his own. Because Captain Owens of the Marion Dragoons had resigned due to failing health and returned to "Rutland," his Orange Lake plantation, the Dragoons were divided into two companies, giving Florida nine independent cavalry companies.[5]

Cypress trees, St. Johns River at Picolata. (Photo by J. Walker Fischer)

On July 2, 1862, General Joseph Finegan, Confederate commander of the Department of East and Middle Florida, authorized Lieutenant Dickison to raise a tenth company. This action gave the state a full regiment, the Second Florida Cavalry, which was mustered into Confederate service for three years or the duration of the war.[6]

Dickison's new company consisted of men from Marion, Alachua, St. Johns, Putnam, Bradford, Duval, Columbia, Clay, Volusia, Sumter, Hillsborough, Nassau, and Madison counties. Mustered in at Flotard's Pond in Marion County in August 1862, it became Company H, Second Florida Cavalry, with Dickison elected captain. Subordinate to Dickison were twelve other officers and sixty-three privates.

Many of the guns in Dickison's cavalry/artillery unit were M1841 Mountain Howitzer tubes mounted on a prairie carriage pulled by two-horse teams with the gunners riding their own horses. Sometimes they were equipped with heavier field guns pulled with six-horse teams.[7]

Due to its light weight and easy handling, the Mountain Howitzer was used extensively by these cavalry units on both sides during the war. It was first introduced into service as a pack gun, broken down and packed over long distances.

While Dickison and others organized, the Federal invasion of Florida became unstoppable. Brigadier-General Joseph Finegan issued a proclamation to the loyal people of Florida requesting they be ready "to destroy their cotton on the near approach of the enemy rather than permit it to fall into the hands of the invaders of our country."[8]

Apalachicola had fallen to the Federals in April, and in May a thousand additional Northern troops had arrived in Pensacola. During a formal ceremony and celebration in the Plaza, the United States flag flew over the city, which had formerly been a Confederate stronghold.[9]

Initially, Federal raiding parties from Fort Pickens, which had been recently reinforced, destroyed the Pensacola Navy Yard's dry dock. A Confederate picket at Fort Barrancas recalled:

> When the signal was given to set fire to government property, the signal was a blue light shown from Ft. McRee. We were ordered (after everything was burning) to meet at the Big Bayou bridge. As soon as the Yanks saw the fire, they began shelling us from Ft. Pickens, and they made it pretty hot for us. It was a very dark night and there was [sic] great many loaded shells laying in and around the camps and as the fire got to them, they would explode in all directions and the shells from Ft. Pickens exploding over here made it quite lively for a while.[10]

Shortly after, a boat's crew from the *U.S.S. Colorado* destroyed the Confederate privateer *Judah* in Pensacola harbor. In November, guns from Fort Pickens and those of Federal warships, nearly destroyed Fort McRee. By May 1862, the Confederate defenders had abandoned their positions, the Federals reoccupied Pensacola, and it soon became a base for important United States naval operations in the Gulf of Mexico.[11]

United States Colonel William Chase, in occupying Fort Pickens, knew that Florida, as a sovereign power, had to keep her harbors open to international commerce. But with the harbor forts in

Attack on Pensacola. (Drawing by Scott Nelson)

Fort Pickens. (Photo by Dave Page)

Federal hands, those forts would become "locks, cell doors—prison guards rather than sentries." All eyes focused on Pensacola harbor, and Chase was out to deliver his ultimatum to the people of Confederate Florida: surrender or fight![12]

Confederate Brigadier-General Braxton Bragg, commander of the Pensacola-Mobile region, reported the attack being made "on a point at the navy yard where the boats of our harbor police were moored, and succeeded in setting fire and destroying a small armed vessel in our service." Although Bragg conceded that the raid had been "a daring exploit," the Union Navy had sent its message that it was ever on the alert.[13]

It was of the utmost importance for Dickison to monitor the disintegrating situation in and around Pensacola. After attacking Federal outposts on the eastern half of Florida, he would always return to his sanctuary on the western edge of the St. Johns River. Now that Pensacola had fallen to the enemy, an overland attack might be imminent at any time, and Dickison might find himself hemmed in from both sides with no direction for an escape route.[14]

With the Federals occupying St. Augustine, with an outpost at Haw Creek, their cavalry conducted hit-and-run raids on the nearby settlers' farms in Volusia County. The blue coats seized all available corn, smoked and salted meats, and any available household supplies. The Federals appropriated herds of cattle and drove them north to Union cattle pens at Pellicer Creek.[15]

Finegan, while trying to remain optimistic, lamented the departure of the Fourth Florida Infantry, which had been summoned to Corinth, Mississippi. Not counting the Dickison men, who were in the process of formation, Finegan was left with 6,350 men, including the Fifth Florida at Camp Leenear, Tallahassee, which was only two-thirds armed. In addition, his Sixth Florida was stationed at the Chattahoochee River; Seventh Florida, only four-fifths armed, under orders for the Jacksonville area; the First Rifles, who had absolutely no rifles nor any weaponry at all; the First Special Battalion at Ricco's Bluff; three batteries of light artillery; and nine companies of cavalry, only partly armed, stationed at different points along the coast. This anything-but-threatening force was backed up by three companies of Missouri Volunteers, six-month enlistees. Only half of the enlistees were armed, and the company was poorly organized for the war effort.[16]

Because of the horrendous manpower shortage, Florida newspapers began carrying advertisements inserted by Captain T. W. Brevard, Jr., of Tallahassee, and Colonel A. J. T. Wright of Lake City. These patriots called for volunteers, announcing the formation of the "Partizan Corps," consisting of six companies. Fully authorized by the Confederate Secretary of War and sanctioned by General Finegan, the "untiring" and "undaunted" were called to do their duty.[17]

"Florida had already given her best blood freely to the cause," the ad read, "and we are called upon to avenge it. Let no man delay. Let all remember that the fate of our country hangs upon the action of her sons. Every man must do his duty."[18]

Meanwhile, the United States Government passed a law for a national draft, the first of four drafts which would last through the end of the war. All physically able men, ages eighteen to forty-five, were inducted into the military. Most of the eligible men complied with the law but tens of thousands resisted. Hundreds of draft officials were beaten and scores killed while attempting to round up recruits.[19]

Others hired substitutes, giving the government $300 to replace them in the draft. Others rushed to Canada, or as in the case of Mark Twain, the Nevada Territory. Yet, thousands of loyal Americans entered the military, and there was anything but a manpower shortage in the Federal army.

The Federal Navy also launched a campaign to procure men and advertised in many newspapers across the country. One of these appeared in a Massachusetts newspaper:

> Our gallant navy, which did such good service in the last war with England, earning for itself the proud title of the "right arm of the nation's defense" has an important part to perform in the present war, and is now in the want of men.
>
> Lieut. Thornton has opened an office in this city for recruits, who are coming forward freely. Having once served in the Navy, I can assure our seamen that they will be sure of good pay, good rations, kind treatment, and the best of medical attendance with full pay in case of sickness. Flogging has long been abolished, and no abuse[s] of any kind are tolerated. Now is the time for Jack to step forward to protect "our flag."[20]

As Florida's active troops continued being ordered elsewhere, General Finegan saw his force in the state shrink to 2,686 officers and men. This small force now consisted of the First Special Battalion Florida Infantry, the Fifth Florida Infantry, eight other companies of infantry, eight companies of cavalry, and two batteries of artillery.[21]

As Tampa underwent shelling, and Federal forces probed the interior from Jacksonville and St. Augustine, Lieutenant C. H. LaTrobe, of the Confederate States Engineers, also placed newspaper ads, citing the urgent need by the military for saltpeter or nitre, which constituted seventy-five per cent of the gunpowder being manufactured. "The Confederacy," he stated, "is perhaps more in need of this than of any of the munitions of War."[22]

Nitre, found in limestone caves, could also be leeched from the soil under "old houses, stables, negro cabins, tobacco houses, etc." and was found on all the plantations. The government said it would pay individuals for the nitre, as well as shipping costs, if taken to the nearest railroad depot and shipped to Tallahassee.

On August 24, 1862, Dickison, with his command now armed and organized, left Flotard Pond and rode into Gainesville where they procured much-needed arms and ammunition. From Gainesville, they proceeded to the heavily-fortified area near Jacksonville where they spent three weeks performing picket duty and various maneuvers, encamped near the old Brick church.[23]

Leaving the Brick church, they camped a week at Yellow Bluff until they were ordered to Camp Finegan. While encamped there, they received word that the Federals were moving down the waters of the St. Johns River, and Dickison ordered his command to Palatka, some seventy miles from Jacksonville.

At Palatka, they captured several runaway slaves and a large number of deserters. Dickison sent a scouting party in the direction of St. Augustine, which resulted in the capture of Lieutenant Cate from the Seventeenth New Hampshire Volunteers, in addition to two noncommissioned officers, and two privates.

After an intense interrogation of the prisoners, Captain Dickison learned that two companies of the Seventh New Hampshire Volunteers, commanded by Colonel Putnam, were encamped at a house one and one-half miles from St. Augustine. Determined to capture the Federals, Dickison left First Lieutenant William H. McCardell and a detachment on the west bank of the San Sebastian River where he expected the enemy to appear.

The Federal troops did not appear, but unbeknownst to Dickison, Lieutenant-Colonel Abbott, of the Seventh New Hampshire Volunteers, and six companies of 350 men, crossed the San Sebastian River four miles below the location of McCardell's men. Abbott's pickets had seen the Dickison men, and the Federals intended to capture their wagon train at the Moultrie Creek encampment and cut off their escape route.

Lieutenant McCardell and his detachment opened fire on the Federals, and while the battle raged, the wagon train was drawn away in safety. Seemingly out of nowhere, Captain Dickison dashed into the Union line and captured the rear guard, consisting of one commissioned officer and twenty-six men.

Still the Federals refused to retreat and held their position for several hours while both sides fired continuously. Finally, the blue-clad army conducted an orderly retreat in the direction of St. Augustine. It was a stunning victory for Dickison, who, with a force of only forty-three men, had repulsed an army superior in numbers. Even more impressive were the statistics: none of the forty-three had been killed or wounded. They returned to Palatka the following evening.

The company enjoyed Palatka only a few days when ordered to the Jacksonville area. Using the St. Johns River for his movements and its lush west bank for cover, Dickison turned the rich old Indian region to his advantage, applying savage tactics, ambushes, night raids, and surprise attacks.[24]

General Finegan had received a report that the Federals were landing in force at Jacksonville and moved forward with detachments of cavalry under Captain Dickison and Captain Chambers. Passing the old brick church, now a familiar landmark to Dickison, they set up a position on a hill, half a mile from the

Vicinity of Federal entrenchments, Picolata. (Photo by J. Walker Fischer)

river. From this vantage point, they could observe both the city and the enemy picket line.

Finegan ordered Dickison to select twenty men and strike the enemy pickets on the plank-road while Lieutenant McCormich waited on the right with his detachment. As the Federals opened fire on Dickison, he directed a charge, chasing his quarry to an old depot.

Waiting in ambush behind the depot was a regiment of infantry who immediately fired on the Dickison men. Stopping to return the fire, the Confederates raced through the streets, which were teeming with Federal soldiers who had just stepped off the gunboats.

Reloading their Enfield rifles, the Confederates rode quietly through the maze of streets, barely escaping the soldiers who hunted them. When they passed safely beyond the picket line, four Federals lay dead and a few wounded. Dickison's guerrillas lost a single horse.

Returning to headquarters, they were greeted by General Finegan and chief-of-staff Captain W. Call who complimented them on their gallantry. Both officers had them given up for dead.

Within a couple days, Dickison and his troop were ordered to the old brick church to relieve the pickets headquartered there. With the Federal picket in sight, Dickison realized his unit was in a vulnerable position with the route of retreat impassable for cavalry.

Dickison reshuffled his unit to a more advantageous position and personally rode along the railroad track past many quaint cottages. He responded when he heard the command, "Halt. Halt." Looking in the direction of the verbal command, he found several Federal troops arresting private citizens. When they fired at him, he spurred his horse to escape.

Directly in his path was a pile of rail stacking, and his only chance was over it. His horse responded, and they cleared the obstacle, which may have even surprised Dickison. In front of him was a high plank fence, but a gate was open, and Dickison, atop his steed, charged in and made his exit through a less substantial opening that led to the street. When he reached his own men, the enemy was held in check and eventually retreated to the depot. Dickison did not ride out alone again that day.

With Confederate goods continuously being smuggled along the St. Johns from New Smyrna and other points, Dickison did everything in his power to offer protection to the blockade runners. Once he escorted a great cargo of arms on the blockade-runner, *Gladiator*, landed ashore on the Indian River, proceeded to the St. Johns, and saw it safely to the boats at Palatka. During the odyssey, Dickison's men held in check six Federal companies from St. Augustine who were attempting to capture the *Gladiator*. When the goods reached Palatka, Dickison and forty-five men galloped back to the Union forces and drove them back to St. Augustine, making prisoners of their rear guard.

For several months after, Dickison and his Company H guarded the triangular area from Palatka to St. Augustine to New Smyrna.[25] In the Palatka area, Dickison and his troops camped near the town at Camp Call, later known as Ravine Gardens.[26]

With such an impossible area to cover and still be effective, Confederate command eventually re-enforced him with Company C, under Captain W. E. Chambers.

Outside those victories by the Dickison men, the picture in Confederate Florida, due to the manpower and arms shortages, looked bleak. Governor John Milton continued his crusade asking the people of Florida to take whatever steps necessary to "insure their rights as free men." He asked all men between the ages of eighteen and thirty-five not already in the service to volunteer with either the First or Second Infantry, whose ranks had been "decimated by the vicissitudes of war."[27]

Milton also expressed his alarm over the slave situation in the state of Florida: "After the most diligent inquiry, I believe the number left in the State capable of bearing arms is insufficient, unless judiciously organized into military bodies, to keep the slaves subject to authority, I am receiving information daily, and from various parts of the State, of an increasing disposition on the part of the slaves to go to the enemy, and unless we shall have a force apparently sufficient to prevent it, they may accomplish their purpose by violence, especially if any attempt shall be made by the enemy to invade the State by land."[28]

To cope with this problem, General Finegan issued a special order authorizing J. J. Dickison to "remove all negroes having no owners with them and free negroes from the St. Johns River into the interior and a safe distance from the enemy, and place them in charge of some white person, to be held subject to the owner's orders, and in case of free negroes to be left in their own charge, subject to the laws of the State."[29]

The concern in Tallahassee was well-founded, for Florida's well-being as an agricultural state depended on slave labor. Trouble now hovered over the seven planting counties of middle Florida, where 40,000 of the state's 60,000 slaves were situated. There was always the fear of a slave revolt, especially at that time, with the majority of Florida's troops outside the state. A Florida state law limited movement of the slaves, and citizen committees had been established to watch the Negroes and cut off a would-be rebellion.

It was unlawful for four or more Negroes to congregate in a confined space, and firearms were confiscated if found on their person. Offenders were punished and made examples to other Negroes who might be planning a similar insurrection. Dickison carried out his orders immediately to curb just such an insurrection.[30]

General Finegan was just as frantic in telegraphing Adjutant General Cooper from Tallahassee: "Can you send me one regiment of infantry from the coast of Georgia or Carolina? I need them very much."[31]

Unable to secure relief, Finegan ten days later cabled Richmond: "There are not enough troops at any one point to prevent invasion by even a moderate force." He hoped troops would be added to prevent a "sudden raid upon the capital" and to protect the batteries along the St. Johns River. His own scant force, he complained, was spread from Tampa Bay to St. Andrew's Bay on the Gulf and from Fernandina to the St. Johns River on the east coast.[32]

General Pierre Beauregard, on November 21, 1862, dispatched General Howell Cobb to Tallahassee to meet with General Finegan. Beauregard sent word with Cobb that he could not spare a single troop from Georgia or South Carolina for the defense of Florida because his own resources were limited. It was his hope, however, that a successful Virginia campaign would make troops available, some of which could be ordered to Florida. Finegan was told to do the best he could with what he had for the present.[33]

On New Year's Eve, Captain Dickison was ordered to lead a party of twenty men with rations and proceed as secretly as possible from his camp in "Dixieland" across the St. Johns River. In the vicinity of St. Augustine, he was ordered to capture, if possible, any Federals or wagons going into or coming out of the city. He was also asked to do everything in his power to prevent communication between the people in the country and the enemy in St. Augustine. As always, he was successful.[34]

The third Federal occupation of Jacksonville on March 10, 1863, was accomplished by Colonel Thomas Wentworth Higginson's First South Carolina Volunteers and Colonel James Montgomery's

Sally port of Fort Marion, St. Augustine. (National Archives)

Second South Carolina Volunteers. These two regiments were composed of emancipated slaves from the Florida area led by white officers. Later, two white regiments—the Sixth Connecticut and the Eighth Maine—reinforced them.[35]

This new occupation of Jacksonville served as an experiment to test the newly organized black regiments. Entering the city, the former slaves were jubilant. According to Colonel Higginson, "When we rounded the point below the city, and saw from afar its long streets, its brick warehouses, its white cottages, and its overshadowing trees—all peaceful and undisturbed by flames—it seemed, in the men's favorite phrase, 'too much good.'" Higginson added that "there were children playing on the wharves; careless men, here and there, lounged down to look at us, hands in pockets; a few women came to their doors and gazed listlessly upon us, shading their eyes with their hands."[36]

Fortifications were constructed to protect the terminus of the railroad in the city. Shade trees were cut down and used for barricading the streets. Many homes, however, were torched and plundered, and the inhabitants abused. These actions led to several clashes between the black troops and J. J. Dickison.

Meanwhile, Federal troops that had landed at Fernandina on January 15, 1863, were contented as long as they stayed in town. There was strength in numbers, and, removed from the battle scene, the Union soldiers enjoyed what was to many, an extended vacation.

"We found peas in blossom and formed, and flowers in bloom," wrote a Federal officer. "The Lantana and English violet were in bloom, the Oleander was in bud; cabbages were fit for the table. In the gardens, on the plantations, and wherever any pains had been taken, flowers were growing in the utmost luxuriance. In fact why should

Fort Clinch near Fernandina, first of the national properties seized by the Confederacy during the war to be retaken by Federals, March 1862. (Photo by Dave Page)

they not be? There was ice only once, that was a mere scale, of almost imperceptible thickness. The winds were indeed sometimes quite bleak, and caused considerable discomfort, but the thermometer was never very low."[37]

The writer was amazed to find the countryside along the St. Mary's River growing cotton in great abundance. He was told by a woman who lived in the area that she had seen ten thousand bales of cotton stacked at Fernandina, waiting for shipments both north and east. He considered Fernandina harbor, with its ideal location on Amelia Island at the St. Mary's River, a port far superior to Charleston.

But not all Union officers were interested in cotton and flowers. General William Birney of the United States Army left Jacksonville on April 26, 1863, and proceeded up the St. Johns River one hundred and fifty miles to Welaka. He had heard more than he cared to hear from scouts and deserters about J. J. Dickison, as well as about the movements of cotton and cattle. He took with him a very large army to crush the enemy and placed pickets at every point where the enemy could possibly cross the river.[38]

Dickison had no troops on the east side of the river, and while he controlled the west bank, his artillery was not in place during the time of Birney's raid. Birney knew Dickison had no troops on the east side of the river, and with their gunboats patrolling the stream between Lake George and the mouth of the St. Johns, they had only to keep an eye on the dangerous west side. Birney was aware, also, there was strength in numbers, and all the numbers were on his side.

Reaching Welaka, the cavalry and infantry left their boats and spread out into the interior. Collecting cotton and cattle as they probed the wilderness, they reached Lake Harney, some two hundred miles from Jacksonville. Cross country to Smyrna, they captured two blockade runners and a large supply of cotton before heading north to St. Augustine and back to Jacksonville. The raid took only ten days and netted the Union a large amount of cotton and five thousand head of cattle.

A. G. Brown, a United States Treasury Agent who accompanied Birney, recorded that the troops were escorted by transport steamers, *Mary Benton* and *Harriet Weed*, the former carrying a large force of negro troops with six large boats in tow. At Picolata, the *Harriet Weed* welcomed a detachment of the Seventy-fifth New York and some mounted infantry aboard. As the procession paraded up the St. Johns, it appropriated every boat on the west bank of the river including one suspected of being used by Dickison's men for laying torpedoes.

In Saunders, they encamped at the home of an elderly Yankee-hating Southerner who swore if he were young, he would "fight them twenty years." When the Federals left in the morning, they took with them his slaves and horses.

The next day they stayed with a more tolerant host who was a deserter from the Confederate army. They also stormed the home of a beef contractor who supplied the Confederate army with meat but were unable to catch him. They did capture, however, a Confederate messenger carrying important correspondence having to do with the blockade runners, which took them to Smyrna. This movement paid off as they captured two blockade runners from Nassau, the *Fannie* and the *Shell*, both crammed with cotton.

Treasury Agent Brown gloated over the taking of two hundred thousand dollars worth of cotton and beef cattle, and because they "had cleared the country east of the St. Johns of rebels." He had not, however, taken into consideration, the west bank, "Dixieland."

Only a couple of days following the Birney raid, the *Governor Milton*, a small steamer the Federals had captured at Black Creek, was returning to Jacksonville with a full load of cotton. Dickison, who was most deserving of his title of Swamp Fox, had monitored Federal activity on the river during and after the Birney raid. Encamped only a mile from the river, he heard the *Milton*'s whistle and set off to intercept her. He was treated to a rare sight; the *Governor Milton* was traveling without the protection of a gunboat.

Taking only thirty men, Dickison waded into the swamp water waist-high and hid behind cypress trees across from a high bluff referred to as Rollston. The Federals, fearing the Confederate sharpshooters might command the bluff, steered away from danger, directly into pistol range of the Dickison men.

Dickison's men opened fire on the unsuspecting steamer and riddled the pilothouse with minie-balls. The pilot and several soldiers on deck were killed instantly and the boat floated on out of control. Other Federal soldiers on board hid behind cotton bales and returned the fire. No Confederates were hit, however, as the steamer continued on its way past the bend in the river known as "Devil's Elbow."

On March 26, 1863, the Federals landed another large force on the east side of the St. Johns River near Palatka. Captain Dickison and his men waited in ambush, and the following day, the transport *Mary Benton*, with five hundred negro troops of General Montgomery's command, under Lieutenant-Colonel Billings, crossed the river and landed.

Wary of any Confederates in the area, Billings dispatched a scout for a safety check. The soldier was permitted to walk into Palatka unmolested and return to his boat with the good news. It was then the Dickison men opened fire, killing Billings with a shot in his back. Twenty-five more Federals were either killed or wounded. The terrified Federals raced

Rebel Steamer *Governor Milton*, captured by the United States flotilla in the St. Johns River. (From *Frank Leslie's Illustrated Newspaper*, Vol. 15, page 141, 1862)

back to Jacksonville, and Dickison received congratulatory letters from Finegan's Assistant Adjutant-General and the Chief of Staff for the Department of South Carolina, Georgia, and Florida in Charleston.

On December 30, Dickison struck again before year's end. With Lieutenants Reddick and McCardell, and detachments of Companies C and H, Second Florida Cavalry Regiment, he attacked a much larger force near Lake City. The Federals were rendered helpless, and Dickison captured thirty-five men and wounded six, including the commanding officer.

For gallantry on this occasion, the sword captured during the engagement was awarded to Sergeant J. S. Poer of Captain Dickison's company by order of General Finegan.

Both coastlines belonged to the powerful Federals, but "Dixieland," along the St. Johns, remained firmly under the control of J. J. Dickison.

Notes

[1]Branch Cabell and A. J. Hanna, *The St. Johns, a Parade of Diversities,* New York and Toronto, Rinehart & Company, Inc., 1943, pp. 9-10.

[2]Vince Murray, "Captain J. J. Dickison Marion County's Civil War Hero," *Ocala Star-Banner.*

[3]*The Tampa Tribune,* Sunday, August 28, 1960.

[4]Zonira Hunter Tolles, *Shadows on the Sand,* Gainesville, Storter Printing Company, 1976, pp. 171-176.

[5]Samuel Proctor Introduction to Mary Elizabeth Dickison, *Dickison and His men,* pp. XI-XII.

[6]Robert Hawk, *Florida's Army,* Englewood, Florida, Pineapple Press, Inc., 1986, p. 103.

[7]"Second Florida Cavalry Horse Artillery," Internet.

[8]Samuel Proctor, "Florida a Hundred Years Ago," May 1, 1862.

[9]Ibid., May 12, 1862.

[10]Frank Suarez, Memoir in manuscript at Pensacola Historical Society.

[11]Peter M. Chaitin, *The Coastal War Chesapeake Bay to Rio Grande,* p. 8.

[12]Thomas G. Rodgers, "Florida's War of Nerves," *Civil War Times Illustrated,* June 1999, p. 30.

[13]Scott Rye, "Burn the Rebel Pirate!" *Civil War Times Illustrated,* June 1999, p. 28.

[14]Samuel Proctor, "Florida a Hundred Years Ago," May 12, 1862.

[15]Harold D. Cardwell, Sr., "Civil War in Voluisa," *The Civil War in Volusia County,* p. 35.

[16]Samuel Proctor, "Florida a Hundred Years Ago," May 21, 1862.

[17]Ibid., June 17, 1862.

[18]Ibid.

[19]David Leon Chandler, *Henry Flagler the Astonishing Life and Times of the Visionary Robber Baron Who Founded Florida,* New York, Macmillan Publishing Company, 1986, pp. 39-40.

[20]*New Bedford Evening Standard,* April 27, 1861.

[21]Samuel Proctor, "Florida a Hundred Years Ago," June 30, 1862.

[22]Ibid., July 8, 1862.

[23]Mary Elizabeth Dickison, *Dickison and His Men,* pp. 46-48, 165-168.

[24]Marjory Stoneman Douglas, *Florida the Long Frontier,* pp. 181-182.

[25]Ibid.

[26]Mary Emily Boyd, "Civil War Stories," Putnam County Clerk of Court.

[27]Samuel Proctor, "Florida a Hundred Years Ago," August 12, 1862.

[28]Ibid., August 18, 1862, and October 31, 1862.

[29]Ibid.

[30]Earle Bowden, *The Pensacola News-Journal,* Sunday, November 4, 1962, p. 7A.

[31]Samuel Proctor, "Florida a Hundred Years Ago," September 19, 1862.

[32]Ibid., September 29, 1862.

[33]Ibid., November 21, 1862.

[34]Ibid., December 31, 1862.

[35]Richard A. Martin, *The City Makers,* Jacksonville, Convention Press, Inc., 1972, p. 50.

[36]Ibid.

[37]*Chelsea Telegraph and Pioneer,* March 26, 1864.

[38]Mary Elizabeth Dickison, *Dickison and His Men,* pp. 169-183.

Chapter 3

The Net Tightens

J. J. Dickison's claim to the interior of Florida may have been a valid one, for he did control the west side of the St. Johns River, and despite heavy Federal vigilance, his movements went almost unrestricted. But both Florida coastlines, the majority of its major rivers and inlets, belonged to the Federal navy, and from these points, many overland expeditions started into the interior.

Rear Admiral John A. Dahlgren, officer of Federal Navy. (National Archives)

Only four days after Fort Sumter had surrendered, Confederate president Jefferson Davis published an announcement authorizing ship owners to turn privateer, and acting as naval vessels, capture United States' merchantman. These privateers could sell captured Union ships and goods for profit as contraband of war. These men were also paid twenty percent of the value of any Union warship they destroyed for the Confederate government. Meanwhile, Davis was buying time to create his own navy.[1]

The Federals openly referred to the Confederate raiders as "pirates," as evidenced by the *Lowell* (Massachusetts) *Daily Courier:*

> A special Washington dispatch to the *New York [H]erald*, says Governor Andrew has notified the Secretary of the Navy of the purchase of the Steamships *Massachusetts* and *South Carolina*, and ask authority to commission commanders, if not employed by the government. They will be used to

protect Massachusetts commerce from Jeff. davis' [sic] pirates.[2]

Not only did the Confederacy lack a navy, but it did not have the industrial facilities to construct hulls, boilers, and other components of warships. Through a blockade, the Federals threatened to halt the flow of goods in an effort to starve the people and its armies. Davis, with a fleet of privateer-owned warships, could confront some Union commerce ships and break the blockade. This action would draw Union ships from blockade positions and increase the chances of blockade-runners beating the Federal net.[3]

Companies were quickly formed in the South and funds were raised by selling shares of stock. Patriotic citizens, at least those with money, were interested in turning a quick, easy profit and purchased as many shares as they could afford. They were also supporting the Southern cause for independence.[4]

Only two days later, President Abraham Lincoln proclaimed his naval blockade on the Confederacy. Lincoln's net spanned the Atlantic coast from South Carolina to Florida, and the Gulf Coast to the Mexican border. When Virginia and North Carolina moved closer to secession, Lincoln widened his net to include the Potomac River. He also warned Confederate privateers, lured to the sea by Davis, that any of them caught in possession of Union merchantmen, would be tried, convicted, and hanged as pirates.[5]

Initially, blockade-running from Europe was attempted, but the open seas were risky and took too much time. A more methodical plan of transshipment was devised. Larger and slower vessels transported the stores across the ocean to intermediate points at Bermuda or Nassau. Then fast runners would take over and run the illegal cargo to the blockaded coast. England supplied the Confederacy with a steady stream of goods in exchange for Southern cotton.[6]

The blockading of the Gulf of Mexico commenced unofficially with a routine cruising of the *Home Squadron* in and about the harbor of Pensacola. Nervous Federal army officers feared that Fort Pickens was in danger of attack from Floridans on the mainland. Not until the last week of May 1861, were blockade vessels ordered to Mobile and New Orleans, and the port of Galveston did not see its first blockading ship until the middle of July.[7]

Initially, the Confederates, not only in Florida, but throughout Southern ports, did not take the blockade seriously. When the *Powhatan* approached Mobile, Fort Morgan met the blockading fleet by "displaying the U.S. flag, with the Union down, from the same staff and below the Confederate flag."[8]

President Abraham Lincon had proclaimed the blockade in May, and Gideon Welles had ordered warships to cruise Confederate ports. A true blockade, however, was unrealistic. Federal ships could not patrol the 3,000 miles of shoreline in sight of each other from the Potomac River to the Rio Grande. Many naval experts felt such action was unnecessary if ships patrolled the key Confederate ports.

When the war began, the United States controlled only four harbors in the South: the stronghold of Fortress Monroe at the tip of Virginia's peninsula, guarding the mouth of Chesapeake Bay; Fort Pickens at Pensacola; Fort Taylor at Key West; and Fort Jefferson off the tip of the Florida Keys. Three of the four harbors were located in Florida. The rest of the South was a new nation at war with the United States. A plan was urgently needed.[9]

One of these, Fort Taylor, was considered a "fetid place of disease" by many

President Abraham Lincoln. (National Archives)

Unionists, and most of these, attempted to keep their men and ships away from Key West. Of the 448 Federal soldiers garrisoned at Fort Taylor in 1862, 331 contracted yellow fever and seventy-one of these died.[10]

The Union had taken Fort Taylor on the night that Florida seceded from the Union. Lieutenant Edward Hunt, who had constructed the fort, led a small group of Federal soldiers to the fort and occupied it. Only fifty men in Florida's largest town held the crucial fortification but Southerners marched away to join the war, not caring about the Union presence in Key West. Not until after the blockade was successful did the Federals bring captured blockade runners, ships, and cargoes before the 200 massive guns of Fort Taylor.

Winfield Scott, however, had advocated the strangling of Confederate harbors a month before the war had even begun. He informed President Lincoln that the blockade should be established and strengthened; the Confederacy should be split in two at the Mississippi River; constant pressure needed to be applied to the armies of northern Virginia; and the Federal navy would be used to support the army through amphibious assault, naval gunfire, and troop transport.[11]

The United States Navy's first task was to replace the pro-Confederate Naval officers who had left to fight for the South. In an attempt to fill these gaps, the Navy Department ordered the three upper classes of the Naval Academy to sea. Volunteer commissions were offered to some of the men.[12]

Welles quickly sanctioned production by private shipyards the manufacture of two dozen four-gunned screw gunboats, each weighing 691 tons. He helped develop a new kind of sidewheel gunboat, and forty were in operation the first year. These "double-enders" boasted a rudder at both bow and stern, making them capable of steaming in either direction. These double-enders were able to move in and out of the sandbar-strewn coastal waters off the coast of Florida and navigate the meandering bayous of the Deep South's swampy river areas.[13]

Welles dispatched his brother-in-law, Charles D. Morgan, to seaports throughout the Union. With an open expense account, Morgan purchased cargo ships, coal barges, ferryboats, yachts, packet boats, tugboats—anything that could float—and turned them over to the United States Navy.[14]

These converted ships were able to meet the test. The *Somerset*, formally a ferryboat, soon captured the blockade runner *Circassian* by hitting her with two shells and sending another into her rigging. The blockade runner surrendered without a struggle.

Early in the war, the fall of 1861, the harbor of Port Royal, South Carolina, was seized by the Federals and became the headquarters and supply depot of the South Atlantic Blockading Squadron under Flag Officer Samuel F. Dupont. At this time, the Confederacy could still effectively run the blockade into large ports such as Charleston, Savannah, and Wilmington, and toward these "northern" ports the Federal navy concentrated its attention.[15]

Officer Dupont summed up the attitude of the United States Navy concerning peninsular Florida in the opening months of the blockade: "The lower coast [below St. Augustine] may be placed under scrutiny of two or more small cruisers, by which its shores will be continually traversed, and its bays inspected. It can hardly be said to be inhabited, and is of no great consequence as a convenient place of resort for pirates."[16]

As the first year of the war was drawing to a close, the Federal policy began to change, and the United States Navy took major steps to tighten the blockade of the lower Atlantic coast—namely Florida. From Port Royal, Federal ships cruised the waters of South Carolina, Georgia, and Florida as far as Mosquito Inlet, which comprised the extreme southern edge of Dupont's command. The East Gulf Blockading Squadron, based at Key West, patrolled Florida's waters as far north as Mosquito Inlet.[17]

Mosquito Inlet was a valuable point then to the Confederate blockade runners since it was located at the edge of the two geographical blockading boundaries. While Federal warships frequently visited its coastline, the inlet often escaped the scrutiny of many of these ships.

As the Federal blockade closed points in South Carolina and Georgia in 1862, the Confederacy depended upon Florida as an alternative entry point for shipments of arms and supplies. Florida was anything but ideal for these activities since it lacked good deep-water harbors and its only railroad did not connect with the lines in Georgia. Still it was close to a pro-Confederate British government in the Bahama Islands. Once a blockade-runner was safely inside the harbor of Mosquito Inlet, its cargo would be unloaded, placed on wagons, and transported overland to the St. Johns River and into the interior. Dickison quite frequently was called upon to protect these activities.[18]

The United States Government had set up its Department of Florida one day after the bombardment of Fort Sumter. The Union Department of Florida included not only Florida, but also contiguous islands in the Gulf of Mexico. Brevet Colonel Harvey Brown of the Second United States Artillery was initially placed in command. At the time, he was in charge of a relief expedition on its way to Fort Pickens. Upon reaching his destination, Fort Pickens became department headquarters.[19]

The raiding of Union vessels became a common Confederate practice in Florida. These ships would drop the goods on the Atlantic coast, and wagons would transport the arms, ammunition, salt and other short-supply items to the rail head at Waldo. These items would be shipped to Southern troops north of Florida and the blockade-runners would go back to sea with cotton to be exported to Europe.[20]

Since the Union had decided to seize all naval bases between Hampton Roads, Virginia, and Key West, Florida, Dickison and other blockade protectors had their hands full. By capturing these ports, Southern blockade-runners would be stripped of repair and fueling centers, and European powers would get the message that the Union was taking care of its own.[21]

Samuel DuPont and his subordinates felt they must cleanse the Gulf of Mexico of blockade-running activity. Of that entire coast, the Federals held only one base, Key West—600 miles removed from Mobile and 800 miles from New Orleans. Florida would need to be squeezed under the Federal thumb.

In January 1862, the Federals had their eye on occupying Cedar Keys.[22] With the exception of Key West, the village had the largest harbor in Florida, and controlling it was a major asset. Traffic came to Cedar Keys from as far away as Havana and New Orleans. It also served as the Gulf terminus of the newly constructed Florida Railroad Company's line that ran across the state to Fernandina Beach.

A month earlier, Confederate Brigadier-General J. H. Trapier ordered all Florida troops to Fernandina Beach as a Union attack was expected. The two companies of Confederate troops stationed at Cedar Keys went immediately. The 100 or so inhabitants of Cedar Keys, however, were afraid that persons in the area, who had been arrested as traitors and set free, might seek revenge on the town. General Trapier sent them a small force, Company F, Fourth Regiment Florida Volunteers, consisting of Second Lieutenant William T. Weeks and twenty-two men.

On January 16, a Federal man-of-war, armed with five guns, steamed into the harbor, destroyed seven ships considered blockade-runners and spiked three cannons. A Confederate lieutenant and fourteen privates attempted to escape on a flatboat using only push poles. At mid-channel, the water became too deep for the poles, and the men were captured by the Federal steamer, *Hatteras*.

A favorite stop for blockade-runners was Bayport, between Cedar Keys and Tampa. Throughout 1861 and 1862, Confederate runners had their way, but in April the following year, a force of United States marines and sailors attacked the battery defending the port. Several runners drove their ships aground to avoid being sunk and set fire to a schooner loaded with cotton to prevent its capture. The Federals destroyed a sloop carrying corn, and when Confederates met them with rifled cannon, the blue-coats retired out of range.[23]

One blockade-runner, however, had trouble with his own government at Bayport because of a cargo of rum.

> "I would have written you long before this but being constantly on the move I had no opportunity [sic]," wrote the runner from Ocala. "We have had a great deal of trouble with our cargo but we have succeed[ed] in getting it all from Bay Port. General Fenigan [sic] ordered the barrels of Rum to be destroyed and Colonel Thomas arrived at Bay Port for that express purpose. When the military authorities seized it we got the Sheriff of that County with a writ of repleavy and had it taken from them just as they were going to destroy it. It will all be here in a few days a large portion is already here. We have disposed of some of the Rum and expect in a day or two to sell the balance."[24]

In the spring of 1862, the Confederacy decided to run a major shipment of arms and munitions into Mosquito Inlet. The timing was poor, however, for it was then the Federal government sent an expedition to occupy the seacoast of northern Florida.[25]

The most suitable craft for blockade running was small, agile and fast and could slip through the shallow coves and rivers, outwitting the Federal gunboats. At Nassau, Bahamas, the goods were transferred to larger, more seaworthy, vessels for the voyage to Europe. Once the ships left Nassau, they were outside the jurisdiction of United States waters, and the trip to Europe was without fear of gunboat molestation.[26]

A blockade-runner, Jacob E. Mickler, wrote his wife from Tampa on December 7, 1862.

> "We are now painting the smacks and when we paint their [sic] names upon the sterns I will let you know which one I and your Father will go in," penned Mickler. "We do not expect to return in the same vessels as they draw too much water and carry too little. We will dispose of them and purchase two others of less drawft [sic]. I expect Darling the one we will return in will endeavor to run into Nassau river with a cargo of Salt—and the other will try and get into St. Marks near Tallahassee. Oh Darling What quantities of Oranges we get here."[27]

Mickler, in another letter to his wife, this one written from Cuba and dated January 22, 1863, began with an account of the "smack" *Silas Henry*. Leaving Tampa, the *Silas Henry* had attempted to run the blockade during the night, but after making but two miles, the crew was forced to burn the vessel and return to Tampa. But despite the obstacles, Mickler was determined to run the blockade.

> "We passed the blockade about 12 o'clock that night with both of our vessels," he wrote to his wife. "We ran close by her without being percerve [sic]. I expected every moment to see her fire a broad side at us. The next day Darling in blew a gale and we got seperated [sic] from the *Primma Donna*. Monday we made the island of Cuba about 50 miles to the westward of this place and did not arrive here untill [sic] Tuesday about 11 o'clock A.M. Tuesday morning very early about 10 or 15 miles from here we saw a large Man of War in the Gulf. As soon as they discovered us She steamed for us and we thought we would soon be taken. All on board began to hide what money they had as best they could. When she came close we discovered she was a Spanish Gun Boat and a few hours afterwards we arrived safe at this place."[28]

The transfer of goods from the inland areas to the Florida coast was almost as dangerous as the sea run. A popular route, employed by Confederate runners, took goods from New Smyrna overland to Enterprise, where they were shipped by small steamers to Fort Brock on the Oklawaha and moved again by wagon to Waldo. Cotton, turpentine, and tobacco, the lifeline of the Florida Confederacy, was passed along in this fashion.[29]

The Federals, however, had an easier task taking control of the Gulf coast. Commodore David Dixon Porter, by taking practice shots at Mobile Harbor, unknowingly aided the Union cause at Pensacola during the summer of 1862. The Confederate commander at Pensacola heard the shots and thought the city was being invaded by the Federal navy. He quickly evacuated his sick and wounded, and set fire to the navy yard and Fort McRee. Then he withdrew his forces.[30]

Seeing the flames, Porter entered Pensacola in the *Harriet Lane* and ferried the Union troops from endangered Fort Pickens to the mainland. Although the navy yard had been mostly destroyed, it remained a sheltered harbor with its wharves intact.

The east coast inlets and offshore areas often became battlegrounds for the blockade trade. The tiny contraband ships, heavily loaded with goods, were very vulnerable as they docked in the coastal rivers, with more room for maneuvering should an attack be mounted. The contraband ships not carrying cotton and other staples, carried important arms and ammunitions, and, on at least one occasion, General Robert E. Lee took a hand

Rear Admiral David Dixon Porter. (National Archives)

in arranging for their protection at New Smyrna.

Lee warned General J. H. Trapier about arrangements being made for "running into Musquito [sic] Inlet . . . arms and ammunition, by means of small fast steamers . . . At least two moderate sized guns [must] be placed at New Smyrna, to protect the landing. . . . The cargoes of the steamers are so valuable and so vitally important, that no precaution should be omitted."[31]

In the spring of 1863, the Mosquito Inlet blockade-running activity came to the attention of the East Gulf Blockading Squadron at Key West. Learning that a schooner was loading goods at New Smyrna, the new gunboat *Sagamore*, stationed off Indian River, below Cape Canaveral, steamed to the inlet to intercept it. Arriving on February 28, it located the Confederate schooner but hesitated to attack, fearing the Confederates had mounted cannons to protect the harbor. Instead they fired a few shots, hoping the Confederates would leave their cargo and flee.[32]

The following day, the Federals searched the inlet, and before dawn, sent four rowboats to surprise the blockade-runner. As they approached, they found the boat set afire, and determined to capture her as a prize. Acting Masters Mate, Jeff A. Slamm, ordered his men to board it.

Immediately, Confederate riflemen on shore opened fire, killing one sailor and wounding five others. The shocked Federals returned fire with the ship's mounted howitzer and their muskets, and the battle lasted twenty minutes. While trying in vain to put out the fire and pull the schooner from the shore, they found it grounded and retreated in their boats amid a hail of fire. The blockade-runner continued to burn.

The next day, Federal gunboats captured the Confederate schooner *Charm*, laden with cotton. Accompanying Volunteer Acting Masters Mate Henry A. Crane, who captured the *Charm*, were former Confederates who had come over to the Federal side in December and were assigned to the *Sagamore*.

Crane knew the area well and was able to assist the Federal gunboats on the inland waterways of the coastal region. While Dickison controlled "Dixieland" on the west side of the St. Johns, the east side was a no-man's land controlled by neither the Union nor Confederacy, and regarded by the former as a haven for deserters, draft dodgers, and renegades.

During the summer months, the South Atlantic Blockading Squadron tightened its net in the area around Mosquito Inlet by sending the schooner *Para* to patrol the waters. It immediately captured the *Emma* attempting to run the blockade and sent her to Philadelphia as a prize.

On July 26, 1863, the inhabitants of Smyrna watched two Federal ships coming up the river. The residents thought it was merely another routine search for cotton-laden blockade-runners. The Federal Government had assured the people in Smyrna that their homes would not be invaded as long as they remained civilians.[33]

The ships, the United States dispatch steamer, *Oleander*, a side-wheeler, with the *Beauregard* in tow, anchored close to the John Sheldon house. As the Sheldon family sat down to dinner, a shell crashed through the house, slicing the top off their piano. As the terrified family fled, there followed what one Federal termed "a good shelling," followed by calm.

The following day, the shelling resumed, as the Federals blasted 280 shells into the house, the woods, and adjacent swamp. Twenty sailors came ashore and began carting off the piano, mirrors, tables, hens, and pictures. While crossing the creek with their booty, they were fired upon by a handful of Confederates. No one was hurt as the looters returned to their ship, leaving their treasure behind.

The official report of Lieutenant-Commander Earl English, United States Navy, commanding the *U.S.S. Sagamore,* takes a different tone:

> "On the afternoon of the 26th July, I attacked New Smyrna with the U. S. dispatch steamer *Oleander* and schooner *Beauregard* and boats belonging to this vessel and the schooner *Para*, which vessel was stationed off blockading that place." He goes on to relate his shelling of the town, the capture of a sloop laden with cotton, and the destruction of several blockade-runners that were about to disembark. He continued: "In landing, the party was fired upon by a number of

Old Stone Wharf, New Smyrna Beach. The wharf dates from the 1770s and was the site of an 1862 skirmish resulting in the town's first shelling by Union gunboats. (Photo by J. Walker Fischer)

Ruins of structure destroyed by Union gunboats, New Smyrna. (Photo by J. Walker Fischer)

stragglers concealed in the bushes. The conduct of all connected with the expedition was praiseworthy. From the handsome dash in which it was made I attribute our success, particularly in coming off without having anyone injured."[34]

Walter Scofield, a young surgeon aboard the *Sagamore*, wrote in his diary, "the greatest punishment for a blockade-runner, would be to take his vessel and put him ashore in the state of Florida."[35]

The average blockade-runner made three or four trips to sea before being captured. Federal policy dictated runners be captured if they could be taken without resistance, rather than be sunk or destroyed. Often blockade-runners carrying arms would be hit by a single shot and blown up.[36]

One blockade runner, Ed Walsh, from St. George's, Bermuda, said he made monthly wages of about $200 in gold as a crew member of a Confederate runner. But running heavily laden cargoes of contraband past several warships guarding

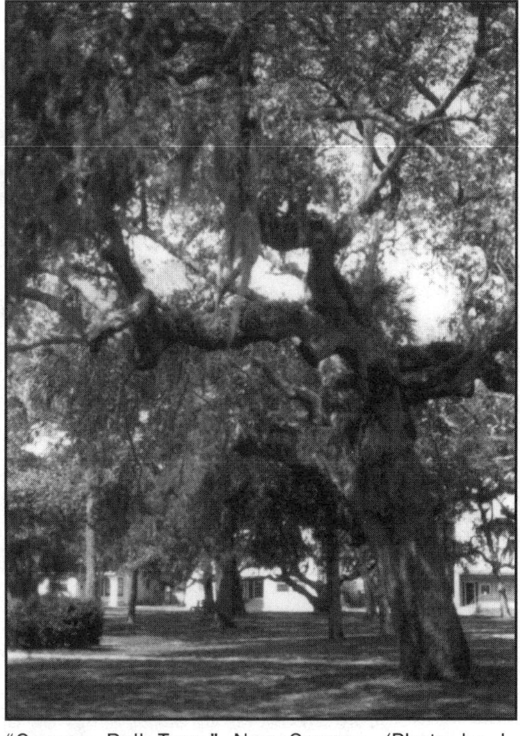

"Cannon Ball Tree," New Smyrna. (Photo by J. Walker Fischer)

Ruins (top and bottom) of the old Sugar Mill, New Smyrna. (Photos by J. Walker Fischer)

the entrances of Southern harbors, was a treacherous employment.[37]

Still, the blockade hampered the Southern supply situation when it was working. Local Confederate manufacturers were progressing in the manufacturing of war materials, and the South was producing enough food, but many of its troops, especially those of Lee's army, were short on rations. The Confederacy's main problem was in the distribution of those goods.[38]

During the hot summer months, fever killed many Federals aboard their ships. When not chasing blockade-runners or destroying salt works, the Federals found blockade duty a tedious job. While anchored for weeks awaiting their Confederate prey, they, in turn, became the prey of mosquitoes, sand fleas, fever, and death.[39]

Other Federal troops kept busy. In Key West, a Martello Tower, an early Corsican means of defense was constructed. This cylindrical tower was frequently referred to as "an upside-down flower pot." Key West constructed two of these towers during the war to assist Fort Taylor in repelling a Confederate landing force. That invasion never came, but blockade runners remained active throughout Florida.[40]

Since cotton was king in Nassau, and the Confederacy needed arms and ammunition, the blockade-runner ignored the odds, and did what was necessary to keep Florida's war effort going. Scanning the sea in fear of his would-be captors, the blockade-runner may have believed the popular verse:

Stand firmly by your cannon
Let ball and grapeshot fly,
And trust in God and Davis,
But keep your powder dry.[41]

Notes

[1]*The Civil War: The Blockade,* Alexandria, Virginia, Time-Life Books, 1983, pp. 11-12.

[2]*Lowell Daily Courier,* May 9, 1861.

[3]Paul F. Bradley, "Rebel Raider of the High Seas," *America's Civil War,* March 1999, p. 35.

[4]Dave Horner, *The Blockade-Runners,* New York, Dodd, Mead & Company, 1968, p. 5.

[5]*The Civil War: The Blockade,* pp. 11-12.

[6]Dave Horner, *The Blockade-Runners,* p. 5.

[7]Ivan Musicant, *Divided Waters: The Naval History of the Civil War,* New York, Harper Collins Publishers, 1995, p. 60.

[8]Ibid.

[9]R. Ernest Dupuy and Trevor N. Dupuy, *The Compact History of the Civil War,* New York, Hawthorn Books, Inc., 1960, p. 31; *Taunton* (Massachusetts) *Daily Gazette,* April 24, 1861.

[10]Joy Williams, *The Florida Keys,* New York, Random House, 1996, pp. 187-188.

[11]Ivan Musicant, *Divided Waters: The Naval History of the Civil War,* pp. 59-61.

[12]*The Civil War: The Blockade,* p. 22.

[13]Ivan Musicant, *Divided Waters: The Naval History of the Civil War,* p. 55.

[14]*The Civil War: The Blockade,* p. 21.

[15]Thomas Graham, "Naval Activities at Mosquito Inlet," *The Civil War in Volusia County,* pp. 22-23.

[16]*Official Records of the Union and Confederate Navies in the War of the Rebellion,* "Third Conference Report for Consideration of Measures for effectually Blockading the South Atlantic Coast," July 26, 1861, Washington: GPO, 1894-1927, Series I, Volume 12, pp. 201-206.

[17]Fletcher Pratt, *The Navy, A History,* Garden City, Garden City Publishing Company, 1938, pp. 260-261.

[18]Thomas Graham, "Naval Activities at Mosquito Inlet," *The Civil War in Volusia*

County, pp. 22-23.

[19]Patricia L. Faust, editor, *Historical Times Illustrated Encyclopedia of the Civil War,* New York, Harper & Row, 1986, no page numbers.

[20]Darrell G. Riley, "The Civil War years," *Ocala Star-Banner,* 1997, Internet.

[21]Ivan Musicant, *Divided Waters: The Naval History of the Civil War,* pp. 62-63.

[22]Glenn Langford, "Action at Cedar Keys," Internet.

[23]Dave Page, *Ships Versus Shore: Civil War Engagements Along Southern Shores and Rivers,* Nashville, Rutledge Hill Press, Nashville, 1994, p. 188.

[24]David J. Coles and Zack C. Waters, "Indian Fighter, Confederate Soldier, Blockade Runner, and Scout: The Life and letters of Jacob E. Mickler," *El Escribano: The St. Augustine Journal of History,* Vol. 34, 1997, pp. 19-20. Mickler's letter to his wife is dated "July Friday 1863."

[25]Ivan Musicant, *Divided Waters: The Naval History of the Civil War,* pp. 62-63.

[26]Harold D. Cardwell, Sr., "New Smyrna: Confederacy's Keyhole through the Union Blockade," *The Civil War in Volusia County,* pp. 15-16.

[27]David J. Coles and Zack C. Waters, "Indian Fighter, Confederate Soldier, Blockade Runner, and Scout: The Life and Letters of Jacob E. Mickler," *El Escribano: The St. Augustine Journal of History,* Vol. 34, 1997, pp. 15-16.

[28]Ibid., p. 17.

[29]Harold D. Cardwell, Sr., "New Smyrna: Confederacy's Keyhole through the Union Blockade," *The Civil War in Volusia County,* pp. 15-16.

[30]Ivan Musicant, *Divided Waters: The Naval History of the Civil War,* p. 238.

[31]Harold D. Cardwell, Sr., "New Symrna: Confederacy's Keyhole through the Union Blockade," *The Civil War in Volusia County,* pp. 15-16.

[32]Thomas Graham, "Naval Activities at Mosquito Inlet," *The Civil War in Volusia County,* pp. 27-28.

[33]Zelia Wilson Sweett, *New Smyrna, Florida in the Civil War.*

[34]*Official Records of the Union and Confederate Navies in the War of the Rebellion,* Series I, Volume 67, Report of Lieutenant-Commander Earl English, U.S. Navy, Commanding *U.S.S. Sagamore,* August 12, 1863.

[35]E.B. Long with Barbara Long, *The Civil War Day by Day, An Almanac 1861-1865,* New York, Da Capo Press, Inc., 1971, p. 392; Zelia Wilson Sweett, *New Smyrna, Florida in the Civil War.*

[36]Alice Strickland, *Blockade Runners,* pamphlet published by *Florida Historical Quarterly,* pp. 85-93.

[37]Dave Horner, *The Blockade-Runners,* p. 113.

[38]R. Ernest Dupuy and Trevor N. Dupoy, *The Compact History of the Civil War,* New York, Hawthorn Books, Inc., 1969, p. 285.

[39]Alice Strickland, *Blockade Runners,* pp. 85-93.

[40]Joy Williams, *The Florida Keys,* pp. 189-191.

[41]Alice Strickland, *Blockade Runners,* pp. 85-93.

Chapter 4

"Tallahassee in the Morning"

Responding to an official report that the Federals had mounted a considerable force in the area of Fort Myers, Captain J. J. Dickison and his faithful, headed south for Fort Meade to reinforce Colonel Brevard. James McKay, leader of the Confederate Cow Cavalry had reported on January 7 that the Federals were planning to destroy the cattle business with the assistance of Southern traitors. McKay was frustrated and forced to suspend operations on account of the poor condition of the cattle and the poor pasture along the way.[1]

One of McKay's men later recalled: "The company began at once to gather beef cattle from all parts of South Florida, drove them to Live Oak, where they were shipped to [Braxton] Bragg's army. We frequently had skirmishes with Yankees and deserters. At one time they landed at the mouth of the Anclote River, with a force of 400 men, one company of Yankee soldiers, one company of deserters, and a Negro company, and they began a raid through the country to Brooksville; they surprised and captured eleven of our pickets, composed of boys and old men, and their horses."[2]

Confederate soldier statue at Brooksville courthouse. (Photo by George Diezel II)

Confederate Major Charles J. Munnerlyn's Cattle Guard Battalion, which patrolled a 300-mile line from Lafayette County to Lake Okeechobee, was also harassed by blockading forces, occupation troops, and traitors.[3]

The Gainesville Cotton States announced, "It is reported that a number of the citizens and deserters from the Confederate army have gone over to the Yankees and have taken the oath of allegiance to Lincoln. It is also said that some have agreed to furnish large numbers of cattle to the enemy, but arrangements are being made to take care of them . . . and we hope to be able to record a brilliant affair before long."[4]

This "brilliant affair" was to be a Confederate attack on Fort Myers, spearheaded by the 160 men of Captain McKay's Confederate cow cavalry and sixty cavalry men under J. J. Dickison. Dickison was ordered to link up with McKay on February 10 at Fort Myers. Unbeknownst to Dickison and McKay, these Federal troops had already left Jacksonville heading for Tallahassee instead.

McKay too had been left in the dark. The courier who reached him in Tampa with news of a Federal occupation of Fort Myers had ridden over a hundred miles to deliver his message. McKay and Captain John T. Lesley gathered 200 men under the command of Major William Footman, and the party traveled two hundred miles to Fort Myers.

The fort consisted of numerous buildings, including a hospital, commissary building, barracks, bakehouse, wharf, and two guardhouses. Most of these structures were intact from the Seminole War days and were surrounded by earthworks. The wharf, hospital, and officers' quarters were situated upon the banks of the Caloosahatchee River, forming a semi-circle around the parade ground. The breastworks towered seven feet high and were about fifteen feet wide at their base.[5]

The Confederates hoped to strike before daylight, but their plan was hampered by weather. Confederate Lieutenant Francis C. M. Boggess later reminisced that "on the night that their anticipated attack was to be made it rained until the water was knee deep over the entire country."[6]

Another Southern soldier gave this account:

> The intention was to surprise and capture the place and troops, and destroy the place, and arriving about eight miles of the place we captured their outside pickets, then onto within sight of the place, we captured their pickets just outside the fort," recalled McKay soldier, T. B. Ellis. "This was just before day, in the morning, when the whole garrison was asleep and not expecting any danger, and notwithstanding the plan was to rush in on them and capture them before they could ready for resistance, and all plans had been carried out, and we at their gates, expecting nothing else but to go right in and capture them, but judge my disappointment when Major Footman sent in a flag of truce and demanded a surrender. Of course, that gave them time to make ready for resistance and of course they declined to surrender, and sent word that if we wanted to come in. So the planned surprise part was a failure."[7]

Major Footman asked his men if they wanted to attack and all but one man were in favor. With Dickison still on his way south, Major Footman declined to attack. He decided he might launch an attack at a later date.

According to T. B. Ellis,

> "I asked the major why he did not make the attempt and he said he did not think a good general would take the risk of having his men slaughtered, so we started our return trip, and when we arrived at Fort Meade, we met couriers with orders for us to report at once to Lake City, as the Yankees were landing at Jacksonville, with the intention of making a raid through the country to Tallahassee, so we moved forward as fast as possible toward Lake City, but when we arrived at Gainesville, we had news that the Yankees had attempted it, and got as far as Ocean Pond and were met by our soldiers, and were whipped and had returned to Jacksonville."[8]

Major General Quincy Adams Gillmore. (National Archives)

Ellis was correct, although the Federal invasion had begun much sooner than he believed. As Dickison pulled out from the St. Johns to link up with the cow cavalry, a large Federal force embarked upon twenty-eight transports with about 7,000 men. Under General Seymour, and with naval support from Admiral Dahlgren, they planned to rendezvous at the mouth of the St. Johns River.[9]

General Quincy Adams Gillmore, who had been frustrated in his attempts to take Charleston, decided in December 1863 that his Federal Department of the South be given a more promising coastal expedition. Gillmore proposed to President Lincoln that he take several of his troops from Charleston to northern Florida where he would impose a pro-Federal government. With Florida left virtually unprotected except for a few bands of Confederate stalwarts such as J. J. Dickison, he expected opposition to be light.[10]

Late the previous year, President Abraham Lincoln had issued an Amnesty Proclamation that he hoped would encourage citizens of Confederate states to return to the Union. Lincoln's proclamation outlined a program for the reconstruction of occupied Southern states. Salmon P. Chase, United States Treasury Secretary, felt the plan would serve to readmit a few Southern states in time for the 1864 Republican National Convention. Chase had desires of his own on the presidency, and he needed these readmitted states to support his nomination. At the conclusion of a study, Chase determined that Florida was the most likely state for early readmission into the Union.[11]

President Abraham Lincoln planned to make Florida a loyal Union state again, and the purposes behind the expedition were: to secure an outlet for cotton, lumber, turpentine, and other products; to cut off a major source of the enemy's supplies; to obtain recruits for the colored regiments; and to restore Florida to her allegiance.[12]

Lincoln had written General Quincy Adams Gillmore on January 13, 1864, directing him to proceed with plans for the reoccupation of Florida. General Truman Seymour, who had commanded the July 18 storming of Fort Wagner, had been chosen to lead the expedition. He took with him a force of about 7,000 men.[13]

General Seymour was more than capable of handling the Florida situation. A former West Pointer, he had served as an artillery captain when the first shots of war were fired at Fort Sumter. Before this, he had been brevetted twice for bravery in the Mexican and Seminole Wars. Following the outbreak of the Civil War, Seymour commanded a division at Seven Days, Second Bull Run, South Mountain, and Antietem.[14]

Troops from as far away as South Carolina were mobilized and put on transports for a faraway port only hinted upon by Union brass. Twenty-four-year-old Lieutenant Tully McCrea, serving with Federal Battery M, First U.S. Artillery, was among those sent south. In a letter to his sweetheart, dated February 5, 1864, the West Point graduate and former roommate of George Armstrong Custer, wrote:

> A large expedition is leaving here today. I think the destination is somewhere in Florida, but that remains for us to find out after we arrive there. There are a large number of vessels in the harbor waiting to load the troops and I suppose we will start tomorrow. General Seymour, my favorite general here, is in command and if we have an opportunity there will be some hard fighting and someone will be hurt."[15]

Other troops in South Carolina began to assemble at Hilton Head on January 4th. A month later, General Gillmore reviewed these troops, and, the following day, the battalion embarked on the steamers *Charles Houghton* and *General Hunter.* Two days later they reached Jacksonville and the *General Hunter* was fired upon by Confederate troops.[16]

On February 7, 1864, Union transports entered the city of Jacksonville "amid the cracking of a few carbine from retiring Confederate troops." There was, otherwise, no organized resistance on the part of the Confederate military or by loyal civilians. By evening, Jacksonville was an armed Federal camp. The Union troops had little to gloat over, as they found the city "pathetically dilapidated, a mere skeleton of its former self, a victim of war. Straggling winter weeds [grew] in the streets and the remains of burned houses [gave] a grotesque, Godforsaken, and dreary aspect to the town."[17]

According to "an unidentified soldier and correspondent," the Independent Battalion of (Federal) Massachusetts Cavalry swept into Jacksonville with a

> "brilliant and successful dash" under the command of Major Stevens. "The battalion landed at the wharf at this place about one o'clock on the afternoon of the 7th," wrote the anonymous soldier in a letter to the *Boston Herald.* "As soon as the steamers *Gen. Hunter, Maple Leaf* and *Charles Houghton* [the latter having on board one company of Company C of cavalry, and the *Maple Leaf* the Fifty-fourth Massachusetts Regiment] attempted to moor at the wharf, they were met by a volley by some mounted rebels. The mate and pilot of the *Maple Leaf* were both seriously wounded, and others slightly. Two companies of the 54th were immediately formed, and Co. C of the cavalry, saddled. All being in readiness to lead, Major Stevens reported to Gen. Seymour, and was ordered by him to make a careful reconnisance [sic] of the city. This detachment immediately started, traveling partly on the railroad and then through the woods, in pursuit of the mounted rebels. We succeeded in capturing five of them. When about seven miles, Major Stevens came suddenly upon a signal station, in full operation. The rebel party not knowing the Yanks were so near, we succeeded in capturing five at the station, with all their implements. After destroying their buildings, Major Stevens went out still further, captured four more (two being mounted) and brought them all into headquarters. There were only about forty-five of our men engaged in the reconnoisance [sic]. Most of the persons hail from Georgia, and all refused to take the oath of allegiance. They have been sent to Hilton Head.[18]

Federal steamers and vessels of all kinds moved down the St. Johns River as women and children flocked to their windows, some assembling on the wharves, to watch the invading Yankees. Most of them recalled the recent burning of their homes during prior Federal invasions but General Seymour had ordered his troops to leave their homes untouched.[19]

General Seymour spent four tedious days in the vicinity of Jacksonville with his men. After General Gillmore departed from the city, Seymour decided to move out, after receiving information that the Confederates were attempting to remove the rails from the Atlantic & Gulf Central. If the Rebels were successful, Seymour's superior, General Gillmore, would see his plans dashed for another Federal advance to the Suwannee River.[20]

General Seymour had about 5,500 men with him, and although he knew the Confederates might have an even larger force waiting at Lake City, he felt they would be mostly harmless state militia. Lincoln had said to him, "I wish the thing done in the most speedy way possible," and Seymour was determined to keep the president happy.[21]

The following day, General Joseph Finegan notified General Pierre Beauregard in Charleston of the arrival of Federal troops in Jacksonville. Finegan, a native of Clones, Ireland, had been a planter and lumber mill operator in Jacksonville, and he had practiced law and built railroads in Fernandina before the war. He now served as commander of the District of Middle and East Florida.[22]

Beauregard's reply to Finegan was a straightforward, "Hold the Federal forces at bay with forces on hand." As the Fortieth Massachusetts Mounted Infantry marched west out of Jacksonville, the Confederates evacuated Camp Finegan, the largest Confederate camp in the St. Johns River area.[23]

General Beauregard had recommended to President Davis that Lieutenant General Daniel Harvey Hill lead a strong force of Confederate soldiers from the Charleston area to take charge of the situation in Georgia and northern Florida.

Brigadier General Joseph Finegan. (National Archives)

After some delay, however, Davis decided against such a move.[24]

The Fortieth Massachusetts Mounted Infantry marched through the countryside, its artillery keeping up the pace. One soldier recalled,

> To one who had never seen artillery keep close up with the cavalry on a march, the feat of Capt. Elder on Monday night would have astonished him beyond measure. No matter where or how fast the cavalry went, Capt. Elder was sure to be up with the spare horses with his artillery. Through ditches, over stumps, turning short corners, walking, trotting, galloping, the artillery never lagged in the rear. Capt. Elder is widely known as one of the most successful and daring officers we have in the artillery service. Gen. Seymour evidently knew his men when he selected officers for this raiding party.[25]

A Southern newspaper, in printing a letter of a rebel defender, was not so complimentary regarding the march of the Fortieth Massachusetts:

> When we reached Starke and found that the enemy had left two hours before, after occupying the place for twelve hours. They searched all the houses for 'armed rebels' but found none. They had all left and escaped. And now you can believe it (for we can scarcely realize it yet) that a troop of the Massachusetts Yankees should occupy a village for twelve hours and not steal a single chicken or pig.[26]

The Federal invaders, led by Colonel G. V. Henry, were attacked shortly after midnight by Confederate troops of the Milton Light Artillery, under Captain Dunham. Losing eighteen men, four cannons, six wagons, and forty-five horses and mules, the Confederates could only slow the Federal advance and were forced to retreat. By early morning, the seemingly unstoppable Union force entered Baldwin, some nineteen miles west of Jacksonville.[27]

A Federal soldier recalled that only about 500 rebels opposed them at Baldwin. Resistance was useless and the Confederate defenders fell back and scattered.

> The surprise was so complete that the rebels did not fire their artillery at all, alas our command would have sorely suffered, as they were compelled to cross a narrow bridge in easy canister range of their guns, and could not have escaped heavy losses. The charge of the Massachusetts battalion was one of the most gallant and brilliant charges that has occurred during the war.

According to the soldier, the Federal columns charged through the enemy's battery "without flinching or holding back, and without firing a single shot."[28]

One of the Confederate soldiers captured at Baldwin was Lieutenant Joseph Barco of the First Florida Battalion. Lieutenant Barco had escaped from Camp Finegan a night earlier and lost all of his extra clothing and equipment in what he referred to as the Confederate "stampede." Federal forces captured about half a million dollars worth of material at Baldwin.[29]

Leaving Baldwin, which the *New York Herald* described as "wretched desolation," the Federal invaders moved on with Confederate prisoners, several pieces of captured artillery, $25,000 worth of cotton, quantities of turpentine, rosin, pitch, tobacco and rice, the telegraph office with all its equipment, a train of cars, a tanning machine, and four-day forage for a thousand men. Assisted by a guide, a Florida resident of twenty years, the units were able to move quickly without getting lost.[30]

A soldier of the Fifty-fourth Massachusetts Regiment wrote that as they marched towards St. Mary's Creek they were prepared for the

> grand march on Tallahassee, and everything had the assurance of complete preparation, and the men seemed in fine spirits, and our success since the landing of Feb. 7th had been marked though more from good luck than good management. The 40th Massachusetts Cavalry, under command of Col. Henry, had inflicted considerable damage on the enemy's property, and we anticipated nothing but victory.[31]

At the south fork of the St. Mary's River, another small force of Confederate cavalry, attempted to check the crossing of Colonel Henry's troops but with little success. The Federal advance, led by a battalion of Massachusetts cavalry, pushed their way into the heartland. One observer recalled:

> Day after day, when the endurance of these now experienced horsemen was taxed to the utmost, the 40th [Massachusetts Mounted Infantry] kept up through all, and night always found the two together. When the sabre and pistol were unable to open the road, forward marched the dismounted skirmishers of the 40th, and the difficulties soon vanished. In the valley of St. Mary's river are buried, side by side, the dead of the Indept. Battalion Mass. Cavalry and the

> 40th Mass. Mounted Infantry. Rebel graves, close by, attest that they did not die unavenged.[32]

The march from Jacksonville to the St. Mary's River had been met with little resistance. Federal troops now, however, discovered that the south fork of the river, about fourteen miles from Baldwin, constituted a very defensible point for the enemy.

"The bugle sounded the call to mount, and the advance of the Massachusetts battalion, under Maj. Stevens, started forwarded [sic] and entered a small defile leading through thick, impenetrable underbrush and pine trees to the bridge across the St. Mary's," wrote a Union soldier. "The platoon of four men of the cavalry which had the advance had just passed a sharp turn in the road, and had approached close on the bridge, without anticipating an attack, when a half dozen reports were heard, and three of the four fell from their saddles, shot by a rebel force ambuscaded [sic] in a strong position beyond the stream."[33]

The Federals took cover, and when they finally advanced, were met with a sharp volley of musketry that killed several of their men. The Union troops offered a volley of their own but they were no match for the Confederate sharpshooters that were concealed behind bushes and stumps.

When they finally advanced to the stream, the Union troops found that the Confederates had blown up the bridge and were entrenched on the other side. Falling back, the men were ordered by Colonel Henry to charge the road and attempt to ford the stream.

Leaving their horses, several Union cavalry men hit the water and were covered by their own skirmishers. Captain Elder's battery, situated on a crest of a little hill in front of the Barber house, was flanked by the cavalry and mounted infantry on either side. The troops fording the St. Mary's River found the stream could not be crossed to the left of the Confederate sharpshooters, but volleys from Elder's battery and from other troops positioned where the river makes a turn, sent the Confederates fleeing. Two of the Southerners were killed, several wounded, and more than sixty horses were captured.

As the Federals crossed the river and moved in pursuit of the enemy, they captured another small group of Confederates. These prisoners swore they were Union men or conscripts in Confederate service, forced to fight against their will.

Charles Remick, a Union officer, wrote a Boston newspaper regarding the almost unstoppable Federal invasion:

> Our regiment has seen several engagements, in one of which five pieces of artillery were captured by us; also a whole rebel camp, the rebels having barely time to get out of their beds, leaving everything behind them and scattering like so many sheep. Not a gun was fired nor a man hurt. Another skirmish was on this stream [St. Mary's River] where we now lay, in which we lost eight or ten men killed and several wounded. The rebel loss was much more serious, and we captured thirty horses. Another skirmish was at Lake City (or Alligator), in which we were over powered, having no infantry support and were obliged to retreat seven miles. The farthest point we went from here was Starke, about in the centre of the State. A few miles south is Fort Hardee, famous in the Indian wars.[34]

By evening, the Federals reached the tiny village of Sanderson and occupied it. One Union soldier reported a number of women assembled near the hotel:

> They were inclined to welcome us because they thought we would be able to prevent the spread of the destructive element. They were nervous and fidgety but managed to give us a tolerably polite reception and to assure us of their sympathy with the rebel cause. . . . Their

features are sharpened and pinched as if the gaunt wolf famine had already been on the threshold of their dwellings."[35]

On the 10th, Henry met resistance from Confederate outposts near Lake City and withdrew five miles in the direction of Jacksonville. The following day, Confederate soldiers promised by Beauregard, left James Island in Savannah, Georgia, to reinforce Finegan. Finegan also sent word to Captain Dickison, who had nearly reached his destination, Fort Myers, asking him to return. With information regarding the impending battle, Dickison at once turned his army northward.[36]

Longtime Palatka resident, Captain Richard Joseph Adams, was relieved as quartermaster at Gainesville, and ordered toward Fort Meade to bring supplies to Dickison and his command. Dickison met Adams at the flat ford of the Hillsboro River and continued north to rendezvous with General Finegan.[37]

Shortly after the meeting with Dickison, Captain Adams was captured by deserters who burned his wagon train. Managing to escape, Adams traveled through Alachua, Levy, and Hernando counties, made it safely to Lake City, and joined General Finegan in time for the campaign at Olustee where he helped with the care of the wounded.

One young Fort Meade man, sixteen-year-old Richard Cabal (Cab) Langford, had walked all the way to Atlanta to aid an older brother helping to hold the city from the Yankees. Upon finding his brother, he was told to go home to "momma," and he walked back to Fort Meade. Following the thirty-day trek, he joined the Bradford County Home Guard under Captain Joseph R. Richard in the Company of Captain J.J. Dickison, who was heading north.[38]

Despite the success of the Federal Florida campaign up to this time, General Seymour wrote his commander, Quincy Gillmore, a shocking letter on February 11.

> I am convinced that a movement upon Lake City is not, in the present condition of transportation, admissible, and indeed that what has been said of the desire of Florida to come back now is a delusion. The backbone of rebeldom is not here, and Florida will not cast its lot until more important successes elsewhere are assured. . . . I would advise that the forces be withdrawn at once from the interior, that Jacksonville alone be held, and that Palatka (upriver from Jacksonville) be also held, which will permit as many Union people [and company], to come in as will join us voluntarily.[39]

While Seymour's enthusiasm for battle returned over the next few days, Gillmore's seems to have waned. In a February 13th letter to Major General Henry Halleck, Gillmore stated:

> I intend to construct small works, capable of resisting a *coup de main*, at Jacksonville, Baldwin, Palatka, and perhaps one or two other important points, so strong that 200 or 300 men will be sufficient at each point. Twenty-five hundred men, in addition to the two regiments that have been permanently stationed in this State (one at St. Augustine and one at Fernandina), ought to be ample in Florida. . . . I have written to the Secretary of the Treasury recommending that the port of Jacksonville be declared open.[40]

On the same day, Joseph Finegan's defending force went into permanent camp at Camp Beauregard, near Olustee, on Ocean Pond. Finegan had selected this location between two small lakes with each flank protected by marsh and open water. Through this gap ran the pike and railway, and immediately upon arrival, his men began digging entrenchments.[41]

General Finegan reported: "In the meantime I used every possible effort to gather re-enforcements, and on the 13th, moved to Ocean Pond, on Olustee,

13 miles from Lake City, and occupied the only strong position between Lake City and Barber's. Here I had field-works thrown up, and for several days, with a force less than 2,000 strong, awaited the enemy's advance."[42]

Finegan planned to skirmish lightly with the Federals before falling back so he could lure the enemy against his fieldworks at Olustee Station. Thus, Seymour would have to choose between two equally unappealing tactical options: a frontal assault on Confederate entrenchments or a withdrawal before a strong opposing army.[43]

At Olustee, Finegan's army consisted of three brigades under his command: General A. H. Colquitt, the Chatham Artillery with four pieces, and the Sixth, Nineteenth, Twenty-third, Twenty-seventh, and Twenty-eighth Georgia Infantry; Colonel G. P. Harrison, First Florida Battalion, Twenty-eighth Georgia Artillery Battalion, Georgia Light Battery, and the First, Thirty-second, and Sixty-fourth Georgia Infantry; and Colonel A. H. McCormick, Fourth Georgia Cavalry, and the Second Florida Cavalry. With the Florida (Leon) Light Artillery Battalion held in reserve, Finegan had a total effective force of 4,600 infantry, slightly less than 600 cavalry, and twelve artillery guns.[44]

Meanwhile, other Federal troops in Colonel Henry's army stormed into Gainesville under Major Stevens, Captain Elder, and Captain George E. Marshall. Gainesville, located on the Cedar Keys and Fernandina Railroad line, was a key Confederate depot for government stores.[45]

Marshall's Federal troops reached Gainesville at 2:00 A.M., Sunday morning, February 14, following several skirmishes with over a hundred Confederate resistors. Occupying the city, Marshall placed pickets in key areas around their camp, but two of these were surprised by Confederate soldiers and captured.

Dickison headed north to reinforce Finegan along with cavalry headed by Captain W. E. Chambers, slammed into Marshall's force at Gainesville. A negro had warned Marshall of Dickison's onslaught forty minutes prior to the attack, and the union commander enlisted the aid of about a hundred negro men. Marshall ransacked Confederate warehouses of 167 bales of cotton and barricaded the crossroads leading into town.

Many of Dickison's men leaped the cotton bale fortification but a seven-fold volley was poured into them by the Federals' new Spencer repeating rifles. The Southern cavalry tried a flanking maneuver but were struck by another disastrous volley. In spite of the enemy fire, Dickison and his men took the city at 2:00 A.M. on the 15th while Marshall's force retreated to Jacksonville.

As other Federal troops poured into the area near Olustee, the Fifty-fourth Massachusetts (Black) Volunteer Infantry Regiment, just heralded for their heroism during the assault at Fort Wagner, South Carolina, sang "We're bound for Tallahassee in the morning" as they marched through the open countryside.[46]

One soldier advancing on Olustee with Company D of the 115th New York Infantry Regiment, penned, "Feb. 20. Marched at 7 a.m. passing Sanderson Station again at 12 (Meridian) eating from our haversacks, no coffee to be had. At 2 p.m. cavalry began skirmishing with the Rebel force."[47]

A soldier in the First Massachusetts Cavalry wrote that his regiment spent the night of the 19th bivouacked "in a magnificent Florida orange grove," some twenty miles from Lake City. There he had expected to meet the enemy, but all was quiet. He added:

"And we smoked, and talked of the fun anticipated at Lake City, which was said to be full of nice people whose husbands and lovers were 'gone to the war,' as we lay under the mighty branches of the live oaks and pines that covered the face of the earth for miles and miles."[48]

Another Union soldier, Lieutenant George E. Eddy, of the Third Rhode Island, described his unit's trek to Olustee:

> Thursday morning, the 18th, we left our camp at Jacksonville, in light marching order, with ten days' rations; marched all day, and as the roads were bad, we only made sixteen miles, when we halted for the night. Friday morning, 19th, started early in the morning, marched all day, made seventeen miles, and stopped over night at a place called Barber's. Saturday morning, 20th, at 7 o'clock, started once more for a place called "Lake City," thirty-six miles distant, which, if we succeeded in occupying, would stop supplies being sent to the western armies of the enemy. Marched eighteen miles, when we met the enemy.[49]

Confederate Corporal Henry Shackelford of the Nineteenth Georgia Infantry, camped near Lake City, saw the Federals coming:

> We rested there about two hours when a scout came in and reported the enemy advancing and were within four miles, tearing up the railroad track as they came. "Fall in" was the word and we moved on down the railroad, which was as straight as an arrow, though keeping in the edge of the woods until we got within about one mile of the Yankee advance skirmishers. We filed off to the right in the woods and formed a line, shucked off knapsacks and all heavy baggage, and threw out skirmishers about two hundred yards in advance.
>
> They were not out long before the enemy made their appearance, advancing slowly. We could see them a half mile, as the country is quite level, and no undergrowth. They soon drove in our skirmishers and firing commenced. One could plainly see the blue coats army in fine order. The order was given to up and at them, which was no quicker said than done, and then what an awful roar of cannon and musketry, men falling and groaning, officers giving commands, the balls flying as thick as sleet. Cheer after cheer went up, onward pushed the rebels firing and yelling.[50]

One of the Federal skirmishers, Milton Woodford of the Seventh Connecticut later wrote:

> As soon as we were deployed, we were ordered to advance, keep cool, take good aim and not waste our ammunition. . . . As we advanced, the enemy retired, keeping just in sight. Whenever we could get near enough to stand any chance of doing execution we would blaze away at them, and they returned the fire in a way that showed they were good marksmen, for their shots came plenty near enough, although none of us were hit.
>
> This kind of running fight was kept up for about three miles . . .[51]

Finegan, received word of the oncoming Federals, and sent cavalry under Colonel Carraway Smith, to skirmish and draw the advance into the works at Olustee.[52] Union skirmishers advanced about 1:30 P.M. on the 20th. As the Federals fired, the Confederate cavalry, as ordered, withdrew to their infantry at the crossing of the wagon road and the railroad. General Colquitt threw out skirmishers and formed his battle line as reinforcements joined him.[53]

One of Colquitt's men from the Twenty-third Georgia Infantry Regiment recalled, "Colquitt's brigade to which I belong, was in camp at the time near Olustee Station, twelve miles east of lake City. At about 8 o'clock on the morning of the 12th [sic, 20th] inst., we were informed that the Yankees were advancing. A part of the brigade was immediately ordered to some rifle pits hastily constructed near at hand; the remainder forming line of battle in the open field. In this position we patiently awaited the coming of the foe for an hour,

Battle of Olustee, 1996 Reenactment. (Photo by J. Walker Fischer)

when our General, who is a fair man, concluded to meet halfway, and two regiments the 13th [sic] and 28th Georgia were sent forward, the 23rd Georgia following soon after."[54]

As the fight began, the Federals' "first line in which all the known tribes were represented, negroes included, after some resistance was broken." Both sides took to the protection of pine trees as the battled waged "Indian style." The Confederates "continued to advance, never halting, making in the meantime the woods ring with the terrible rebel yell, and as a negro or a Yankee ran from tree to tree muskets enough were generally leveled at them to stop their career."[55]

This was nothing new to General Colquitt, a veteran of the Mexican War and some of the Civil War's most decisive battles. He had fought well on the Peninsula during the Seven Days Battles, and at Sharpsburg, Fredericksburg, and Chancellorsville.[56]

"It was found that the enemy were in force on each side of the road, near where the railroad crossed it, with each flank protected by strong entrenchments, some works in the center, and three batteries of field artillery," wrote a Union soldier from Colonel Hawes' brigade. "They had a strong cavalry force, and at this time it is supposed they had in the engagement from twelve to fifteen thousand men, a superior force to our, in their own chosen position."[57]

While the Confederates did not have the superior numbers believed by many Federals, they did have an edge in position of troops. The Federals sent the Seventh Connecticut forward as skirmishers on the right, towards the enemy's left flank, which was protected by a swamp and a small pond. Meanwhile, the Seventh New Hampshire deployed to the right in line of battle. The Eighth United States Colored Troops moved to the left where the Confederates' right flank was protected by another marsh. Langdon's Battery, Battery M, First United States Artillery, and Elder's Battery, stood ready on the left, supported by the Eighth United States Colored Troops. Elder's Battery began firing and all hell broke loose.

Newly arrived Confederate soldiers witnessed signs of a fight in progress. One of these soldiers, George Dorman, later recalled his feelings, "when we were first introduced in a sure enough fight . . . that while it was sickening and heart- rending, it was just the commencing of hardening the hearts of men."[58]

Scenes from the Battle of Olustee, 1996 Reenactment. (Photos by J. Walker Fischer)

Dorman further recounted: "Just about four hundred yards this side of where we went into the battle of Olustee, which had been going on for about two hours, we began to meet the litter-bearers bringing the wounded to the rear. We passed a house with a yard fence around it. On the inside of that yard were nine dead men. . . . From then on it never was a sight to see dead men."[59]

A Union soldier recalled:

The rebels opened with their batteries, a large force of sharpshooters picked off infantry officers and our artillerist, and vollies of musketry were poured in with great accuracy and rapidity on our two front regiments. The rebel fire was quite low, so that our men were wounded in the feet and legs a good deal, but they were brought down and disabled as effectually as though shot in the head, and they toppled over with most disheartening frequency. The rattling of musketry, the roar of artillery, the

Scenes from the Battle of Olustee, 1996 Reenactment. (Photos by J. Walker Fischer)

Scenes from the Battle of Olustee, 1996 Reenactment. (Photos by J. Walker Fischer)

> shrieks of wounded horses, the groans of dying men, the defiant shouts of those engaged in the combat, the dense smoke lighted up with flashes from the belching guns, tree-tops falling, grape shot flying, companies and regiments depleted from the iron storm—these were the characteristic of the four hour scene which followed. To the soldiers it was exciting—to the mere spectators appalling. The fight grew hotter as it continued—the charges got desperate. Those who had trembled with fear at first, trembled with solicitude now, and neglected entirely the dangers which it was impossible to avoid.[60]

As the Federals advanced through the pine woods, they met heavy resistance, and General Seymour, personally leading the Seventh New Hampshire, ordered a deployment under fire, to avoid the small pond.[61] With the noise and confusion, the Seventh misunderstood the order, and scattered for the rear lines.

The Seventh New Hampshire was not the same regiment as when heroic Colonel Pitman led it over the parapets of Fort Wagner. Its reduced ranks had been filled with unwilling conscripts and mercenary substitutes, and the left wing had been deprived of their Spencer seven-shooters. When their muskets proved unserviceable, they retreated despite orders from their commander to stand and fight.[62]

An unidentified correspondent wrote about the Seventh's bad rifles at Olustee:

> Some two months ago our regiment was furnished with Spencer Carbine with the expectation of being mounted. The horses had not been furnished at the time we left St. Helena for this expedition. The 40th Massachusetts were mounted and supplied with Springfield rifles. A few days before this engagement by order of the officer in command (General Seymour), half of our men were obliged to exchange their favorite pieces for the old guns of that regiment, many of which were so damaged as to be perfectly useless. I counted more than twenty in our company that were entirely useless. Many of them had no ramrods and others no locks. By this our entire regiment was disheartened. To be drawn up in line of battle to be shot down by the enemy and no effective weapon in their hands was truly discouraging.[63]

With or without bad rifles, the retreat of the Seventh was viewed by their fellow soldiers, most of whom became confused. The Eighth United States Colored Troops were hit with deadly fire on the left, and they quickly retreated following the Seventh. The Federal artillery, left unprotected, took a heavy pounding.

"It was our misfortune to have for support a negro regiment, who, by running, caused us to lose our pieces," wrote an officer of the Third Rhode Island. "The fight lasted three hours, when finding his small army so much cut up, the General ordered a retreat. We returned to Jacksonville, 58 miles distant; reached there last night at 12 o'clock. We had 5000 men engaged on our side, and, lost 1200, as near as I can learn. The enemy had 15,000 [sic] men opposed to us, and of course, whipped us badly."[64]

The Federals rallied and placed six guns under heavy fire, only one hundred-fifty yards from the Confederates. A regiment of colored troops went into line on the left, and Colonel Guy V. Henry's Fortieth (Mounted) Massachusetts and the Massachusetts Cavalry Battalion held the flanks.[65]

As the Confederates maintained a heavy fire, more Federal units, sustaining heavy losses, were forced to retreat. Two of the Union guns were also abandoned.

"The Yankees were giving back and on our pushing forward, pitched three negro regiments against us, and all acknowledged that they fought well," recalled Confederate Corporal Henry Shackelford. "We walked over many a wooly head as we drove them back. The

Yanks couldn't stand before 'Georgia Boys' and finally gave way and ran, our boys pursuing. We got all their artillery, eight pieces, took about 400 prisoners and killed about the same number. How our boys did walk into the niggers, they would beg and pray but it did no good. We drove them about five miles when a halt was ordered, we built big fires and then how we did enjoy captured coffee, sugar, hams, bread and everything else. We remained about three hours in this position, and then returned to our camps 'kivered' with honor and glory."[66]

According to a report from Brigadier General John Porter Hatch, Commanding Officer, United States Forces, District of Florida, a list of wounded and prisoners in the hands of the Confederates was compiled by the Southern commander and forwarded to his attention. "The very small number of colored prisoners attracted immediate attention," stated General Hatch, "as it was well known that the number left wounded on the field was large. It is now known that most of the wounded colored men were murdered on the field."[67]

Barton's brigade reinforced the fleeing Federals and took up their former position on the right side of the road.[68] Colquitt, with Confederate reinforcements, directed several battalions to the line and opened a murderous fire as they advanced. They were backed by a piece of artillery mounted on a railway car, and Barton's brigade was pushed back.

"Yesterday was one of the most anxious days of my whole life," wrote one of the Union soldiers engaged in the campaign.

Scene from the Battle of Olustee, 1996 Reenactment. (Photo by J. Walker Fischer)

"I heard of the fight early in the morning, and that Col. Barton's whole command had been captured."[69] He also stated that "Barton's brigade were in front, and of course suffered badly. Colonel Barton had two horses killed under him, and received several balls through his hat, coat, etc., yet he was unhurt."[70]

One member of the Second Florida Confederate Cavalry recalled that General Finegan had ordered General Colquitt to fall back during the fight, but Colquitt replied it was no time to fall back. Instead Colquitt asked for more men and then quickly took care of the Federals.[71]

According to Corporal Henry Shackelford, "Proud old Georgia will never have cause to be ashamed of Colquit's brigade."[72]

General Montgomery and a staff officer of General Seymour were at the tracks, trying to rally the Federal troops. Shouting their battle cry, "Three cheers for Massachusetts and seven dollars a month," the Fifty-fourth Massachusetts Colored Troops advanced against a hail of bullets. General Seymour rode up and told Colonel Hallowell the day was lost, and everything depended on the Fifty-fourth.[73]

The Fifty-fourth settled in a grove of pine, and the First North Carolina (Federal) formed on the right side of the road. The Confederates continued to pour a heavy fire into these troops, but at one point, with no order given, the Fifty-fourth mounted a charge. Colonel Hallowell, realizing the entire regiment might follow them to destruction, called them back.

With all Federal units in retreat, no order had been given to the Fifty-fourth, who stood alone against the now overpowering Confederates. Darkness came at 5:30, and the Fifty-fourth, like the other regiments, had lost heavily.

Scene from the Battle of Olustee, 1996 Reenactment. (Photo by J. Walker Fischer)

General Montgomery shouted, "Now, men, you have done well. I love you all. Each man take care of himself."[74]

Ammunition had run short after four hours of fighting and "the men were wearied with their seventeen mile march, and their afternoon of hot fighting under the warm sun. At 7:00, they began to retreat a short distance, then formed another line. When the Confederates did not follow, the men began their weary march back to Jacksonville."[75]

A black soldier of the Fifty-fourth Massachusetts Regiment later wrote: "I cannot account for the rebels failing to harrass our retreat, the 54th Regiment being the last to leave the field, and leaving it in such good order led them to suppose that we intended to renew the attack. Had our utter helplessness been known, few of the officers or men of this army would have been able to have returned to Jacksonville."[76]

According to a *Boston Journal* report:

> Our artillery fired handsomely, but uselessly, owning to the character of the attack. It could not, however, have done much service owning to one of those unaccountable blunders that so frequently occur in this war. At the most critical juncture in [undecipherable word], a supply of ammunition sent from the rear for the batteries was discovered to be of the wrong size, and the retreat had to be a more precipatate [sic] one than it otherwise might have been, but while for such a blunder it could have been so deliberate, after leaving the swamp, as to have saved many lives, prevented the wounded from falling into the enemy's hands, and have given to the movement the name of a repulse instead of a disaster."[77]

The Fifty-fourth was the last Federal unit to retire, and with fixed bayonets, repeating cheers to make the Confederates believe they were being reinforced, they followed the long line of disappearing bluecoats. The Confederates pursued them in the direction of Jacksonville.

General Finegan, who came on the field during the later action, ordered Colquitt to pursue the Federals and occupy Sanderson. With the men fatigued and without food, the pursuing drive was not effective.

General Truman Seymour dispatched his initial report the same day of the battle to his superiors: "Have met the enemy at Olustee and now falling back. Many wounded. Think I may be compelled to go to Baldwin, but shall go to Barber's immediately. Fribley, killed; Sammon, Hamilton, Myrick, wounded, seven guns lost. A devilish hard rub."[78]

Retreating Federals were hammered by rain during the night following the battle. One soldier wrote, "The night was passed in quiet, though the torrents of rain did not add to the comfort of the soldiers, who were lying on the ground, which was before morning nearly covered with water."[79]

Union Lieutenant Nicholas DeGroff wrote later that day, "While dreading the onslaught, the excitement of the battle so engaged my attention that I did not realize my peril and now it all seems like a hideous dream, rather than authorized warfare."[80]

Confederate Lieutenant Winston Stephens wrote his wife that "I am now writing with a Yankee pen, Yankee ink and on Yankee paper captured on the battlefield." But after describing the horrors of the engagement, he added, "I never want to see another battle or go on the field after it is over."[81]

One Confederate soldier did ride over the field the next day and was shocked to find so many soldiers killed. "At least two hundred negroes and Yankees lay dead on the field, and as to the captured I have no reliable information, I suppose about three hundred," he later stated. "We captured eight pieces of artillery, thirty-four hundred stand of small arms, canteens, oil cloths, knapsacks, watches, & c., any quantity. It was a complete victory. We are now distant from Jacksonville some twenty miles, and have just received marching orders. I think we will advance."[82]

Private James Matt Jordan of the Twenty-seventh Georgia Volunteers wrote his wife:

> It is again through the hand of a kind providence that I am spared to address you a few lines, which will inform you that I am well but almost broken down as we have all been in another fight. The Feds. Advanced on our pickets yesterday and drove them back until about five o'clock O. M. at which time our brigade and 32 Ga. Regt. And 6th Ga Regt and some Florida troops were sent to reinforce the picket line, and from then until night some desperate slaughtering by both Rebel and Fed.
>
> The Rebels drove them back and now hold the battle ground and 2 or 3 miles below. The white troops were New Yorkers. We captured several prisoners and 6 pieces of artillery. Our casualties is [sic] very heavy. Of our Regt some 5 or 6 killed dead on the ground and several badly wounded but I don't know how many, but Co. A had remarkably good luck. We had only one man hurt and it was Capt. R. Patton. He was shot slight in the cheek of his stem. The Talbot County Company lost 2 killed dead. It was the two Carlisle boys.
>
> The Yankee prisoners say they had no idea of meeting with such a force here. They said they did not expect to meet nothing but cavalry here. The negroes were badly cut up and killed Our men killed some of them after they had fell in our hands wounded."[83]

Captain John C. Richard of the First Florida Special Battalion wrote that Confederate troops faced an enemy "much larger than ours, but we whipt them badly." Richard added, "I feel very thankful that we suffered so little. Some of the boys have Yankee overcoats, caps, canteens etc. Some good blankets. Many little things taken, this paper among them."[84]

The Confederate victory was decisive, and while they were unable to push the Federals from the East Coast, they managed to save the rich agricultural areas of the state. The Battle for Florida, as Olustee is commonly referred to, cost the Federals 1,861 men killed, wounded, or missing, out of a total of 5,500. A smaller Confederate force had defeated a larger Northern army and the interior of Florida was saved for the time being.[85]

The diary of Susan Bradford Eppes reads: "Yesterday a terrible battle was fought at Ocean Pond, or Olustee, both names are used in the news sent to us of the fierce struggle between the Yankees and our troops. Many are dead on both sides and our loss would have been heavier if the Yankees had been better shots."[86]

Recalled from Fort Myers and Gainesville, J. J. Dickison and his tiny army marched day and night covering 575 miles, only to reach the battle twelve hours after it ended. Although fatigued and hungry, they joined in the pursuit and managed to capture forty or more enemy soldiers who were leaving the battlefield. Although he missed most of Florida's biggest battle through no fault of his own and made an exhausting march to bring aid, he would, from this point on, be heavily engaged in battle until the end of the war.[87]

Part of the Second Florida Cavalry to which Dickison belonged, however, had protected the Confederate right flank in the Battle of Olustee. Lieutenant Colonel Abner McCormick commanded 202 men from the regiment, and at one point in the action, these Dickison men dismounted and stopped a Union effort to turn the flank. Not surprising, the Second Cavalry suffered no known losses in the engagement.[88]

And that war would go on, and Olustee would not be the last battle fought in the state of Florida. Captain James W. Grace of the Fifty-fourth Massachusetts wrote, "We were badly beaten that night, and the next day we kept falling back, until we reached Jacksonville." But the Federals were regrouping, and Captain Grace, added, "The total loss of the regiment, I am unable to give you at this time. All we want now is more troops; with them we would go forward again and drive the rebels from the State."[89]

The Boston Herald reported that the Federal thrust to advance beyond Sanderson was a disappointment and General Seymour and his troops had slowly retreated back to Jacksonville, closely pursued by the enemy. The report, however, attempted to justify the withdrawal, stating that, "We have had no casualties since Olustee, and our withdrawal towards Jacksonville is not a retreat, but only a common-sense result of the failure to proceed beyond that point."[90]

The newspaper had stated earlier that the expedition had failed because General Seymour had exceeded General Gillmore's orders, by "going to hunt up a fight with an unknown enemy, instead of holding certain points and awaiting attack."[91]

Another Eastern newspaper blamed General Seymour for not keeping his army in a state of constant preparation:

> In the meantime vigilant enemy had pushed a strong force down ten miles this side of Lake City, and formed, an important strategic point, an intrenched [sic] camp, covering rifle pits. This had been done so quietly, so skillfully and secretly, that our officers knew nothing of it till they found themselves in the nicely prepared ambuscade. Whilst on the march, many companies not having their guns loaded, much of the artillery empty, and with scouts and skirmishers with but a short distance in advance of the main force, our army was greeted with shot, shell, grape and cannister and we were in such close range that the gunners to some of our artillery were killed with buckshot, whilst loading their guns for the first time in the action.[92]

General Seymour, on the other hand, later stated that he had "received information of the enemy's whereabouts and plans, which led him to believe that by pushing rapidly forward his column, he would be able to defeat the enemy's designs and secure important military advantages." *The Boston Journal* commented: "What ever that information may have been, the events of Saturday would indicate that it was by no means reliable, or that general Seymour acted upon it with to [sic] much haste."[93]

A black soldier of the Fifty-fifth Massachusetts wrote to an Anglo-African newspaper of his distrust of General Seymour:

> We are being reinforced pretty heavily, now as the re-enlisted veterans are coming down to rejoin their regiments. One or two colored regiments have arrived this week; the 7th U.S., I have understood, is one of them. I think from appearances, that we will see some active operations, ere long, and perhaps may be successful, but more probably will be butchered as at Olustee. Our officers and men place but little confidence in the Commanding general, and among troops of all arms can be heard expressions of distrust regarding him. He has never been successful, and has, in different instances, been the means of having men uselessly slaughtered, but we earnestly hope that his next offensive will be attended with different results."[94]

The seriousness of the battle reached General Gillmore, who on the morning of the twenty-third was attending a ball in Beaufort, South Carolina. A steamer carrying wounded men from Jacksonville reached Beaufort shortly after Gillmore's arrival at the ball. Still, the dancing continued until about ten o'clock, when one of the ladies present received word that her husband had been killed in the battle.[95]

According to the *Herald*: "The dancing was then stopped. The removal of the wounded men from the boat occupied the entire night. It was reported that their [sic] was enough wounded men at Jacksonville to make two more boat-loads for Beaufort."[96]

Most of the wounds were serious. One Federal officer was hit by a ball that entered his right side, deflected off his shoulder blade and lodged against his spine, paralyzing his legs. He babbled incoherently during the night, but the next day was "more like himself," wrote a surgeon to his wife, knowing death was inevitable. The officer died the next day.[97]

James Flynn, who entered the Union army as a substitute for one Arthur Baily, served with the Seventh New Hampshire at Olustee. Flynn joined the army to search for his fifteen-year-old son, Thomas, who had run away to serve in the Union army. In a letter to his wife Susannah, written from Tallahassee, James Flynn wrote of his injuries and capture:

> I also sent you another few lines from Barbers Plantation Florida with a 5 dollar bill Which I gave to the Chaplain to post for me that was on the 18th Febry 2 days before the battle near Lake City I was wounded just on the lower Ribs and the ball passed out Within 2 inches of my back bone near my two shoulder blades I am getting on first rate Rate do not fret. Keep good courage If you were to see the wounded men you would pity them We are treated very kindly by the enemy as much so as the Circumstances care to admit I hope soon to be moved I suppose to Georgia to be paroled or exchanged God willing I will soon see Ye I now hope that your health is good and Jacks' [one of Flynn's sons] Tell him from me to be a good boy And to keep to school And please God I will soon see him and send him a present When ever you go out bring Him also I do Not like 9th Street Do not allow Him to wander on the streets I suppose Tom was home Since I heard from you last Give my respect to Mr Gifford This letter goes by Flag of truce You need not write as it wouldn't likely come Keep up you Courage Thank God I am myself again And do not neglect yourself or Jack I am a Prisoner of war I hope Soon to be Paroled or Exchanged.[98]

James Flynn was never heard from again.

His son Thomas fought with Anderson's Zouaves, later the Sixty-second Infantry, and charged up Fisher's Hill at the Battle of Winchester under General Philip Sheridan. He called Sheridan "a grate [sic] man." Like his mother and brother Jack, he, too, never heard from his father again.[99]

The Battle of Olustee was a serious setback to the Union forces, happening

James Flynn. (Photo courtesy Gerard Flynn)

at a time when Federal victories were taken for granted. Because of the Olustee outcome, the Northern press was very critical of the Lincoln administration and General Seymour. The *New York Herald* maintained the Florida invasion was undertaken to bring the state back into the Union "in order that Mr. Lincoln might have three more delegates for him in the nominating convention and Mr. Hay might go to Congress."[100]

Lincoln, however, was "deeply wounded" by the allegation that he had paid in blood for votes. The president likened the situation to a backwoods traveler caught in a violent storm. "O Lord," said the president, "if it's all the same to you, give us a little more light and a little less noise!"[101]

The *Boston Journal* was outraged by such accusations and carried the following editorial:

> The Florida Expedition. The opposition press seek to throw upon the President the responsibility for the recent disaster to our arms in Florida. They say that the expedition was undertaken, under his directions, to "organize" that State under emancipation proclamation, and bring in back in season to vote in the next Presidential election. This has been repeated so often by a reckless partisan press that we have no doubt they have begun to believe it to be true. At all events, they are determined to act on the principle that "a lie well stuck to is as good as the truth." It is well for the public to understand that there is no substantial basis for this statement of the objects of the expedition. It was originally a flying rumor in Washington connected with the departure of Col. Hay, the Private Secretary of the President, for Hilton Head, and had no other foundation than the fertile imagination of an enterprising correspondent.[102]

According to the *Journal* editorial, the purpose of the expedition was to cut off the supply of beef cattle that the Confederates had in abundance in the state.

Thomas Flynn. (Photo courtesy Gerard Flynn)

General Gillmore had intended, stated the article, to advance his lines to Baldwin, twenty miles west of Jacksonville, on the main railroad line in central Florida. The article did concur, however, that General Truman Seymour had "exceeded his instructions, and instead of fortifying himself at Baldwin went in search of a fight and got whipped."[103]

A letter that appeared in the *Boston Journal* perhaps sized up the Florida situation best. The writer, obviously a participant in the Battle of Olustee, blamed much of the Union's woe on their marching too far into the interior of Florida: "The expedition in Florida, from which we expected to hear such good results, has, so far, proved a failure; in our words, our troops have been badly whipped."[104]

A sergeant in the Fifty-fourth Massachusetts agreed with that assessment of the Confederacy's Florida defenders at Olustee, stating, "I fear the rebels . . . have out-generaled us. They chose the battleground . . . and managed it so adroitly that no man in the Union army knew anything about it."[105]

But many Federals simply shrugged their shoulders and looked the other way when it came to the defeat at Olustee. These "realists" considered the battle as one of no importance to the Union and called the fight a waste of manpower in a sector of the country that had no valid strategic importance.[106] In addition to a Confederate victory, the Union troops were "engaged by flies, snakes, and endless boredom."[107]

But the Confederate victory at Olustee over a Northern invasion force of equal strength gave President Jefferson Davis assurance that his country's hopes were still alive. Early in 1864 also, William Tecumseh Sherman and William Sooy Smith embarked upon a joint thrust of Meridian, Mississippi, and on to the great cannon factory at Selma, Alabama. But at Okolona, Mississippi, Smith was whipped by Nathan Bedford Forrest and the expedition failed. Smith, in fact, was forced to retire. Two months after Olustee, Davis had the pleasure of congratulating and promoting Brigadier General R. F. Hoke for capturing the Union naval base at Plymouth. These victories indicated to the president that progress was being made to take Federal pressure off the North Carolina coast. It reassured him, certainly, of his belief in the superiority of Southern manpower and the inevitability of a Southern victory. The main problem before him was the attempt to keep his troops adequately supplied.[108]

Notes

[1]Canter Brown, Jr., *Florida's Peace River Frontier,* Orlando, University of Central Florida Press, 1991, pp. 160-161; Dorothy Dodd, "Florida in the War, 1861-1865," in Allen Morris, comp., *The Florida Handbook 1961-1962,* Tallahassee, Peninsular Publishing Company, 1961, p. 261; James W. Covington, *The Story of Southwestern Florida,* Volume 1, New York, Lewis Historical Publishing Company, 1957, pp. 145-146.

[2]T. B. Ellis, "Short Record of T. B. Ellis, Sr.," unpublished manuscript in Zack C. Waters Collection, p. 12.

[3]Alfred Jackson Hanna and Kathryn Abbey Hanna, *Lake Okeechobee, Wellspring of the Everglades,* Indianapolis, Bobbs-Merrill Company, 1948, p. 78; Joe A. Akerman, Jr., *Florida Cowman: A History of Florida Cattle Raising,* Kissimmee, Florida Cattlemen's Association, 1976, pp. 91-93.

[4]Canter Brown, Jr., *Florida's Peace River Frontier,* pp. 160-161.

[5]Karl H. Grismer, *The Story of Fort Myers,* St. Petersburg, St. Petersburg Printing Company, Inc., 1949, p. 80; Rodney E. Dillon, Jr., "The Battle of Fort Myers," *Tampa Bay History,* date unknown, in Zack C. Waters Collection, p. 28; Zack C. Waters, "Tampa's Forgotten Defenders The Confederate Commanders of Fort Brooke, *Sunland Tribune: Journal of the Tampa Historical Society.*

[6]Francis C. M. Boggess, *A Veteran of Four Wars, the Autobiography of F. C. M. Boggess,* Arcadia, Champion Job Rooms, 1900, pp. 67-69; Rodney E. Dillon, Jr., "The Battle of Fort Myers, *Tampa Bay History,* p. 31.

[7]T. B. Ellis, "Short Record of T. B. Ellis, Sr.," pp. 14-15.

[8]Ibid.

[9]Luis F. Emilio, *A Brave Black Regiment,* New York, Bantam Books, Reprinted from the 1894 Boston Book

Company edition, 1991, pp. 155-166.

[10]Peter M. Chaitin, *The Coastal War: Chesapeake Bay to Rio Grande,* p. 139.

[11]"135 Years Ago," *The General's Orders,* The Newsletter for the Joseph E. Johnston Camp #28, February 1999, pp. 8-9.

[12]Luis F. Emilio, *A Brave Black Regiment,* pp. 155-166.

[13]Corporal James Henry Gooding, edited by Virginia M. Adams, *On the Altar of Freedom: A Black Soldier's Civil War Letters from the Front,* Amherst, The University of Massachusetts Press, 1991, pp. 108-109.

[14]Shelby Foote, *The Civil War: A Narrative Fredericksburg to Meridian,* New York, Random House, 1963, p. 902.

[15]Lieutenant Tully McCrea letter to his sweetheart dated February 7, 1864, Thomas Hayes, "Letters from Olustee," unpublished manuscript.

[16]Benjamin W. Crowninshield, *A History of the First Regiment of Massachusetts Cavalry Volunteers,* written for the First Massachusetts Cavalry Association, Cambridge, Houghton, Mifflin and Company—The Riverside Press, 1891, pp. 258-259.

[17]Samuel Proctor, "Florida a Hundred Years Ago," February 7, 1864.

[18]*Boston Herald,* February 22, 1864.

[19]Corporal James Henry Gooding, edited by Virginia M. Adams, *On the Altar of Freedom: A Black Soldier's Civil War Letters from the Front,* pp. 112-113.

[20]Shelby Foote, *The Civil War: A Narrative Fredericksburg to Meridian,* pp. 902-903.

[21]Ibid.

[22]Ezra J. Warner, *Generals in Gray: Lives of the Confederate Commanders,* Baton Rouge, Louisiana State University Press, 1959, pp. 88-89; Patricia L. Faust, editor, *Historical Times Illustrated Encyclopedia of the Civil War,* New York, Harper & Row, 1986, no page numbers.

[23]Samuel Proctor, "Florida a Hundred Years Ago, February 8, 1864.

[24]Douglas Southall Freeman, *Lee's Lieutenants: Gettysburg to Appomattox,* Volume 3, New York, Charles Scribner's Sons, 1972, pp. 318-319.

[25]*Boston Herald,* February 22, 1864.

[26]*Augusta (Georgia) Chronicle & Sentinel,* March 1, 1864.

[27]Samuel Proctor, "Florida a Hundred Years Ago," February 8, 1864.

[28]*Boston Journal,* February 22, 1864.

[29]David James Coles, "Far from Fields of Glory: Military Operations in Florida During the Civil War, 1864-1865," A Dissertation submitted to the Florida State University Department of History, 1996, p. 52.

[30]Samuel Proctor, "Florida a Hundred Years Ago," February 8, 1864.

[31]*Weekly Anglo-African,* April 23, 1864.

[32]*Chelsea* (Massachusetts) *Telegram and Pioneer,* March 12, 1864.

[33]*Boston Herald,* February 22, 1864.

[34]Letter Charles Remick of the Fourth Massachusetts Mounted Infantry to editor dated February 18, 1864. The letter was published in the *Boston Journal,* February 29, 1864.

[35]Samuel Proctor, "Florida a Hundred Years Ago," February 9-10, 1864.

[36]Ibid.; Richard P. Weinert, "The Confederate Swamp Fox," Putnam County Archives and History.

[37]Captain Richard Joseph Adams, "Civil War Stories," Putnam County Clerk of Court.

[38]Celia Langford Christensen, "Richard Cabal (Cab) Langford," January 10, 1999, Internet.

[39]David James Coles, "Far from Fields of Glory: Military Operations in Florida During the Civil War, 1864-1865," pp. 57-59.

[40]Ibid., p. 60.

[41]Samuel Proctor, "Florida a Hundred Years Ago, February 13, 1864.

[42]Final Report of Brigadier General Joseph Finegan, commanding Confeder-

ate Forces, final report on the engagement at Olustee, February 26, 1864.

[43]Don Hillhouse, "From Loustee to Appomattox: The 1st Florida Special Battalion," *Civil War Regiments: A Journal of the American Civil War,* Vol. 3, No. 1, 1993.

[44]Samuel Proctor, "Florida a Hundred Years Ago," February 19, 1864.

[45]*Chelsea* (Massachusetts) *Telegraph and Pioneer,* March 5, 1864, p. 1.

[46]Luis F. Emilio, *A Brave Black Regiment,* pp. 166-177.

[47]Letter from Lieutenant Nicholas DeGroff, February 20, 1864, Thomas Hayes, "Letters from Olustee."

[48]*Army and Navy Journal,* July 24, 1875, Volume 12, p. 798.

[49]*Boston Herald,* March 1, 1864.

[50]Letter from Corporal Henry Shackelford to his mother dated February 20, 1864, *Atlanta Intelligencer,* March 2, 1864.

[51]David James Coles, "Far from Fields of Glory: Military Operations in Florida During the Civil War, 1864-1865," pp. 118-119.

[52]Luis F. Emilio, *A Brave Black Regiment,* pp. 166-177.

[53]*Atlanta Intelligencer,* March 2, 1864.

[54]Letter from H. W. B. to editor, *Athens* (Georgia) *Southern Banner,* March 9, 1864.

[55]Ibid.

[56]Ezra J. Warner, *Generals in Gray: Lives of the Confederate Commanders,* p. 58.

[57]*Boston Herald,* March 2, 1864.

[58]Don Hillhouse, "From Olustee to Appomattox: The 1st Florida Special Battalion," *Civil War Regiments: A Journal of the American Civil War.*

[59]Ibid.

[60]*Boston Herald,* March 2, 1864.

[61]Luis F. Emilio, *A Brave Black Regiment,* pp. 166-177.

[62]*Boston Herald,* March 2, 1864.

[63]*Boston Journal,* March 4, 1864.

[64]Lieutenant George E. Eddy, Third Rhode Island, *Boston Herald,* March 1, 1864.

[65]*Boston Herald,* March 2, 1864.

[66]Letter from Corporal Henry Shackelford to his mother dated February 20, 1864, *Atlanta Intelligencer,* March 2, 1864.

[67]Report from Brigadier General Jno. P. Hatch Commanding Officer, United States Forces, District of Florida, on the engagement at Olustee, Florida, concerning Union wounded and dead, September 25, 1864.

[68]Luis F. Emilio, *A Brave Black Regiment,* pp. 166-177.

[69]*Boston Journal,* February 29, 1864.

[70]Ibid.

[71]Letter from Winston Stephens to his wife dated February 27, 1864, Thomas Hayes, "Letters from Olustee."

[72]*Atlanta Intelligencer,* March 2, 1864.

[73]Luis F. Emilio, *A Brave Black Regiment,* pp. 166-177.

[74]Ibid.

[75]*Boston Herald,* March 2, 1864.

[76]*Weekly Anglo-African,* April 23, 1864.

[77]*Boston Journal,* February 24, 1864.

[78]Initial Report from Brigadier General Truman Seymour, Commanding Officer, United States Forces, District of Florida, on the engagement at Olustee, Florida.

[79]*The Boston Journal,* February 22, 1864.

[80]Letter from Lieutenant Nicholas DeGroff dated February 20, 1864, Thomas Hayes, "Letters from Olustee."

[81]Letter from Lieutenant Winston Stephens to his wife dated February 21, 1864, Thomas Hayes, "Letters from Olustee."

[82]H. W. B. letter, *Athens Southern Banner,* March 9, 1864.

[83]Letter from Private James Matt Jordan, Volume 2 of *Letters from Confederate Soldiers,* United Daughters of the Confederacy Collection, Georgia State Archives.

[84]Don Hillhouse, *Heavy Artillery & Light Infantry,* p. 73.

[85]Rembert W. Patrick, *Florida Under Five Flags,* Gainesville, University of Florida Press, 1955, p. 54.

[86]Susan Bradfor Eppes, *Through Some Eventful Years,* pp. 233-234.

[87]Mary Elizabeth Dickison, *Dickison and His Men,* p. 48.

[88]Wakulla County, Florida Civil War Page, Internet.

[89]Letter from Captain James W. Grace to editor dated February 25, 1864, *New Bedford* (Massachusetts) *Mercury,* March 9, 1864.

[90]*Boston Herald,* March 9, 1864, p. 4.

[91]*Boston Herald,* March 1, 1864.

[92]*Boston Journal,* March 10, 1864.

[93]*Boston Journal,* March 2, 1864.

[94]*Weekly Anglo-African,* April 23, 1864.

[95]*Boston Journal,* March 2, 1864.

[96]*Boston Herald,* March 1, 1864.

[97]Joseph T. Glatthaar, *Forged in Battle: The Civil War Alliance of Black Soldiers and White Officers,* New York, The Free Press, 1990, p. 161.

[98]James Flynn, Seventh New Hampshire, letter to his wife, Susannah, dated March 30, 1864, courtesy of Gerard Flynn.

[99]Thomas Flynn, Army of West Virginia, letter to his mother dated September 23, 1864, courtesy of Gerard Flynn.

[100]Samuel Proctor, "Florida a Hundred Years Ago," February 23, 1864.

[101]Shelby Foote, *The Civil War: A Narrative Fredericksburg to Meridian,* p. 906.

[102]*Boston Journal,* March 2, 1864.

[103]Ibid.

[104]*Boston Journal,* February 29, 1864.

[105]Bruce Catton, narrator, James M. McPherson, editor, *The American Heritage New History of the Civil War,* New York, Penguin Books, 1996, p. 404.

[106]Henry E. Simmons, *A Concise Encyclopedia of the Civil War,* New York, Bonanza Books, 1964, p. 156.

[107]Frank E. Vandiver, *Their Tattered Flags: The Epic of the Confederacy,* New York & Evanston, Harper & Row, 1970, p. 273.

[108]Ibid.; R. Ernest Dupuy and Trevor N. Dupuy, *The Compact History of the Civil War,* pp. 284-285.

Chapter 5

Palatka, Welaka, and Saunders

As the fleeing Federals retreated from the battlefield at Olustee, Colonel Scott, C. S. A., conferred the honor of outpost duty on Captain Dickison's command.[1] After only a few days of outpost duty, Dickison and company were ordered again to follow the enemy in the direction of Palatka, and the commanding officer of the Fourth Florida Cavalry, would "hold himself in readiness to support him with his whole company if necessary."[2]

Bronson-Mulholland House, Palatka. Built in 1854 by Judge Isaac Bronson, it was used by Confederate soldiers as a lookout on the St. Johns River. (Photo by J. Walker Fischer)

At this same time, General Seymour, who had led the Federal disaster at Olustee, was advised he was not authorized to advance beyond his command at the present time and should be concerned only with securing his position at Jacksonville. Seymour was also urged to strengthen his communication along the St. Johns River so Dickison and guerilla forces could not ambush their transports. Seymour's other instructions involved exploring a little of the interior, but under no circumstances to make another advance. If he were to find a concentration of Confederates, he was to garrison and fortify Palatka.[3]

Confederate General James Patton Anderson arrived in Florida on March 1, and assumed command of the district with headquarters outside Jacksonville. He remained there operating against the enemy at Jacksonville and on the St. Johns River that summer until he was ordered back to the Army of Tennessee. General Anderson later recalled:

> We were able to confine the enemy closely to his entrenchments around Jacksonville, and by blowing up two of his armed transport above Jacksonville and one below, put a complete stop to his navigation of the river above that city, and caused him to evacuate Palatka and to use the river below Jacksonville with the greatest caution.[4]

Union troops hastily began fortifying Jacksonville by constructing a line of entrenchments around the town, supported by redoubts. They built signal towers not only in Jacksonville but in Yellow Bluff and Mayport, providing a means of communications between these points. Gillmore hurriedly ordered the brigades of Adelbert Ames and Robert S. Foster to reinforce Jacksonville, and by February 25, Seymour had organized his forces into two divisions under Israel Vogdes and Ames.[5]

Confederate soldiers studied the Federal activity in and around Jacksonville, watching for any troop movements. One

Yellow Bluff Fort, Confederate entrenchments near Jacksonville. (Photo by J. Walker Fischer)

Confederate marker, Yellow Bluff Fort near Jacksonville. (Photo by Dave Page)

of these soldiers wrote his wife from Trout Creek. "I am station[ed] here permently [sic] that is as long as the Yankees remain in Jacksonville. It is one of the most important post[s] in the army (so says Genl. Anderson) Darling and I am proud I have charge of it. From here Darling I can see all the Yankee movements on the river."[6]

The soldier informed his wife of a narrow escape he and some fellow soldiers experienced one night. He stated that a Confederate officer, a Captain Bryant, had planned to place twelve torpedoes on the river below Jacksonville. But the Federals landed some two to three hundred troops in the area, and Captain Bryant and his party were forced to depart with their wagons and torpedoes.

"The yankees landed Darling not over a hundred yards from where we were encamped and march[ed] close by us," wrote the soldier. "I thought Darling my horse was gone that night certain. The night was dark—We could here [sic] them talking as the[y] marched by. I can tell you Darling after they got by we got out of this neck in a hurry and have returned here [Trout Creek] today."[7]

But, for the most part, time passed slowly and unevntfully, especially for Union troops in the area. An officer of a Massachusetts regiment stationed in Jacksonville following the engagement at Olustee, wrote to a Boston newspaper:

> Everything is quiet now, our forces are now entrenching themselves about ten miles from here. No sign of the enemy following. We are fortifying the town. We have a strong position; intrenchments [sic] in front, gunboats in the river on our flanks and open communications in our rear down the river, which the enemy cannot blockade as they did Little Washington in North Carolina, and men enough to man all the defences [sic] thoroughly. It does not appear probable that we shall be attacked. If the rebels come we are ready.[8]

A report from another Boston newspaper concurred:

> Large reinforcements are already on there [sic] way to Florida, so that we shall hold our position, and finally succeed in our expedition without doubt. It will interest many of your readers to know that among the force now in Florida is Foster's Brigade, of which I have spoken in a previous letter. At Hilton Head there was "mounting in hot haste," and the most energetic preparations to send men, stores and munitions to Florida. The Sanitary Commis-

> sion was already on the ground, and dispensed valuable aid. I have never seen evidence of greater energy that I saw at Hilton head all day the 22nd. There is a recompense in store for the rebel force in Florida if Gen. Gillmore [sic] can accomplish it.[9]

A report of March 12 stated that the defense of Jacksonville remained unchanged. "Our lines extend only six miles out of the city. The rebels are constructing earthworks at Cedar Creek, which doesn't look much if they intended attacking us, but if they do see fit to, they will have a sweet time of it."[10]

A gale and tornado struck the coast around Jacksonville that week, and many ships dragged their anchors in the harbor, many losing them. Jacksonville was totally isolated for three days with no communication, for the St. Johns Bar was difficult to get over. One ship, the *Burnside,* was lost and other ships remained in the harbor.

Within days, Seymour was given word that Dickison's cavalry was roaming the area, and he decided to occupy Palatka at once. Colonel William B. Barton, Forty-eighth New York Infantry, was ordered by Seymour, to proceed to Palatka at once and set up defensive works. He was to maintain a force of at least 500 men.[11]

A Confederate soldier hastily wrote his wife: "I am sorry I was not on the river yesterday as the day before two verry [sic] large transports propellers went up and I know they must have went down yesterday loaded with troops. A very large propeller transport has just gone up light and a large schooner came down this morning loaded. They are leaving Jacksonville fast—I sometimes think Darling they will leave a Gun boat or two there with negroe [sic] troops—but time will tell."[12]

On the 10th, Federal troops entered Palatka and occupied the town. Barton's troops met no resistance but were aware of Confederate cavalry pickets only nine miles away. Barton was also furnished information relating to other Confederate activity in the area: a small force at Gainesville, a thousand cavalry at Starke, pickets at Nine Mile Hammock on the Orange Springs Road, and more imposing pickets near Rice Creek Road, only four miles away.[13]

Learning of Barton's shaky position, General Gillmore ordered Palatka "fortified so that the position can be held against great odds. A fieldwork, enclosed with a formidable obstacle on all sides, will perhaps suffice, and no offensive operations involving the possibility of [another] defeat shall be undertaken till these defenses are in efficient condition."[14]

General Seymour visited Palatka the following day and ordered two or three siege guns for the redoubt in the center. Believing St. Augustine to be impregnable against any Confederate attack, he ordered some of its less important guns sent to Palatka.

Following the enemy toward the town of Palatka, Dickison and his force were informed that Union troops had occupied the town and were holding it with a force of over five thousand men. Since his own "invasion force" consisted of only 145 men, Dickison requested reinforcements from Lieutenant-Colonel Harris, of the Fourth Georgia Cavalry Regiment.[15]

Colonel Harris' command consisted of not more than one hundred and twenty-five men, but he answered Dickison's call by moving his force to Sweetwater Branch, only twelve miles from Palatka. Scouts were sent out by Dickison and Harris to ascertain the enemy's actual strength and position, and the following day Dickison and his company, with a detachment of the Fourth Georgia Cavalry, moved to the front to drive in the enemy's pickets.

One eighteen-year-old Floridian rode into Dickison's camp at Rolleston on the banks of the St. Johns River, six miles above his home, and enlisted in the company. Dickison's men were preparing to move camp across the river by Sweetwater Branch back of Palatka. The young man was called to picket duty the following morning with his squad and was ordered to move to a landing at the Rosignol place at the mouth of Rice Creek, five miles below Palatka.[16]

A couple days later, a picket reported a Federal gunboat steaming up the river about twenty miles below them. Dickison instructed his men to hold themselves in readiness and prepare for action should the gunboat attempt to land at Palatka. Dickison divided the company into two detachments, taking half his men to the right upon a river bluff; the others gathering in a ditch, back of Teasdale and Reid's wharf and warehouse.

All night, as the soldiers waited, they could hear workmen constructing a temporary wharf for the landing of one thousand Negro troops with white officers. These troops had been camped at Federal Point, Cornelius Dupont's wharf.

James M. Dancy, who rode with Dickison's men, recalled:

> As soon as the Federal gun boat approached this wharf, Cornelius Dupont, a neighbor living there, mounted his horse and rode as fast as he could to the plantation, where he notified my father of the landing of the troops. My father sent little William Dancy and one of the small Negro boys to the top of a corn house nearby to watch the road to the river, and to notify him when the troops came in sight. Instead the boys became busy at play and forgot their mission. Father was talking to Mr. Dupont, who was still on horseback, when the latter looked up. There in full sight were the glistening rifles of the oncoming troops."[17]

Confederate monument, Town Square, Palatka. (Photo by J. Walker Fischer)

The Federals wasted little time in unloading their cannon on the landing. According to Dancy's reminiscences, the enemy did not see Dickison and his men watching from the ditches nearby. Dickison opened fire with small arms. Dancy recalled:

> The men ashore ran for their lives. Capt. Dickinson [sic] could see cannon being unloaded; consequently, he decided to put a stop to this and opened fire. Hawsers were chopped in two aboard ship. Engines began to turn, and the ship moved out into the chan-

ALTHOUGH THE FLAG THEY DIED TO SAVE
FLOATS NOT O'ER ANY LAND OR SEA
THROUGHOUT ETERNAL YEARS SHALL WAVE
THE BANNER OF THEIR CHIVALRY.

Inscription, base of Confederate monument, Palatka. (Photo by J. Walker Fischer)

> nel. The next moment, shells began to explode. Capt. Dickinson's [sic] squad, after firing, started for our camp. We were the last to pass under the shell fire, one shell exploding under a corner of the building behind which we took refuge. About half way to our camp a twenty-inch shell struck a large pine tree about thirty feet from the ground, exploded, and tore that tree to splinters. That was the last shell fired, and we were safe in our camp.[18]

Dickison, however, was not to be outdone. He returned to camp with three captured pickets. Dr. R. B. Burroughs, the young surgeon of the Fourth Georgia Cavalry, was so overwhelmed with the Swamp Fox's fearlessness, he was moved to write about it. Although the Federals had followed Seymour's orders and had the town heavily fortified, Dickison's company skirmished with them continually over the six weeks they held the town.

On one occasion, Dickison and sixteen of his men were attacked by a battalion of Federals who moved on them unexpectedly. The skirmish lasted forty minutes, but Dickison held his position against the superior force. Only when the enemy was reinforced did Dickison order a slow and orderly retreat. Five Federal troops were killed during the skirmish, and another eight wounded.[19]

Tombstone in Westview Cemetery, Palatka. Alleged site of Battle of Palatka. (Photo by J. Walker Fischer)

Only a couple days later, Dickison took a position on a hill overlooking the city, which offered a full view of the occupied town. After again successfully driving in the Union pickets, Company H was ordered to outpost duty, keeping an eye on enemy movements in and around the town.

Gravestone of William Robertson, Company E, Twenty-fourth United States Colored Troops, Westview Cemetery, Battle of Palatka. (Photo by J. Walker Fischer)

Dickison then dispatched Second Lieutenant W. J. McEaddy with a small detachment to move close to the enemy pickets and obtain a better look at their movements. Following McEaddy's mission, Captain Dickison ordered a secret night expedition involving McEaddy and ten other men. The little mission proved very successful as McEaddy captured the entire picket of eight mounted soldiers.

Dickison was then ordered by department commander Colonel Tabb, to take his company and one from the Fourth Georgia and move to the front. If the enemy had changed its position, Dickison was to again drive in the pickets.

In capturing the Federal pickets, Dickison was fired upon, and two enemy regiments advanced on him. Confederates formed a line and held the advance in check, and the battle lasted four hours. Dickison then received orders to fall back to the Branch but disobeyed, believing the large force in front of him would route them.

The stalemate lasted until nightfall when Federal troops retreated, leaving eleven of their men killed and twenty-two wounded. None of Dickison's troops were hit, and he received a congratulatory letter from Colonel Tabb's adjutant.

On April 28, the Confederate command at Fort Milton received a report concerning the Federals, who, with a force of at least one regiment, were in the vicinity of Fort Butler. Authorities immediately notified Captain Dickison of the troop movement and instructed him to be on guard and to be prepared to move. On May 11, the Swamp Fox was informed another company of grey-clad soldiers would be arriving soon to assist him in strengthening his position.[20]

On May 20, Dickison learned the enemy had shifted its forces to the town of Welaka, and, taking two of his men, he hid in the swamp opposite the town. In observing Federal activity from the swamp for a full day, Dickison saw the possibility of a surprise attack.[21]

At sundown, the following day, Dickison, McEaddy, and thirty-five of their men, plus Captain Grey with twenty-five men, trekked nine miles to the banks of the St. Johns River. Under cover of darkness, they crossed the river, with sixty men in three rowboats. After walking another seven miles, they reached the Federal position at Welaka by daybreak.

Dividing his force, Dickison sent two units on the flank, while he attacked, capturing the pickets and completely surprising the enemy. The Swamp Fox had been given information from local residents who informed him the enemy had been using a building for their barracks. They also implied to him that the

Yankees were careless in their defensive precautions, since three roads intersected near the building, and no guards were posted on the northern road.

It was from this unguarded northern road that Dickison's forces attacked, and he ordered the commander of the Welaka garrison to surrender or face total annihilation. Without a single shot fired by the confused Federals, the garrison was surrendered at sunrise, and the Confederates entered the garrison just in time to appropriate the large, much welcomed Union breakfast.

Also appropriated by the Confederate raiders was a large bag of outpost mail, which was to be sent off the following day. This they read with great enjoyment, especially one letter from the company orderly sergeant, who, boasted to friends up north of an arranged and sure-fire plan to capture the Swamp Fox the following evening.

The next morning, a large Union cavalry force learned of the fall of Welaka and hurried to reclaim the town. Dickison, however, had been warned of the rescuing army and recrossed the river with sixty-two prisoners, including two officers who would later be sent to the prison camp at Andersonville, Georgia.

After a much-deserved rest in "Dixieland's" west bank, Dickison called his men to formation and asked for twenty-five volunteers to accompany him to the isolated outpost at Saunders, where another small Union force was encamped. The entire command stepped forward and volunteered, but Captain Dickison could only choose the number requested, since he had few boats to transport the men.

Selecting the twenty-five, Dickison, McEaddy, and company boarded the boats and, after crossing little Lake George, dropped anchor. Leaving three men to guard the boats, the Dickison men marched toward the unsuspecting Federals under cover of night. Dickison planned a surprise attack using the darkness as a cloak.

As they crept up on the enemy camp, Dickison anticipated an easy victory and had already composed a surrender document for the Federal commander to sign. Watching the enemy, they witnessed a Federal cavalryman some fifty yards away riding from a farmhouse. The startled Confederate marksmen drew their rifles, but their captain ordered them not to fire.

Instead, Captain Dickison's oldest son, Charlie, a sergeant in his father's company, led a detachment to storm the farmhouse. Meanwhile, Captain Dickison and others raced in pursuit of the retiring horseman, but they were unable to overtake him.

With his troops separated, Dickison sought the Federal encampment in the direction in which the rider had gone. After a ride of two miles, they sighted the Federal campfires and crept within two hundred yards of the enemy. A single rider, Lieutenant McEaddy, rode forward and demanded a surrender.

McEaddy was confronted by six confused Union cavalrymen but not until he was nearly among them. Detaining McEaddy, the Federal horsemen brought the document to their commanding officer, who was informed the camp was surrounded. The Federal officer, believing the deception, agreed to surrender, and Captain Dickison stepped from the bushes.

Dickison immediately had the captured arms and goods loaded safely on the boats with orders to push off without delay. Only then did the Federals learn they had surrendered their garrison of twenty-six men and six cavalry to only ten Confederates. Furthermore, their embarrassment increased with the realization they had done so without firing a single shot.

Recapturing twelve slaves and taking two wagons, the boats loaded with prisoners reached Dickison's camp the following morning. To avoid the federal cavalry patrolling the St. Johns, Sergeant Dickison, the captain's son, and his detachment, marched fifteen miles through the river swamp and reached the camp the next evening. Amid shouts of joy, their safe return was celebrated by Dickison and his men.

For his strategic victories, Dickison received two congratulatory letters from Assistant Adjutant-General W. G. Barth for his "gallant expedition against the enemy's detached post on the St. Johns," namely, Welaka and Fort Gates. The Dickison men were lauded for accomplishing this feat in only forty-eight hours and marching eighty-five miles, without the loss of a man. Barth added, "Such an exploit attests more emphatically the so truly courageous qualities of the gallant men and skillful leader who achieved it than any commendations it would be possible to give them."[22]

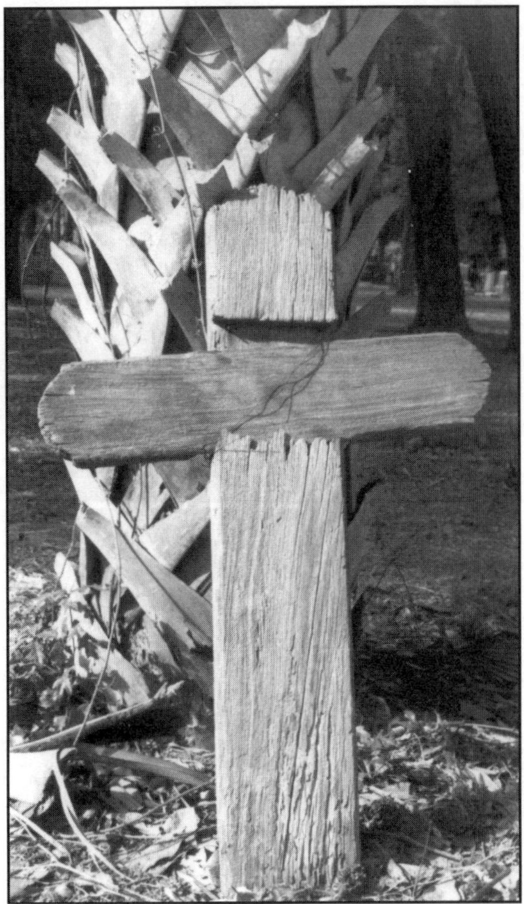

Rough-hewn marker, Westview Cemetery, alleged site of the Battle of Palatka. (Photo by J. Walker Fischer)

Notes

[1]Mary Elizabeth Dickison, *Dickison and His Men,* p. 49.

[2]Samuel Proctor, "Florida a Hundred Years Ago," March 5, 1864.

[3]Ibid., March 7, 1864.

[4]General James Patton Anderson, "Civil War Stories," Putnam County Clerk of Court.

[5]David James Coles, "Far From Fields of Glory: Military Operations in Florida During the Civil War, 1864-1865," pp. 187-188.

[6]David J. Coles and Zack C. Waters, "Indian Fighter, Confederate Soldier, Blockade Runner, and Scout: The Life and Letters of Jacob E. Mickler,"*El Escribano: The St. Augustine Journal of History,* pp. 22-23.

[7]Ibid.

[8]*Boston Journal,* March 1, 1864.

[9]*Boston Journal,* March 2, 1864.

[10]*Boston Herald,* March 18, 1864.

[11]Samuel Proctor, "Florida a Hundred Years Ago," March 9-10, 1864.

[12]David J. Coles and Zack C. Waters, "Indian Fighter, Confederate Soldier, Blockade Runner, and Scout: The Life and Letters of Jacob E. Mickler," *El Escribano: The St. Augustine Journal of History,* p. 23.

[13]Samuel Proctor, "Florida a Hundred Years Ago," March 9-10, 1864.

[14]Ibid., March 12-14, 1864.

[15]Mary Elizabeth Dickison, *Dickison and His Men,* pp. 49-52.

[16]James M. Dancy, *Florida Historical Quarterly,* Vol. 37, page 69.

[17]Ibid., p. 70-71.

[18]Ibid.

[19]Mary Elizabeth Dickison, *Dickison and His Men,* pp. 49-52.

[20]Samuel Proctor, "Florida a Hundred Years Ago," April 28, 1864 and May 11, 1864.

[21]David J. Coles, "Volusia County: The Land Warfare 1861-1865," *Civil War in Volusia County: A Symposium,* pp. 47-50; Mary Elizabeth Dickison, *Dickison and His Men,* pp. 57-61.

[22]Samuel Proctor, "Florida a Hundred Years Ago," May 23, 1864.

Chapter 6

Knight of the Silver Spurs

The fall of Welaka and Saunders was a shock to Federal leaders, and it was even more upsetting to the Volusia detachment, which was now totally cut off from support. Expecting to be attacked by Dickison at any moment, the defenders hastily began implementing defensive measures in the town. The Federal command at St. Augustine quickly sent out reinforcements to bolster the town's defenses.[1]

Justis Silliman of the Seventeenth Connecticut Regiment recalled having only "one broken shovel, one spade, two axes, and an old Southern bag with three tools," with which they, "commenced construction of a little fort on the crest of a little knoll . . . "[2]

Contrary to Federal fears, Dickison did not attack the Volusia garrison. Observing the number of enemy in the redoubt, and the reinforcements adding to that number, he felt his own force too inferior to mount such a foolish attack. He moved instead to intercept reinforcements from St. Augustine forming a new lifeline to Volusia, Welaka, Saunders, and other outposts in the vicinity.[3]

When their security was realized, the Federal commander at Volusia sent Lieutenant Albert Peck to scout on the conditions at Welaka, and attempt to aid another detachment that had somehow eluded capture by Dickison. With Sergeant D. S. Garritt and fourteen men, Peck set off on foot a little before midnight in the direction of Welaka.[4]

On route, the tiny expedition was met by a courier from the Seventy-fifth Ohio Mounted Infantry who informed them Welaka was in Dickison's hands. He added that Peck's men should get off the road as a great number of "Johnnies" were using it.

Making a hasty retreat, Peck's men stopped at a farmhouse, "appropriated" some horses, and rode four miles to where the Seventy-fifth Ohio was moving toward the front. Peck was advised by the Ohioans, to make his way to St. Augustine for there was a strong Confederate force under Captain Dickison in the immediate area.

"It was getting almost night and we found we would have to camp out somewhere," Peck later wrote in his memoirs. "We came to a small stream called Little Haw Creek, and we stopped there awhile to rest and posted a Picket across the stream while we were resting. One of our men named Kelly went up to a house a short distance from the creek to see if he could buy some milk to drink. He soon came running back and said they told him at the house that there were 40 Rebel Infantry coming right down the road, so we got the men posted so we could defend our position if we were attacked, and awaited their appearance, but they did not show up."[5]

Evading the would-be attackers, Peck's men returned to their regiment and marched with them to St. Augustine. Dickison had thoroughly confused them as to the locations and size of his force.[6]

Peck wrote: "We finally came into camp for the night after detailing a strong picket and got through the night without any trouble. The next morning the Ohio boys went on to follow up their Regiment and we marched on to St. Augustine and arrived there all right."[7]

Enraged by the attack on his outposts, Colonel William Noble, Commander of the troops at St. Augustine, ordered the Union gunboat *Columbine* to proceed to Volusia with a detachment of the Thirty-fifth United States Colored Troops. The *U.S.S. Columbine* had been supporting Federal movement up the St. Johns for several months and had gained a reputation as a powerful warship. The Confederates were in awe of it.[8]

A Massachusetts newspaper described the typical Federal gunboat being built at the time:

> It is built so that, when ready for service, little will be presented above the water line save the muzzles of the guns and the top of the smoke-stacks. All the machinery is under water, and this part is so divided into water-tight compartments, that, in case a ball should enter one, it can do no material damage. The sides are sloped at an angle of 45 degrees, and are covered with iron plates two and one half inches in thickness, securely bolted to each other and through the heavy timber beneath. Each plate has been submitted to adequate tests, and is calculated to resist any missile known to modern warfare.
>
> The bow is pierced with four port holes, through which will protrude the muzzles of four 32-pound Parrot guns; the stern will have two pieces of the same sort; the sides will have each, six of those formidable 10 inch columbiads, whose range is only equaled by anything a trifle less than infinity. The magazine is perfectly inaccessible to accidents of any kind, and placed below the water line.[9]

On March 13, the *Columbine* had been successful in capturing the Confederate river steamer *General Sumter* on Lake George, carrying passengers to the Oklawaha River. Acting Master John C. Champion, commanding a launch, took charge of the *Sumter.* Together, the *U.S.S. Columbine* and the *U.S.S. Pawnee*, pushed on up the St. Johns to Lake Monroe. At Deep Creek, they captured the steamer *Hattie Brock.*[10]

On the 21st of May, however, things were different. Confederate Lieutenant Mortimer Bates, from Captain Dunham's battery, reported to Captain Dickison at his headquarters near Palatka. With him was a detachment of twenty-five men, one section of artillery, one twelve-pound howitzer, and a Napoleon gun.[11]

Captain Dickison, anticipating heavy traffic in Federal gunboats due to his recent victories in the area rode out with Lieutenant Bates to find a suitable spot on the river to attack one of the gunboats. They had not ridden far when they were met by a courier who informed them the river was full of gunboats headed in their direction.

The Swamp Fox and another officer had been inspecting the terrain along the west bank of the river for gun placements when they saw the courier approaching at a rapid pace. As soon as the courier was within hearing distance of the two officers, he began shouting: "The river is full of Yankee gunboats coming up."[12]

Dickison ordered Bates to ride three miles back to camp, bring back his battery, and meet him on the hill overlooking Palatka. He also sent orders to second-in-command Captain Grey to gather all his cavalry and also meet them at the hill.[13]

As the command reported in full, they witnessed two gunboats and four transports coming up near Palatka. Captain Dickison quickly dismounted his cavalry and led his men at a run into Palatka where they concealed themselves in the very breastworks constructed by the Federals when they had occupied the town.

Two regiments of Federal troops landed in full view of the Confederates waiting in ambush, and, after moving into formation, they marched away in search of Dickison.[14] The Federal troops were those of Brigadier General George H. Gordon, Union Commander of the District of Florida, who had withdrawn his men from Volusia County because of Dickison" victories at Welaka and Saunders. Gordon's men consisted of troops from the 157th New York, reinforced with six companies of the Thirty-fifth United States Colored Troops. About 600 to 700 Union soldiers landed opposite Palatka. A frustrated Dickison watched from across the river, unable to reach them with his two light field guns.[15]

Moments later, the gunboat, *Columbine,* loaded with troops, passed by the breastworks. The Ottawa and transport Charles Houghton were still unloading troops at Palatka's landing. Dickison's men had only small arms and were not close enough to make any kind of assault, so he ordered them to lie quiet and just observe the ship.

When the gunboat had passed, Dickison took fifty men up the hill to where they had hidden their horses. Captain Grey was left at the breastworks with his men, while Dickison and company raced to Brown's Landing, three miles away, hoping to intercept the gunboat. They arrived only five minutes late.

With Captain Dickison was his good friend Reverend J. W. Thomas of Peniel. Like the Swamp Fox, Reverend Thomas had moved to Florida from South Carolina, and, also like the captain, he was considered a "gallant Confederate soldier."[16]

Dickison rode up river and located the *Columbine* once more. Hiding himself behind a large cypress tree, Dickison watched the boat as it passed only fifty feet from him. Then he dashed back to Palatka.[17]

On the way to town, Dickison was met by one of Lieutenant Grey's couriers, who conveyed news to him that the largest and most-feared vessel on the St. Johns during the war, the gunboat *Ottawa*, was coming up the river. The *Ottawa*, carrying twelve guns, two of them 200-pound rifles, was escorting the transport *Charles Houghton,* which had just landed the troops on the east bank of the river.

Dickison ordered all his men back to Brown's Landing where he instructed Lieutenant Bates to move his artillery into the swamp near the landing. Here they had a full view of the *Ottawa*, at anchor some two hundred yards from the landing. At dusk, the Federals lighted up their boats, making them an easy target. The Confederates fired on both the gunboat and the transport.[18]

According to one of Dickison's soldiers: "The boats anchored not more than 200 yards from the landing where with the coming of darkness Dixie had unlimbered his field pieces. He got in some 30 rounds before the gunboat was ready for action. The gunboat hoisted anchor meanwhile and although badly crippled left the scene."[19]

The surprised Federals reacted in a state of confusion, and a full twenty-eight rounds (not thirty) were fired by the Confederates before the enemy responded with fire power of its own. The transport was hit and, badly crippled from the Confederate shelling, moved away without firing a single shot.[20]

"Before the *Ottawa* answered with a heavy broadside Dixie had his guns moved to a new position," continued the Dickison man. "The Ottawa was so badly damaged she did not move off until some time the next day."[21]

The *Ottawa* then poured a heavy retaliation into the concealed Confederates but, in the darkness, could only locate the attackers by the flash of their guns. Yet, it was more than enough to discourage the Dickison men who were not armed for this type of conflict.[22]

Ordering Lieutenant Bates to gather his men and artillery, the Confederates slipped away into the night. The *Ottawa* had been hit badly enough to be detained for thirty hours, with several of its crew killed or wounded. There was not a single casualty among the Confederates.[23]

The *Houghton* returned to Jacksonville while Commander S. Livingston Breese and his crippled *Ottawa* followed the next day after repairs had been made.[24]

According to a Dickison's man, the gunboats were passing along the St. Johns River and Dunn's Creek to Dunn's Lake, and into the mouth of Haw Creek. The owners of river steamers had sunk their boats in this deep water and the Federal expedition was sent to raise them for use.[25]

The following day, May 23, Dickison ordered Lieutenant Bates to gather a battery of sixteen sharpshooters, four men from each of the four companies. After leaving Captain Grey to guard their camp, Dickison and his troops marched to Horse Landing, some six miles from the scene of their engagement with the *Ottawa*.[26]

At Horse Landing, Dickison's sharpshooters positioned themselves behind cypress trees, with the bigger guns placed on the wharf. Concealment was difficult because the low, flat land was

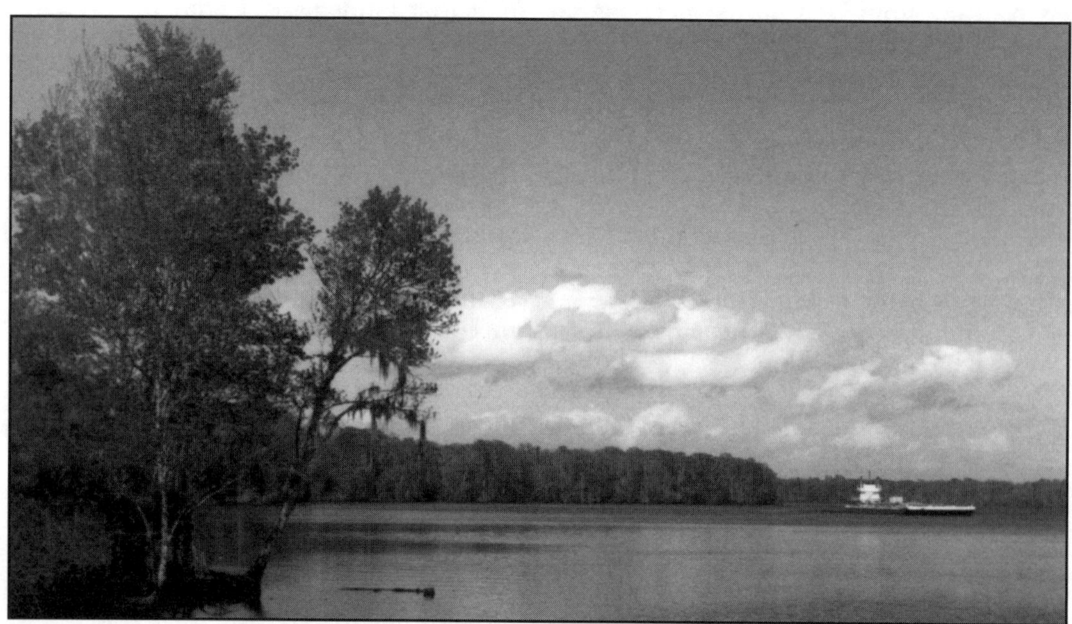

Horse Landing, St. Johns River, looking north from west bank near Palatka. (Photo by J. Walker Fischer)

but inches above the water although the men took positions behind low bushes and tall pines.

According to one of Dickison's men: "There was no ambush, from the fact that Horse Landing is low and flat, the land being but a few inches above the level of the water, and surrounded by low bushes and tall pines. The cannon were placed in the open space used for the landing in plain view of the river."[27]

Dickison stood by the side of the wharf where he could see any naval activity a half mile off. Since the *Columbine* had passed up the river the night before, Dickison was sure the vessel would be returning before long.

The men waited patiently from their concealment with their eyes on the river for the *Columbine*. Noon came with still no sign of the vessel. As the afternoon wore on, the men began to get restless. Dickison, however, continually shouted encouragement, instructing the men to hold their positions.[28]

At three o'clock in the afternoon, the gunboat came in sight, as smoke from the funnels was spotted. Soon the hull loomed large before them, and all eyes watched Captain Dickison to give the command to fire.

As one writer penned, "On the horizon, a spreading band of black smoke heralded the fast approach of the *United States Gunboat Columbine*. Somewhere in the thunderheads to the east, destiny must have smiled and settled back for this incident of war."[29]

The Federal Government had purchased the *Columbine* on December 12, 1862, from Peter Schultz for $25,800. The gunboat weighed 133 tons with a twenty-foot beam and a draft of six feet. Alterations had been made by Howe and Copeland of New York at a cost of $6,233.10.[30]

The *Columbine* was a converted steam tug 117 feet in length, drawing only six feet of water. This side-wheeler was armed with two twenty-four-pound Naval howitzers, protected by sandbags. She carried a force of black troops with white officers besides her own crew. As she neared Dickison, the *Columbine* began firing shells at Horse Landing. The crew had been warned to expect trouble at the landing once rounding the turn at Possum Bluff north of Welaka.[31]

Dickison permitted the *Columbine* to pass within sixty yards of the landing, and, then, ordered his men to open fire. The Swamp Fox's timing was perfect; when the gunboat passed opposite his guns, they were ready to fire again.[32]

"Hearing the boat approaching the men were ordered to climb into branches of the trees, and as soon as the boat came within range, opened fire on her, which was promptly returned from the steamer with shot and shell," recalled a Dickison man. "The sharp shooters killed several on the boat, but the trunks of the trees furnished them ample and safe protection."[33]

Acting Ensign Frank Sanborn, commander of the *Columbine*, had a premonition he might be attacked by infantry at Horse Landing, but he never expected Confederate artillery. "I could discover nothing suspicious until directly abreast the landing, distant about 100 yards, when two pieces of artillery, concealed by the shrubbery and undergrowth, almost simultaneously opened fire on me."[34]

The second volley of Confederate fire cut the wheel chains of the *Columbine*, taking out the steering and soon stranding it on a sandbar in the river.[35] The *Columbine* carried a pair of thirty-two-pounder cannons and 148 men, all with small rifle arms, and these weapons returned the fire on the concealed Confederates. The battle lasted about forty-five minutes.[36]

According to the Dickison man who participated in the capture: "When the boat got directly opposite the landing, the six-pounders were fired, but two shots were enough. One cut the rudder chain, while the other struck the piston rod on its descending stroke and flattened it so useless. There was a large number of negroes on board, and as they had been taught that Dickison would kill them as soon as they fell into his hands, they became thoroughly panic-stricken, and as soon as the boat was disabled twenty-nine of them jumped overboard and were drowned."[37]

Sanborn had rushed to the *Columbine*'s forward gun, but the steam was gone, and Dickison's riflemen and Bates' grapeshot had cleared the quarterdeck. With the aft gun abandoned, Sanborn ordered Acting Master's Mate W. B. Spencer to rally the men, but most had already jumped over the side. Under heavy Confederate fire, the wheel jammed, and, his engine gone, the Federals ran up the white flag.[38]

A 12-pound case shot, fired into
the vessel by Dickison's men.

A twelve-pound case shot, fired into the *Columbine* by Dickison's men, Jacksonville Maritime Museum. (Photo by J. Walker Fischer)

Upon being grounded on the sandbar the *Columbine*'s pilot jumped ship and ran into the woods. The Federal sailors and soldiers, without the benefit of ship or captain, were unable to withstand the scorching blast of the Dickison men, and many more of them jumped overboard to save themselves.[39]

Sanborn valiantly remained with his ship, refusing to give up the fight, but

Model of Union gunboat similar to the *Columbine* at Jacksonville Maritime Museum. (Photo by J. Walker Fischer)

when his guns were abandoned, he had no choice but to surrender the *Columbine*.[40] Dickison recalled:

"We continued to pour canister and solid shot, while our sharpshooters kept a constant and well-directed fire until she [the *Columbine*] became unable to manage her guns. Our battery shot with much precision, nearly every shot taking effect, riddling her very badly."[41]

With the raising of a white flag, Sanborn went ashore in a launch and discussed terms of surrender with Captain Dickison. Sanborn was concerned that both his black and white soldiers might not be treated well, but Dickison gave his word they would be treated with all due respect. Then, Sanborn surrendered himself, officers, vessel, and crew to the Confederate States of America.[42]

When Lieutenant Bates received the surrender, he found only sixty-six of the one hundred forty-eight men alive, and a third of these were badly wounded. Sanborn represented the only officer not killed or wounded, and requested the body of his first lieutenant be wrapped in a United States flag and returned to Federal headquarters for internment. Dickison complied with the request.[43]

Since many of the Federals from the *Columbine* jumped ship, took to the woods or were met by the two infantry squads then scouring the countryside in search of Dickison, mortality figures in this conflict tend to be a matter of conjecture. Sanborn claimed to have lost seventeen men killed or missing, and five wounded, a much more modest figure than that set by Dickison. In addition to the sixty-four Yankees taken prisoner, Dickison's men captured forty-two rifles, twenty-eight cartridge boxes, 2,000 rounds of ammunition, five swords, two boats and much more needed equipment.[44]

The two Dahlgren Naval howitzers captured by the Confederates were likely quite crude. One of the sailors, Drover

Dickison's capture of the Union gunboat *Columbine* on the St. Johns River near Horse Landing, May 1864. (Courtesy Florida State Archives, reproduced from *Dickison and His Men*)

Edwards, who swam the river and escaped, later recalled that the forward gun, before the grounding, had to be shifted from one side to the other.[45]

One of the officers captured, Major General Foster, was in command of the Union forces operating in the St. Johns Valley. Major Foster related to Dickison that the Union was making an all out effort to capture him, and that two regiments had landed at Palatka and were scouring the countryside looking for the Swamp Fox and his command.[46]

In a letter to Octavia Stephens from her sister-in-law Augustina Stephens, written just after the capture of the *Columbine*, the writer stated:

> As the boat approached the wharf area, Captain J. J. Dickison had his men hide in the brush. *Columbine,* moving slowly, was visible a half mile away; although she carried dread missiles of destruction, she was still truly a thing of beauty. When *Columbine* was within sixty yards of the hidden men, they opened fire, then used the moments of sudden confusion on board to reload their guns. As she came directly opposite the ambushers, they were ready to fire again, disabling the boat. She struck a sandbar, where her crew battled the Rebel bushwhackers [forty-five] minutes before she surrendered. After the prisoners, the dead and wounded were removed, *Columbine* was set afire to keep her out of the hands of the Federal soldiers, in several gunboats further down the river. The *Columbine* had been almost entirely new and considered a very fast and superior boat."[47]

Dickison reported that "never did a command fight with more gallantry than the artillery and sharpshooters, every man displaying remarkable coolness and bravery."[48]

The capture of the *Columbine* was doubly rewarding for Dickison since soldiers from that ship had harassed citizens of Palatka during the past year. William D. Moseley, former Florida governor and oldest citizen in Palatka, had been taken aboard the *Columbine* and interrogated. When asked if there were any rebel soldiers in town, he replied that all able-bodied men had gone off to war leaving only women and old men. Shortly after, one of Dickison's men was discovered walking down Lemon Street. Angry Federals threw ex-Governor Moseley in jail and destroyed considerable property belonging to him.[49]

With the now-mended gunboat *Ottawa* still in the area, Dickison found it necessary to burn the *Columbine* for fear of its falling back into enemy hands. He did, however, make preparations for appropriating the two Dahlgren guns and various boat machinery. The guns, he hoped, could be repaired and used against the Federal gunboats.[50]

Fifteen Federal prisoners from the *Columbine* were sent by train to Savannah. Between fifty and sixty Negro troops from the ship, most of whom were runaway slaves from North Carolina, were imprisoned at Lake City. The *Savannah News* reported, "the white prisoners who have arrived were surprised to find that they were so well treated, and that their fare should be so abundant. They were under the impression that the people of the South were on the verge of starvation."[51]

Following the capture of the *Columbine*, Dickison was forced to move out, according to one of his men: "Around the bend in the river, below the landing, another gunboat was anchored, and fearing that it would come to the relief of the *Columbine*, General Dickison quickly took off the prisoners from the captured boat. The boat drifted ashore, when all the combustable [sic] material at hand was gathered and piled on deck and fired, when the boat was left to burn. The other gunboat, fearing a similar fate, quickly steamed up and left for Jacksonville."[52]

With his prisoners secured, Dickison was able to focus his attention on other Federal activities in and about the St. Johns River. His capture of the *Columbine* was a major embarrassment to the Federal Government, and coming directly after his victories at Welaka and Saunders, Dickison appeared to roam "Dixieland" at will.

Returning to Horse Landing from Lake City, Dickison ordered that his wagons were to be loaded with any machinery of value and taken to their camp. A false rumor was circulated by one of the men who thought the machinery was being taken to the Suwannee River to be placed in a gunboat for breaking the blockade at Cedar Keys.

A Dickison man recalled years later:

> The bodies of the negroes who had jumped overboard were washed ashore, and when the wagons returned to the landing for the machinery they presented a horrible sight, the most of their flesh having been eaten by buzzards. One of the soldiers with the wagon train, Dr. Stringfellow, of Gainesville, cracked the thigh bone of one of these deceased brothers who fought so well, and oiled his rusty rifle while waiting. The heavy machinery was hauled through the woods, as Mud Mill Bridge was too weak for such a load, and Rossignol of Palatka was the pilot who led the way under the direction of Captain R. J. Adams.[53]

Following their capture of the *Columbine*, Dickison and his men rode into Orange Springs and attended worship services at the Orange Spring Community Church. Built in 1852, the church also served as a Confederate hospital and burial place for both Confederate and Union soldiers.[54]

To the women of Orange Springs, and for that matter, all over Florida, Dickison was more than a hero; he had become a legend. Indebted to Captain Dickison for the defense of their homes, chastity, and household goods, the ladies of Orange Springs presented him with a pair of silver spurs. These tokens of gratitude were made from old family heirlooms and relics of silver long preserved with scrupulous care, melted in a crucible cut from a firebrick, and fashioned entirely with a hammer in their own little village.[55]

In receiving the gift, Dickison expressed his gratitude for the kindly remembrance and the touching expression of friendship from the fair maids and matrons of Orange Springs. He went on to describe the "sweet breathings of sympathy which arose from their pure souls," and "in a pious and heart-thrilling refrain, were particularly soothing to man's spirit in an hour when Fate, treacherous to Nature, seemed to conspire with the powers of Darkness, and to give to Might the sacred privilege of Right. Even at an instant when the star of peace was shedding no beauteous light upon the oppressed Southland's darkened pathway, their gracious smiles and their generous plaudits were, to the very best of his judgment, a most precious guerdon."[56]

He added that the memorials of their virtue would be engraved upon his heart forever, and their names would be recorded in Lamb's "Book of Life." This, he went on, "is the earnest prayer of your loyal friend and obedient servant."[57]

The ladies of Orange Springs were mesmerized. The Confederacy was honored. And from that day forward, Captain J. J. Dickison, the only cavalryman in history to capture a gunboat, was revered throughout Florida, and even beyond its borders, as "the Knight of the Silver Spurs."[58]

Notes

[1]David J. Coles, "Volusia County: The Land Warfare 1861-1865," *Civil War in Volusia County: A Symposium,* p. 47.

[2]Edward Marcus, Editor, *A New Canaan Private in the Civil War: Letters of Justis Silliman, 17th Connecticut Volunteers,* New Canaan, Connecticut, New Canaan Historical Society, 1984, p. 71.

[3]David J. Coles, "Volusia County: The Land Warfare 1861-1865," *Civil War in Volusia County: A Symposium,* pp. 47-49.

[4]The Albert Peck Papers, Florida State Archives, Bureau of Archives and Records Management, Tallahassee, Florida.

[5]Ibid.

[6]David J. Coles, "Volusia County: The Land Warfare 1861-1865," *Civil War in Volusia County: A Symposium,* pp. 47-49.

[7]The Albert Peck Papers, Florida State Archives.

[8]David J. Coles, "Volusia County: The Land Warfare 1861-1865, *Civil War in Volusia County: A Symposium,* pp. 47-49; David James Coles, "Far From Fields of Glory: Military Operations in Florida During the Civil War, 1864-1865," p. 215.

[9]*Worcester Aegis and Transcript,* December 7, 1861.

[10]Samuel Proctor, "Florida a Hundred Years Ago," March 13, 1864.

[11]Mary Elizabeth Dickison, *Dickison and His Men,* p. 62.

[12]Untitled manuscript in Putnam County Archives and History.

[13]Mary Elizabeth Dickison, *Dickison and His Men,* p. 62.

[14]Ibid.

[15]Vince Murray, "Captain J. J. Dickison Marion County's Civil War Hero," *Ocala Star-Banner,* 1997, Internet.

[16]"Rebels of Palatka," Internet, p. 6.

[17]Mary Elizabeth Dickison, *Dickison and His Men,* p. 62.

[18]Ibid.; Jack Harper, "He Drove Yankees from St. Johns River," *Florida Times Union,* February 6, 1984.

[19]*The Tampa Tribune,* August 28, 1960.

[20]Mary Elizabeth Dickison, *Dickison and His Men,* p. 62.

[21]*The Tampa Tribune,* August 28, 1960.

[22]Mary Elizabeth Dickison, *Dickison and His Men,* p. 62.

[23]Ibid.

[24]Vince Murray, "Captain J. J. Dickison Marion County's Civil War Hero," *Ocala Star-Banner.*

[25]James M. Dancy, "Reminiscences of the Civil War," *Florida Historical Quarterly,* pp. 77-78.

[26]Mary Elizabeth Dickison, *Dickison and His Men,* p. 62.

[27]*Palatka Daily News,* Tuesday Morning, May 24, 1887. Transcribed copy at Putnam County Archives and History.

[28]Untitled manuscript in Putnam County Archives and History.

[29]Gene Gallant, "The Gray Fox of the Confederacy," Putnam County Archives and History.

[30]Frederick Williams, "The *Columbine*—Legends, Facts and Artifacts," October 1979, Putnam County Archives and History.

[31]Frederick Williams, "The Action at Horse Landing," talk delivered to Kirby-Smith Camp, Sons of Confederate Veterans at Jacksonville, on October 6, 1979. Transcript Putnam County Archives and History.

[32]Mary Elizabeth Dickison, *Dickison and His Men,* p. 62.

[33]*Palatka Daily News,* May 24, 1887.

[34]*Official Records of the Union and Confederate Navies in the War of the Rebellion,* 30 volumes, Series 1, Volume 15, pp. 441-454.

[35]David J. Coles, "Volusia County: The Land Warfare 1861-1865," *Civil War in Volusia County: A Symposium,* p. 49.

[36]Mary Elizabeth Dickison, *Dickison and His Men,* p. 66.

[37]*Palatka Daily News,* May 24, 1887.

[38]Vince Murray, "Captain J. J. Dickison Marion County's Civil War Hero," *Ocala*

Star-Banner; Ianthe Bond Hazel, "A Unique Battle," *The Civil War in Volusia County,* p. 20.

[39]David J. Coles, "Volusia County: The Land Warfare 1861-1865," *Civil War in Volusia County A Symposium,* p. 49.

[40]Richard P. Weinert, "The Confederate Swamp Fox," Putnam County Archives and History.

[41]*Official Records of the Union and Comfederate Navies in the War of the Rebellion,* Series 1, Volume 15, pp. 441-454.

[42]David J. Coles, "Volusia County: The Land Warfare 1861-1865," *Civil War in Volusia County: A Symposium,* p. 49.

[43]Mary Elizabeth Dickison, *Dickison and His Men,* pp. 66-67.

[44]David J. Coles, "Volusia County: The Land Warfare 1861-1865," *Civil War in Volusia County: A Symposium,* pp. 49-50.

[45]Frederick Williams, "The *Columbine*—Legend, Facts and Artifacts," Putnam County Archives and History.

[46]J. J. Dickison, "Civil War Stories," Putnam County Clerk of Court.

[47]MatiBelle Reeder, *History of Welaka 1853-1935,* Welaka, Privately Printed, no publication date given, p. 5.

[48]Vince Murray, "Captain J. J. Dickison Marion County's Civil War Hero," *Ocala Star-Banner.*

[49]Frederick Williams, "The Columbine—Legend, Facts and Artifacts," Putnam County Archives and History.

[50]David J. Coles, "Volusia County: The Land Warfare 1861-1865," *Civil War in Volusia County: A Symposium,* p. 50.

[51]Samuel Proctor, "Florida a Hundred Years Ago," May 30, 1864.

[52]*Palatka Daily News,* May 24, 1887.

[53]Ibid.

[54]"History of Florida's Oldest Remaining House of Worship 'The Orange Spring Community Church,'" Putnam County Archives and History.

[55]Mary Elizabeth Dickison, *Dickison and His Men,* pp. 216-221.

[56]Ibid.

[57]Ibid.

[58]One of the Columbine's spent shells sits at the base of the Confederate Soldier Memorial in Palatka on the courthouse lawn. An inscription reads:

"Although the flag they died to save floats not over land or sea

Throughout eternal years shall wave the banner of their chivalry."

Chapter 7

"Joe, I Am Killed"

Repeated setbacks on the part of the Federals kept the interior of Florida in Confederate hands. By May 1864, following the capture of the *Columbine*, the Federals had almost completely withdrawn to the coast, and many departed Florida soil for good to fight in major campaigns north of the state. Instead of pushes by major Federal armies, marauding parties swooped down on tiny communities destroying anything in their way, and moving on to vent more terror.[1]

General Finegan reported, "They [Negro troops] are making prisoners of all male citizens found in Jacksonville, on the St. Johns River, who refuse to take the oath of allegiance, and holding them as hostages for their Negro troops. They are robbing and plundering everything on the east bank of the St. Johns River, which is protected from us by their gunboats, and the river at almost all points above here is very wide and impassable without large boats."[2]

One female Floridan physician, Dr. Ellen Fitzpatrick McCallum Hazel, was arrested as a spy when a Federal gunboat landed at Orange Mills. She was suspected of giving information to her husband, John Bland Hazel, who was under the command of Captain Dickison. Taken sixty-five miles by gunboat to Jacksonville, she disembarked and began walking ahead. Ordered back by the officer, she defiantly informed him that she needed to purchase some clothing and then exclaimed, "You can't hold me prisoner. I am a British subject." Fearing an international incident, the officer released her. She purchased her cloth and returned to Orange Mills and continued administering to Dickison's troops.[3]

Also by May, the problem with deserters became completely out of control. Some deserters, conscripts and Union men, organized into armed groups, and one of these, the "Independent Union Rangers," even boasted a constitution. Many of these mercenaries, recruited from the illiterate backwoods areas of western and central Florida, raided the wealthy plantations, stealing and inciting Negro slaves.[4]

Lieutenant-Colonel John W. Pearson, a friend of Dickison's, and like him a former South Carolinian, also led a company of "irregulars" or guerrillas. In a report to Brigadier-General Richard F. Floyd, commanding Florida state troops, Pearson was appalled by the cooperation shown between Floridians and Federal troops during his campaign along the St. Johns River:

> I regret very much to report to you that at least three-fourths of the people on the St. Johns River and east of it are aiding and abetting the enemy; we could see them at all times through the day communicating with the vessel in their small boats. It is not safe for a small force to be on the east side of the river; there is great danger of being betrayed to the enemy.[5]

But Dixieland, the Dickison-controlled west bank of the river, remained solidly in Confederate hands. Following his capture of the *Columbine* of May 23, and his disposition of prisoners and arms, Dickison returned to his headquarters at Palatka. During the critical months of June and July, Dickison's command patrolled the St. Johns, continuing to wage guerilla warfare.[6]

One grateful Floridian woman, Mrs. Julia Simmons Haisley, praised Dickison for his courage against the always larger Federal force. "There was a commander here with a company of brave men, and at every point he [Dickison] met them. When they thought they had informed themselves of his whereabouts and started in a contrary direction, they would suddenly be confronted by the ubiquitous Captain J. J. Dickison and [be] driven back."[7]

On June 9, Union General William Birney dispatched a letter to the "Commanding Officer of Confederate Forces," inquiring as to the fate of prisoners taken by Dickison from the *Columbine*: "The relatives, friends, and comrades of the men in that unfortunate vessel are anxious to know their fate. I will promptly communicate to them such information as you may think proper to give."[8]

General William Birney had risen through the ranks after participating in the battles of First Bull Run and Chancellorsville. Birney had expedited emancipation for blacks in Maryland by recruiting slaves into seven colored units, and commanded his own units in South Carolina and Olustee, Florida. His brother, Union Major General David B. Birney, one of the most ardent enemies of slavery among Federal leaders, served in several major campaigns.[9]

Following a small but bitter engagement on McGirt's Creek, Birney received general instructions detailing the disposition of Federal troops, which would be used to stave off attacks by Dickison and other Confederate leaders in the area. Conceding the west bank to Dickison, Birney was ordered to hold as much of the east bank of the St. Johns River as possible. Jacksonville was set up again as a base of operations for that mission, and also Fort Clinch, which commanded the entrance to St. Mary's Sound. The main Federal force would be concentrated at Jacksonville, with a regiment of white troops at St. Augustine, and a regiment of mounted troops picketed at the junction of roads leading from Picolata and St. Augustine southward. In addition, forces would be stationed at both Yellow Bluff and St. Johns Bluff with pickets guarding railroad bridges and crossings to annoy the enemy as much as possible.[10]

Still, General George H. Gordon of the Union army was not completely satisfied with the way in which the St. Johns and its tributaries were patrolled. More gunboats were given assignments on the St. Johns, and two boats, one from Jacksonville and one from Mandarin, would meet, turn back, and repeat the operation.[11]

By June 20, General William Birney felt so secure with his Federal occupation policy, he journeyed from Jacksonville to St. Augustine without a guard. "On the whole, I consider the line as safe certainly as the one between New York and Philadelphia."[12]

Considering the state of affairs, it was a ludicrous statement. Not even three months earlier, Confederates had placed twelve torpedoes in the St. Johns River near Mandarin Point, and the United States transport *Maple Leaf,* carrying three regiments of Federal troops, was blown out of the water. On April 16, the transport *Hunter* was destroyed by a torpedo near the sight of the *Maple Leaf,* and on May 9, the *Harriet A. Weed* met a similar fate in the same location. Federalization of the St. Johns was anything but complete.[13]

A Confederate artillery officer wrote, "This will be a wholesome lesson to the Rascals, and their future navigation of the St. Johns will be with fear and trembling."[14]

Dickison's conquests, coupled with the torpedoing of Federal transports, made light of Birney's theory. In the past month, he had successfully harassed the redoubt at Palatka, forcing a Federal withdrawal; won easy victories at both Welaka and Saunders; and captured the Federal gunboat *Columbine.* He had been a thorn in Birney's side and would continue to be until after the war.[15]

It is unlikely Federal Headquarters at Hilton Head, South Carolina, agreed with Birney's assessment, judging from the order sent him on July 16, less than a month after his statement:

> If you cannot properly guard the St. Johns River you must prepare to make St. Augustine your base, keeping Jacksonville and Picolata as advanced points of defense if practicable. In case of immediate danger of the St. Johns River being rendered impracticable for navigation by reason of their planting a great number of torpedoes in the river, the communication from Jacksonville to St. Augustine must be by ferry across the river, which you must provide in season, and by land across the country.[16]

On July 31, Confederate Brigadier-General John K. Jackson, requested Adjutant-General Cooper to confer the rank of Colonel to Captain Dickison. According to the communication, "Captain Dickison, in his recent operations against the enemy in South Florida, displayed in an unusual degree, the qualifications necessary for an efficient cavalry leader."[17]

The communication went on to praise Dickison's capture of the Union gunboat *Columbine*, a feat almost unheard of by a small force of infantry and artillery. Dickison, it continued, "has given his troops and the citizens of South Florida the most unbounded confidence in him. The citizens," it went on, "will rally to him more freely than to any other officer, and with the command to which I could assign him as Colonel, the richest cattle and sugar regions of the state can probably be protected."[18]

Since beef cattle were vital to the Confederate army, Jackson had hoped, by promoting Dickison, he would be able to ward off Union troops, who were continually raiding the cattle drives in an effort to starve the Southern army.

Due to this pressure, the Confederacy had dropped draft exemptions for cattlemen early in February, and scores of area men had rushed to join the Florida Second Cavalry. With their own horses and riding expertise, they were a welcome addition to the tiny bands of Confederate faithfuls who were defending Florida.[19]

Captain James McKay proposed a special Confederate unit known as the "Cow Cavalry," which offered local men a way out of the draft and service on a remote battlefield, by keeping them in the area to defend cattle operations. Cattle supply operations had been suspended for months, but by the fall of 1864, the Cow Cavalry had reestablished an uneasy control over the ranges, taking some pressure off Dickison, who was already guarding some of these drives. Dickison, and the other irregulars, protecting the interior, were thus able to concentrate their efforts on more pressing matters.

When Dickison and his constituents were engaged in these more pressing operations, some loyal citizens, unlike those who conspired with the Federals, had to fend for themselves.

A number of Dickison's band hailed from the Tomoka Settlement in Volusia County, an area which remained pro-Confederate throughout the war. Enlistees included boys as well as men. Typical of these recruits was Private Francis M. Clifton, who had joined Dickison's band in 1862 at the age of fourteen.

However, many women in the Tomoka Settlement had husbands and sons involved in the struggle in other theaters north of the Florida border and were left on their own. One woman, Mrs. Mary Harper, was visited by Federal raiders who appropriated her cattle for the Union cause.

Mrs. Harper cleverly outwitted the military force. The Federal detachment, unsure of the way back to camp, trustingly accepted directions offered by Mrs. Harper.

The cattle trampled into a miserable swamp and were lost. The conquering Federal army had been bettered by a Florida housewife.[20]

Having received orders from headquarters to report immediately with his command, Captain Dickison rode in the direction of Lake City. Enroute, he was stopped by a courier, who reported the enemy had landed another large force at Palatka. Sending Captain Grey forward with his command to Lake City, Dickison retired to his camp.[21]

Finding Palatka, his home base, again occupied by the enemy, Dickison ordered his entire command back. Upon awaiting their return, Dickison took a small detachment, under Lieutenant Dell from Captain Rou's company, and with fifteen men, attempted to prevent a move on the part of the Federals into the interior.

A skirmish with Federal cavalry followed, but in finding the enemy's numbers too great, Dickison fell back, pursued by his adversaries. The Federals pursued Dickison for half a mile, captured three of his pickets and took over his camp. Refusing to evacuate the area, Dickison dispatched Lieutenant Dell to Orange Springs for reinforcements from Captain W. A. Owens' State Militia.

During the night, Company H returned from Lake City. In the early hours of the morning, Dickison sent Lieutenant McEaddy out to scout the enemy. McEaddy was informed at a farmhouse that the enemy was at the next plantation and called Dickison forward.

Tomoka Settlement Cemetery, near Ormond Beach. Graves of Mary Harper and a Dickison man. (Photo by Audrey Parente)

Moving slowly, Dickison's advance caught up with the Federal rear guard, and a battle ensued. Dickison quickly rode up in front of his troops, well in the line of fire, and the 280 cavalry men, brandishing Spencer rifles, navy pistols, and sabers, charged the Federal line. Several Confederate charges were made before the Federals began to retreat.

It was vital for Dickison to strike fast and end the contest. Only six miles away, in the town of Palatka, a force of infantry and artillery, with from three to four thousand troops, lusted for action.

There were more charges and counter-charges with about thirty men on each side engaging in hand-to-hand fighting. In the midst of the furor, a Union officer ordered a cease-fire, and while many Confederates were halfway through the enemy lines, they were under the impression the Federals were surrendering. Captain Dickison, also believing the Federals were surrendering, called a cease-fire and dashed down the lines to cut off any would-be escape routes.

But the Federals had no intention of quitting, and seeing the Confederates fall for the ruse, opened a deadly fire upon them. Sergeant Charlie Dickison, son of Captain Dickison, with four other Confederates, were on the opposite side of the enemy's column from the captain, and were caught in a hail of bullets.

Young Dickison was hit. Shot through the heart, he fell from his horse, and called out to his comrade, Sergeant J. C. Crews, "Joe, I am killed." Crews, oblivious to his own dangerous position, leaped from his horse and took young Dickison in his arms. Crews shouted for Captain Dickison, who worked himself around the Union column toward his dying son. When the captain got to him, Charlie Dickison was dead.[22]

Almost as if on cue, the Federals retreated. Dickison ordered Lieutenant McEaddy to take the command and pursue the force, all the while guarding the Confederate rear. Captain Dickison, crushed and silent, carried his dead son on horseback back to their encampment six miles away. Here, Dickison chose a detail of six men under Sergeant Crews to transport the remains of his firstborn son to the ladies of Orange Springs for care and burial. Fearful the enemy would return with a larger force the next day, the grieving father returned to his post and responded to his sense of duty by keeping watch for the enemy attack.

Instead of mounting another offensive, the large Federal force evacuated their stronghold during the night, fearing Dickison's troops were an advance of a larger force that would, in turn, launch a full-scale attack. Dickison took possession of the town and held it for six weeks. Once again, both sides of the St. Johns belonged to the Swamp Fox.

One loyal Southerner, who witnessed the Battle of Palatka from his home, recalled:

> The Yankees would come to Palatka and then go out in every direction looking for Captain Dickison and his men. One night they came our way and met Dickison's men, and they fought all around our home. Mother was confused and worried, mostly about her little children. She finally decided to make a palmetto mound near our house and hide us there. Just as we got settled, the Yankees came by, chasing Barsley Lovell. He was a brave soldier and rode a fine horse, which sailed over the palmettos by leaps and bounds.
>
> Lovell lay along his horse's neck, leading and shooting his gun at 10 or 12 men in full chase. And even though wounded in the hip and his horse shot in the mouth, he maneuvered the men right into Dickison's boys, who took them prisoners.
>
> After the fight, all gathered at Uncle Jacob Thomas's home near our house, and my brother and I went over there. Our men were bringing in their dead and wounded, and one of the dead was Captain Dickison's own son. I remem-

ber seeing a soldier (Dickison) riding his horse, with the battle across the saddle in front of him. Dickison kept pacing back and forth saying that if he knew which one killed his son he would have him executed immediately.[23]

Dickison's victory at the Battle of Palatka on August 2, 1864, had been hard-fought, but the territory east of him was facing deadly peril and total annihilation. Brigadier General Alexander Asboth had left the Pensacolà perimeter and was leading an expedition up the Alabama and Florida Railroad.[24]

On August 1, Confederate Headquarters in Tallahassee had received a dispatch from Lake City confirming a report that other Federal armies had crossed the St. Mary's River and were only eight miles from a Confederate encampment guarding Gainesville and Tallahassee. Firing had been heard, and there was very little doubt, the Federals were marching on Lake City.[25]

Notes

[1]Kathryn Trimmer Abbey, *Florida Land of Change,* Chapel Hill, University of North Carolina Press,1941, p. 286; *Official Records of the Union and Confederate Armies in the War of the Rebellion,* Series 1, Volume 14, p. 838.

[2]Mary B. Graff, *Mandarin on the St. Johns,* Gainesville, University of Florida Press, 1963, pp. 38-39.

[3]Ellen Fitzpatrick McCallum Hazel, "Civil War Stories," Putnam County Clerk of Court.

[4]Kathryn Trimmer Abbey, *Florida Land of Change,* pp. 290-291.

[5]Zack C. Waters, "Florida's Confederates Guerrillas: John W. Pearson and the Oklawaha Rangers," The Florida Historical Society, Volume LXX, Number 2, October 1991, pp. 138-139.

[6]Mary Elizabeth Dickison, *Dickison and His Men,* p. 75.

[7]Vince Murray, "Captain J. J. Dickison Marion County's Civil War Hero," *Ocala Star-Banner.*

[8]Samuel Proctor, "Florida a Hundred years Ago," June 9, 1864.

[9]Patricia L. Faust, editor, *Historical Times Illustrated Encyclopedia of the Civil War.*

[10]Ibid., June 6, 1864.

[11]Mary B. Graff, *Mandarin on the St. Johns,* p. 42.

[12]*Official Records of the Union and Confederate Armies in the War of the Rebellion,* Series I, Part II, XXXV, p. 122.

[13]Mary B. Graff, *Mandarin on the St. Johns,* pp. 40-41.

[14]Keith V. Holland, Lee B. Manley, and James W. Towart, eds., *The Maple Leaf: An Extraordinary American Civil War Shipwreck,* Jacksonville, St. Johns Archaeological Expeditions, Inc., 1993, pp. 16-17.

[15]Mary B. Graff, *Mandarin on the St. Johns,* pp. 40-41.

[16]*Official Records of the Union and Confederate Armies in the War of the Rebellion,* Series I, Part II, XXXV, p. 176.

[17]Samuel Proctor, "Florida a Hundred Years Ago," July 31, 1864.

[18]Ibid.

[19]Leland Hawes, *The Tampa Tribune,* Sunday, May 3, 1992, p. 4, Bay Life.

[20]Alice Strickland interview with author October 15, 1992, Ormond Beach, Florida.

[21]Mary Elizabeth Dickison, *Dickison and His Men,* pp. 75-79.

[22]Ibid.

[23]William Henry McConn interview with Frances Sheppard DeVore of the *Ocala Star-Banner,* 1951, *Ocala Star-Banner,* Sunday, June 3, 1951. McConn added, "I was only a kid but I sure felt sorry for Captain Dickison that day."

[24]Edwin L. Bearss, "Asboth's Expedition up the Alabama and Florida Railroad," *Florida Historical Quarterly,* Vol. XXIX, October 1960, pp. 159-166.

[25]Mary Elizabeth Dickison, *Dickison and His Men, pp. 75-79.*

Chapter 8

"Remember Charlie Dickison"

On August 1, 1864, the government in Tallahassee received the following report from Confederate headquarters in Lake City: "The enemy crossed the St. Mary's River yesterday, eight miles north of Colonel McCormick's camp at the trestle at 12 o'clock. This information was communicated to this place at 1 o'clock this morning. Since then we hear firing. The report is, they are marching on Lake City. Most of the public property has been removed up the road. Communication by wires with McCormick cut off."[1]

With all communications cut off between would-be defenders in the area, Governor John Milton sent a frantic telegram to Secretary of War J. A. Seddon in Richmond: "We have comparatively no force to defend even this place [Tallahassee] from the enemy. If troops with an efficient commander are not sent here promptly, all will be lost."[2]

General John P. Hatch, newly assigned commander of the Federal District of Florida, arrived in the state with an ambitious plan to occupy the area between the St. Johns and the Suwannee Rivers. He also asked for more troops from his army, stating Seymour's embarrassing defeat at Olustee had truly hurt the Union cause. He stated his force consisted of between 1,000 and 2,000 men, with 500 Union men, deserters, and Negroes leaving Cedar Key, raiding villages on their way to Gainesville.

His own plan was to "advance the force at Baldwin to Barber's and take up the rails of the road from that point to Baldwin. If you think I had better try the raid through Alachua and Marion I will by that time be reinforced and will try the thing."[3]

General J. K. Jackson, in charge of Confederate forces in Florida was warned of the situation by the government in Charleston but was told nothing could be done to supply him with additional troops. Jackson was also informed, "the destruction of railroads and the capture of Tallahassee will be the main objectives of the enemy. Use the force you have to the best advantage to defeat them. This is all you can do; all that can be expected of you."[4]

With the exception of J. J. Dickison's irregulars, there were no other troops on Florida soil in a position to meet the attacking Federals. General Finegan's army, only three months after their brilliant victory at Olustee, and all other infantry in Florida, were sent to Virginia to aid Robert E. Lee's disintegrating Army of Northern Virginia.[5]

Finegan's troops had successfully reached Virginia and joined Lee's army at Hanover Junction on May 28. This new Florida Brigade consisted of the Ninth Florida Regiment, First Florida (Special) Battalion, Second Florida Battalion, Fourth Florida Battalion, and the remnants of several other companies. No reinforcements were left behind to back up Dickison.

On May 16, Hatch's siege began, as Federal troops moved out of Jacksonville and Green Cove Springs with a powerful force of five thousand infantry, Negro troops, four hundred cavalry, and several batteries of artillery. Striking Confederate forces at Baldwin, they easily pushed the tiny Floridian force back across the Little Suwannee River and made a flank movement toward Lake City, Fort Butler, and Starke.[6]

After pillaging the town, the Union force continued on and flanked Waldo, where Captain Dickison and his troops were headquartered. In the course of their raid, these Federal forces had severed the telegraph wires and ripped up railroad track, leaving Dickison without communication with Lake City.

Shortly after dark, two local citizens rushed into Dickison's camp, and reported the Federals were at their plantations, burning Boulware's mill, ginhouse, and other buildings where cotton was stored. Captain Dickison reacted quickly.

Dickison and his guerrillas had enjoyed little rest that summer and were used to moving out at a moment's notice. John W. Pearson of the Oklawaha Rangers, summed up their role: "I am now a guerilla in every sense of the word; we neither tell where we stay nor where we are going, nor when we shall return; assemble the company at the sound of a cow's horn."[7]

Dickison's command consisted of one hundred thirty cavalry of his Company H, twenty-five men from the Fifth Battalion Cavalry, one section of artillery, and ninety brand-new recruits mustered into his unit as infantry. They moved out at once in the direction of the Federals.[8]

The Confederates were confused as to who was really in command as Dickison was outranked by a senior officer. A parley was held between the two officers, and, since Dickison was in command of all South Florida forces including the State Militia, the other officer, a Captain Rou, very generously replied, "I waive my rank in your favor and will follow you."[9]

Dickison left Colonel Elias Earle of Governor John Milton's staff in command of the infantry while he decided to move ahead with the cavalry and artillery.[10] The order was given to move out, and, while they moved very rapidly, they also rode cautiously, since a large force lay directly in front of them. The enemy cavalry moved toward Gainesville leaving five thousand colored infantry troops with substantial artillery at the Boulware plantation.[11]

Locating a Union raiding party, Dickison followed them from plantation to plantation observing the pillaging. The raiding party consisted of four hundred troops of the Seventy-fifth Ohio and the Fourth Massachusetts regiments.

At a plantation belonging to Colonel Edward Lewis, the sacking Federals appropriated one hundred and twenty-five slaves. Mrs. Lewis and her servants, quickly loaded four wagons with her most valuable furniture, bedding, and clothing, and her teamsters hid them in the woods. The captured slaves, however, were easily intimidated and showed the Federals the location of the concealed booty.

When Captain Dickison rode by, a sobbing Mrs. Lewis told him of her plight. Dickison, hoping to comfort her, pledged, "Be hopeful, and before the sun rises again I will send back all that you have been despoiled of."[12] That same evening, following a bitter skirmish, Dickison returned all her property.

Moving on, Dickison learned the Federals were heading for Gainesville, only twelve miles away, and again took up pursuit. Along the way he was met by Captain W. A. Owens with some fifteen State Militia. Owens had been one of the organizers of the Marion Light Dragoons, to which Dickison had served, and due to failing health, the former general had retired. He did, however, secure a commission as captain, and each time the state was invaded, he would report to Dickison with his tiny force.

Dickison realized the importance of the upcoming battle, and while following the enemy in the direction of Gainesville, addressed his men:

> We will meet the enemy very soon; we must win this fight or the country is gone. I can see in my brave men a determination to sacrifice their lives or win the fight, and I know they will win it. They have seen their homes invaded, and the sore distress of their helpless families and neighbors. Such men may be killed but never conquered.[13]

The outcome of the battle had little to do with the outcome of the war, for the war was in reality already lost, and while Dickison's speech was both patriotic and a bit too dramatic, it did assure him of the continued loyalty of his men. His reputation as a warrior of the first magnitude had reached mythical proportions, and whether the war was lost or not, it would not be due to his own shortcomings.[14]

Like Dickison, his superiors refused to give up on the war, but General John K. Jackson in a report to Richmond, conveyed the same sense of urgency as the guerilla leader:

> There are other troops of all arms amounting to about 180 men, under the command of Captain Dickison, in the neighborhood of Gainesville, acting as a core of observation and for protection. In order to concentrate the force I now have, and which is stationed on the South Fork of the St. Mary's River, I have been obliged to strip Middle and West Florida of all forces, even for their defense against raiders of deserters and Negroes.[15]

Gainesville was important to the approaching Federals as it was a prominent supply center, where cattle and agricultural products from further south were stored and shipped northward. The citizens of Gainesville had discovered, however, that "the railroad[,] which had

Samuel Warren Mays (May 10, 1831 to May 3, 1914). Samuel enlisted May 3, 1862 at Gainesville and later served as captain of Company B, Second Florida Battalion at Palatka. He was wounded at Cold Harbor June 3, 1864 and hospitalized then furloughed. He was listed as AWOL on the last roll. His father had represented the St. Augustine vicinity at the Florida Secession Convention. (Photo courtesy Robert Lionel Baldwin—SCV #1282)

been so instrumental in the growth of [the town] now appeared to be an avenue of destruction."[16]

Colonel Andrew Harris of the Seventy-fifth Ohio had left Baldwin on August 15 with just under 200 men. Upon reaching Starke the following day, his force was joined by a detachment of the Fourth Massachusetts Cavalry under Captain Joseph Morton and a company of Florida Unionist troops. After "destroy[ing] a lot of Confederate commissary stores and six [railroad] cars, the troops marched into Gainesville.[17]

It was about 6:30 A.M. on August 17 when the Federals reached the city after an all-night march. About 70 Confederate militia were in Gainesville, but Company B, Fourth Massachusetts Cavalry, drove them from the town. Harris' horses badly needed rest and forage. Harris ordered his men to keep on their accouterments but to slip the bridles and feed the mounts. Cooks were also given word to begin preparing coffee for the troops.[18]

Concentrating on the center of town, the Fourth Massachusetts Cavalry began their defenses, placing their artillery piece to their rear. The Seventy-fifth Ohio settled to the rear of the artillery north of the railroad grade. The units set up in open lots, while mounted and dismounted pickets assembled on all sides.

The Rhode Island artillerymen took a walk through the town after settling in a small grove and feeding their horses. Some of these Federal soldiers procured corn cakes, rock candy, and Confederate money for souvenirs.

Only two miles from Gainesville, Dickison's scouts located the enemy's rear guard, which told him the main force was already in the city. After disposing of the enemy pickets, Dickison moved cautiously to the main line and ordered his artillery to fire two shells.[19] The Rhode Island men, just sitting down to relax with their corn cakes, ran for cover as one of the shots went crashing over their heads.[20]

William Southerton of the Federal's Seventy-fifth Ohio later recalled:

> By the time I reached the railroad that bordered the town on the east, enemy pickets were firing upon our rear guard. A hundred-yard battle line had been drawn up; our one piece of artillery, a Howitzer, with the caisson, was in the middle. My company was on the right flank. All around us was open ground, not a tree, not a fence. Every fourth man took the horses, led them off to one side. A furious attack opened up.[21]

The enemy held the railroad at both crossings and was in the depot and along the tracks. Ordering all his men except one platoon to dismount, Dickison again divided his army, one force moving in on the left to take the depot, the others moving in from the right and center to drive the enemy from the road.[22]

Confederate artillery pounded the enemy on the railroad tracks but was answered by Federal artillery posted near Beville's Hotel. Dickison, pistol in hand, remained on his horse giving orders from the saddle, and as the gray-clad soldiers advanced, the Federals retreated from the railroad and depot.

Dickison's men managed to strike with a crossfire on the enemy's piece of artillery, hitting five of the six horses on the caisson and killing the soldier holding them. The Rhode Islanders fired back, finally finding the range of Confederate guns. Lieutenant T. J. Bruton informed his Confederate gunners, "This is no place to fight. Limber up."

Bruton quickly moved his artillery creating a hornet's nest for the Rhode Islanders. The Federals had only one load of canister and a single shot left, and the corporal commanding their gun had been wounded.[23]

Dickison always carried three six-shooters, two in his holsters, and one on his sword-belt. As he pursued the fleeing Federals from the town, he caught up with an enemy cavalryman, and ordered him to throw down his arms and surrender. The man refused, and Dickison hacked him from the saddle with a blow from his saber.[24]

Dickison, six-guns blazing, ran to another fleeing Federal, this soldier a captain, and ordered him to surrender or be shot. The captain's reply was, "Shoot and be damned."[25] Dickison complied with the captain's wishes.

As Dickison and his troops raced through the streets, many of the women of Gainesville did too, chanting, "Charge, charge." Some Federals made a stand and fired a volley of minie-balls at Dickison in front of a residence where several women stood. The Swamp Fox quickly got the women inside to safety, while other spirited ladies entered the street with buckets of water for the famished Confederates.

The fighting spread from one end of town to the other and lasted about two hours before the enemy retreated in two full columns. Since the town was nearly surrounded, Dickison dashed through the streets calling for his men to mount their horses and pursue the retreating Yankees. As they reached the woods in full flight, the Confederates continued to strike from every side along the road, and the cry of "Remember Charlie Dickison" rang out above the gunfire.

Union soldier William Southerton recalled:

> The rebels . . . circled to the north of town. We were surrounded. Some of our men were killed. A number of our horses [were] killed or disabled. Ammunition was fast dwindling. Harris called in our line. A complete rout followed. Mounting our horses we backed off into town, then out on the road to the west where the Massachusetts cavalry held the enemy in check for a short time. A woman standing in the doorway of a shack fired at Colonel Harris. In a flash she was shot down. Harris escaped out by the road to the west. That was the last time I saw him for a long time.[26]

The chase continued on into Newmansville, some fifteen miles distant, while many Federals were killed or captured along the road. Captain Dickison's horse had been wounded twice, and he ordered a halt. The men were nearly exhausted, and the hot sun had grown unbearable for men who had been fighting for several hours.[27]

During their flight, Harris never had the chance to form his men back into a column. Captain Morton mistakenly led his command out the Newsmanville Road rather than the Waldo Road. Private George H. Luther of the artillery detachment later recalled that the soldiers were confused when given orders to retreat. Following the Newmanville Road, Luther and several others turned into a cart path, hoping to pass around and find the road by which they had entered Gainesville.[28]

With the Confederates on their heels, the Federals ran blindly through the thicket. Several of the men fell over a log across the trail guiding their artillery piece. Moments later, one of the wheel horses was hit, and the gun came to an abrupt halt.

When Harris realized Morton had taken the wrong road, he dashed after him. By making a circular path around the town, he brought a portion of his command back to the Waldo Road. About a mile from Gainesville, Harris discovered the disabled gun and the Rhode Islanders. According to George H. Luther: "Colonel Harris, who was near us at the time, said: 'Boys, I am sorry for you; I have stayed by you till the last minute; good bye;' and away he went through the dust on his splendid horse."

Dickison's men moved in and captured the entire Rhode Island detachment.[29]

The single piece of artillery, belonging to Colonel Andrew Harris and the Seventy-fifth Ohio, had been captured by Dickison and his pursuing Confederates. Of the seventy-five men fleeing with Harris, many had been killed or captured during the chase.[30]

Four of Dickison's men out on scouting patrol ran directly into thirty Federal soldiers in the woods. The Federals, believing the four men to be the advance of reinforcements on the way to Dickison, surrendered and were taken to Confederate headquarters in Gainesville.

Along the way, Colonel Harris and ten Federals who had fled into the woods, rode up. Seeing their men held prisoner by the four Dickison men, they turned, rushed around a plantation and sped to the troops he had left stationed at the Boulware plantation the evening before.

With five thousand Federals at the camp, Harris would have had a strong force to fight Dickison; instead, they returned to their headquarters at Green Cove Springs on the St. Johns River. As they did so, the four Confederates under Sergeant Poer brought their prisoners to Dickison in Gainesville.

Dickison's command had captured two hundred Federals including several officers. One of these captive officers, whose name was Major Fox, had taken his battalion into the area specifically to capture Captain Dickison. Deciding to have a little fun, Dickison pleasantly asked his captive, "Major Fox, how is it you allow this Gray Fox to outrun and capture the Red Fox?"[31]

Dickison's victory at Gainesville immensely enhanced his reputation. He had killed or captured nearly four hundred Federals, and while the enemy at no time could estimate his strength in numbers (but believed it to be between 1,200 to 1,500 men), Dickison's official report lists 175 men in the fight. This glorious little struggle had saved East and South Florida.

The Lake City Columbian, on September 1, 1864, lauded Dickison and the defenders of Gainesville: "Though suddenly and hastily assembled, the citizen soldiery emulated the example of their comrades, the sturdy veterans and victors of many fields of carnage, and by their valor and intrepidity contributed much to the glorious result. Captain Dickison has a fine command, and no officer is more universally beloved by the officers and men under him than he is."[32]

General Hatch, whose ambitious plan had met disaster, had little good to say regarding his "superior" Federal army: Dickison's "force is represented at from 500 to 700, with three pieces of artillery. From what I can learn the attack must have been a surprise. The men, however, fought well, but their ammunition being expended they were ordered to cut their way out. It would appear to have been a thorough rout."[33]

A few days later, General Hatch, revamped his report: "The more I hear of the affair the worse it appears. Colonel Harris undoubtedly allowed his men to scatter through the town and, I fear, to pillage. He was undoubtedly surprised, and although the men individually acted pretty well, I do not believe they were at any time under control. . . . Colonel Harris has always borne the reputation of a brave man, but his regiment was without discipline."[34]

At Green Cove Springs, the large Federal army that had been outwitted by Captain Dickison, encamped under the protection of gunboats. Dickison remained in Gainesville for a few days to keep an eye on a suspected Federal attack from Cedar Keys and to verify a report of a gunboat and several barges in the mouth of the Suwannee River.

A jubilant Confederate Major Sam Jones applauded Dickison in his August

20 report to Richmond: "Captain Dickison, with greatly inferior numerical force, engaged enemies' cavalry and artillery at Gainesville, Florida, on the 17th, and completely routed them, captured 150 prisoners, one piece of artillery, and one hundred stolen Negroes. The enemy was pursued fourteen miles, and scattered. This is the third instance of successful gallantry on the part of Captain Dickison I have had occasion to report to you by telegraph."[35]

Notes

[1]Samuel Proctor, "Florida a Hundred Years Ago," August 1, 1864.

[2]Ibid.

[3]Ibid., August 4, 1864.

[4]Ibid.

[5]J. J. Dickison, *Florida Confederate Military History,* Volume XI, Atlanta, Confederate Publishing Company,1894, Reprint edition New York, 1962, pp. 157-158.

[6]Mary Elizabeth Dickison, *Dickison and His men, pp. 87-88.*

[7]Zack C. Waters, "Florida's Confederate Guerrillas: John W. Pearson and the Oklawaha Rangers," p. 138.

[8]Mary Elizabeth Dickison, *Dickison and His men,* pp. 88-91.

[9]Ibid.

[10]Richard P. Weinert, "The Confederate Swamp Fox," Putnam County Archives and History.

[11]Mary Elizabeth Dickison, *Dickison and His Men,* pp. 88-91.

[12]Ibid.

[13]Ibid.

[14]David J. Coles, "Volusia County: The Land Warfare 1861-1865," *Civil War in Volusia County A Symposium,* p. 50.

[15]Samuel Proctor, "Florida a Hundred Years Ago," August 12, 1864.

[16]David James Coles, "Far from Fields of Glory: Military Operations in Florida During the Civil War, 1864-1865," p. 227.

[17]Ibid., pp. 227-228.

[18]Richard P. Weinert, "The Confederate Swamp Fox," Putnam County Archives and History.

[19]Samuel Proctor, "Florida A Hundred Years Ago," August 12, 1864.

[20]Richard P. Weinert, "The Confederate Swamp Fox," Putnam County Archives and History.

[21]David James Coles, "Far from Fields of Glory: Military Operations in Florida During the Civil War, 1864-1865," pp. 228-229.

[22]Mary Elizabeth Dickison, *Dickison and His Men,* pp. 91-106; Marjory Stoneman Douglas, *Florida: the Long Frontier,* p. 192.

[23]Richard P. Weinert, "The Confederate Swamp Fox," Putnam County Archives and History.

[24]Mary Elizabeth Dickison, *Dickison and His Men,* pp. 91-106.

[25]Ibid.

[26]David James Coles, "Far from Fields of Glory: Military Operations in Florida During the Civil War," p. 229.

[27]Mary Elizabeth Dickison, *Dickison and His Men,* pp. 91-106; Marjory Stoneman Douglas, *Florida The Long Frontier,* p. 192.

[28]Richard P. Weinert, "The Confederate Swamp Fox," Putnam County Archives and History.

[29]Ibid.

[30]Mary Elizabeth Dickison, *Dickison and His Men,* pp. 91-106.

[31]Ibid.

[32]*The Lake City Columbian,* September 1, 1864; Samuel Proctor, "Florida a Hundred Years Ago," September 5, 1864.

[33]Ibid., August 19, 1864.

[34]Ibid., August 22, 1864.

[35]Ibid., August 20, 1864.

Chapter 9

Cradle and Grave

On September 22, 1864, the Confederate War Department wrote to Major-General Sam Jones regarding his recommendation that Dickison be promoted in rank. Despite Dickison's gallantry at Palatka and Gainesville, they could not honor that request. "The services of this officer," it stated, "are highly appreciated by this department . . . there is no position known to which he could be appointed."[1]

Dickison, the following month, however, had been given command of all state troops, soldiers whose ages ranged from fifteen to fifty-five.[2] These troops had been drafted in the spring by Governor Milton and were only to be used in case of a Federal invasion. The first three years of the war, most inland-directed attacks originated from Jacksonville and St. Augustine on Florida's eastern seacoast. Suddenly, raids were also originating in Pensacola, on the state's western coast, and with Dickison continually engaged in middle and eastern Florida, four or five companies of cavalry at Marianna, comprised the only Confederate forces in the west.[3]

A smattering of Confederate troops were still putting up resistance in the Fort Myers area where Dickison had served just prior to the Battle of Olustee. Troops of the Second Florida [United States] Cavalry Regiment were experiencing dreadful August heat in their camp on the Caloosahatchee River. The Federals, however, had made good progress in securing the area against blockade running and cattle driving.[4]

Sergeant James Henry Thompson went to check an apparent distress signal from the north shore of the river across from the fort. With seven men, the Federal troops rowed across the river in two boats to investigate the signal. As they approached the shoreline, carefully watching out for Confederate snipers, Sergeant Thompson recognized the black man who was signaling them.

Thompson told his men to land the boats and not make the black man wade out to them. Without warning, a heavy volley of gunfire erupted from about sixty-five Confederate soldiers concealed in the bushes. The black man had been a decoy, and both Sergeant Thompson and a colored trooper were killed. The remaining Union men pulled away from the shore and dashed to the fort. The jungle belonged to the Confederates.

Rumors circulated in Pensacola that Union prisoners had been hanged in Walton County, and Brigadier-General Alexander Asboth, the Union commander in Pensacola, decided to act. Knowing the Confederacy had but few troops in the area, he marched overland with four battalions of cavalry and two companies of mounted colored infantry. This force was accompanied down Santa Rosa Sound by the steamer *Lizzie Davis*, which supplied the army with provisions.[5]

The tiny, ill-equipped Confederate force in and near Marianna was aware of the Federal move and hid their women and children in nearby caves.[6] Rifles were given to some of the older children in the caves, to be used strictly in defense. The only "regular" troops in the area were those of Company E, Captain William A. Jeter, at Hickory Hill, some twenty miles west of Marianna; Company G, Major William H. Milton (son of Florida State Governor John Milton), twenty-five miles south of town; and Company I, Captain Robert Chisholm, in the town of Marianna.[7]

The town of Marianna received news of the attack from Confederate Colonel A. B. Montgomery, and a meeting was immediately called in the Court House. At the meeting, it was discovered the Jackson Home Guards, organized in 1861, had disbanded and were now defunct. A new company of youths, sixteen years of age and younger, and old men, fifty years and over, was organized immediately, calling itself the "Cradle and Grave Company."[8]

The Cradle and Grave Company consisted of a hundred or more boys and elders, self-armed with shotguns, old flintlocks, and pistols. Jesse J. Norwood, a prominent pro-Unionist with no military training or experience, was elected captain to lead the Confederate defense of their city. Norwood accepted the role only because his town, comprised of civilians, was about to be attacked by an organized army.

This group of unlikely defenders was backed by the Club Company of Home guards from Greenwood, a few home guards from Campbellton, and six or eight regular Confederate soldiers home on sick leave.

When the Federals attacked Marianna on September 27, the regulars of the Fifth Florida (Confederate) Cavalry had not reached the city, and the attackers were resisted instead by two militia companies of boys and elders with squirrel rifles, who had barricaded the road between houses and St. Luke's Episcopal Church.

The Cradle and Grave Company, and other militia men, fought General Asboth's advancing Federals to a standstill. The gallant and heroic fight of the Home Guards was hopeless from the beginning, but, nonetheless, they repulsed two charges and fought desperately for half an hour, while encircled and outnumbered by the superior main body of Asboth's Federals.[9] Asboth led the second Federal charge himself but only after he was certain his flankers had reached the rear of the Home Guards.[10]

As the Federals took the city, they set fire to houses, churches, and barricades, while Colonel Montgomery and his tiny force retreated. A local newspaper, lamenting Montgomery's poorly managed retreat, declared that it was "too disgraceful for us to dwell upon." Montgomery should have sent the Cradle and Grave defenders in retreat after the initial repulse, instead of leaving them to fend for themselves.[11]

Although Asboth and several Union officers were wounded, the city was surrendered. Following the surrender, it is alleged many Southerners were butchered, beaten to death or forced into the burning church by Negro troops. Some of the defenders were spared by deserters from the First Florida Cavalry who were acquainted with them.[12]

The prisoners were assembled in the courthouse along with non-combatants who lived in Marianna. Family members were permitted to visit them, and some of the prisoners were paroled.

Due to the seriousness of Asboth's wound and their precarious position with Confederate reinforcements on the way, the Federals retreated toward Pensacola. General Asboth was placed in a carriage, and the Federals moved through Vernon to Port Washington. The forced march brought the men to Port Washington that same day. The Federal report stated they had captured eighty-one prisoners, ninety-five stand of arms, 200 horses and mules, 400 head of cattle, and seventeen wagons. The sole Marianna resident who left with Asboth's army was the telegraph operator, who had furnished the general with messages that had been sent to Tallahassee.

The same evening, Major William H. Milton arrived with reinforcements, followed the next day by Captain Jeter. Bridges were repaired, scouts sent out, and the Confederate force followed in pursuit of the retreating Federals.[13]

As the Federals reached Pensacola without mishap, Florida State Governor John Milton telegraphed the Confederate War Department in Richmond:

> The enemy captured Marianna yesterday; made Colonel Montgomery with many other prisoners. If we had arms and ammunition we might have resisted them. Two militia companies were captured, unarmed and willing to fight. Unless promptly assisted, West Florida, with abundant supplies of corn, bacon, etc., will be irrecoverably lost. Send arms and ammunition if you cannot send us reinforcements; but if possible, send them. We will fight every inch of the ground.[14]

The same day it was reported to General J. K. Jackson that the Federals were concentrating a large force at Hilton Head intending another invasion of Florida's east coast. On the west coast, Mobile and Pensacola were also active, and Dickison and his men faced a possible two-fronted invasion.[15]

There was little time to consider the alternatives, however, for, on October 23, Dickison received a dispatch from Lieutenant Haynes of the Fifth Battalion of Cavalry, stationed at the outpost at Green Cove Springs. Their position was again in peril as Haynes' men had been attacked by a considerable force of Federals and had been pushed back a distance of three miles.[16]

Dickison and his faithful returned to the saddle, and, with great haste, returned to the scene of battle. Told the enemy was on the move out of Magnolia, he arrived with his men and a single piece of artillery and prepared to attack. The Federals, however, were also on the move, and had crossed the creek five miles north of him at a place called Finegan Ford. A Confederate scout learning of this movement, related to Dickison that the enemy cavalry had made the crossing and taken the road to Middleburgh on Black Creek.

Dickison immediately marched to cut off their return, and finding two roads the Federals might use, placed detachments at both. As the Federals approached, Dickison found them driving a large herd of cattle, which the Yankees termed "rebel beef."

Spotting the Confederates in their path, the Federals mounted a charge and were met by a volley of fire. Forced to halt by the intense barrage, the Federals slowly withdrew, but quickly reformed their line, raised their sabers, and charged again. This time, the Confederates unleashed their artillery, and the enemy fell back in great confusion with Dickison's men on their heels, killing and capturing the unfortunates.

The battle lasted forty to sixty minutes over two miles of woodland only six miles from the town of Magnolia. Only three Federals were believed to escape, one of them a Union officer. Sixty-five men were taken prisoner, but more significant to the Confederates was the capture of seventy horses.

The Dickison men barely caught their breaths after the battle when a scout from the east side of the St. Johns River appeared with news of more enemy movement. From St. Augustine, a considerable Union force marched two miles every day to the abandoned Fairbanks place, situated between the San Sebastian and North Rivers.

St. Augustine had become a Union rest camp, and so secure was the standing army, they were confident the city could not be attacked. Used primarily as a base for raids into the interior of Florida, its only danger lay in attacks on work details from Captain Dickison.[17]

David Levy Branning (October 29, 1842 to April 29, 1910). A Seminole War veteran, Branning enlisted May 8, 1862 at Tallahassee and transferred to Company B, Second Florida Calvary September 24, 1863. He was ill in a hospital on the last roll and was paroled at Waldo May 20, 1865. He became a reverend after the war. (Photo courtesy Robert Lionel Baldwin—SCV #1282)

The abandoned Fairbanks place, where Federal detachments marched every day, was typical of farms throughout the area. Nearly all the people living along the St. Johns River, as well as along the Floridian coast, had fled with their slaves and light possessions long before when the Federals had gained control of the river. Their homes were left unprotected, and in most cases, filled with family furniture and cherished heirlooms, since there had not been sufficient time for the fleeing owners to remove them.

The commanders of Federal gunboats cruising the St. Johns and infantry commanders of troops marching out of St. Augustine took good advantage of these abandoned homes between Jacksonville and Enterprise, a distance of 150 miles. Union troops looted the homes of those valuables that could be carried away, and officers ate, drank, and slept in comfort before continuing up the St. Johns. Many of these homes were burned or shelled and the magnificent orange groves destroyed.

Taking one hundred cavalry on only one flatboat, Dickison engineered another of his secret moves and reached the St. Johns early the following morning. Leaving a detachment in view of St. Augustine to cut off additional troops, which might be marching to the Fairbanks place, Dickison crossed the San Sebastian River at its headwaters with the rest of his men.[18]

Reaching the Fairbanks place at sunrise but finding no one occupying the house, Dickison divided what remained of his army. He and several troops positioned themselves to engage the enemy in front of the house, while the rest of his men circled back to block any would-be retreat.

The quiet was suddenly broken when distant drums signaled the approach of the Union army marching toward the house, but the Union advance force reached Dickison some distance ahead of the main battalion. Since the main Union force had not yet passed, Confederates circling back were unable to attain their position behind the Federals.

Dickison, in front of the advancing Federals, waited until the enemy was about a few yards from him and confronted them, demanding a surrender. His request was met with a volley of fire, and the dismounted Confederates answered with fire of their own.

The Swamp Fox quickly ordered a charge, and most of the Union advance force were killed or captured. The main battalion turned and retreated, but by then, the other half of Dickison's army had altered its own position and charged the fleeing enemy on horseback. Among those killed was the commanding officer of the Union force.

As Dickison rode slowly through the carnage, he came upon a dying Union officer, and since no surgeon was in either camp, he bound the soldier's wound with his own handkerchief and made a pillow for him with his own blanket. The man was wounded in both his neck and shoulder, and, Dickison, in finding a gold watch and chain on his patient, reminded his men they never robbed their prisoners. The next day, the soldier was dead, and Dickison had recrossed the St. Johns to safety.

The situation in Florida, like the rest of the Confederacy, was now critical, and the people of the state depended solely on guerilla bands like those led by J. J. Dickison and Charles J. Munnerlyn for protection. On November 13, Governor Milton, in a letter to President Jefferson Davis, announced he had formed forty-two companies with over 3,000 troops for the defense of Florida since requesting aid the previous July. The Confederate Government had shipped in 1,500 arms for use by these defending Floridians but refused responsibility for any general support.[19]

Secretary of War Judah P. Benjamin was much concerned with the failing Confederacy. In a letter to Edward Porter Alexander, Benjamin referred to a system of signals that Porter had devised, some of which included Florida.

> The President [Davis] is much interested in your system of signals and attaches high value to it, and is disposed to adopt your suggestions in relation to the details of officers instructed by you for duty at their points. I have therefore to request in his name that you will be good enough to send me a list of such persons as you would recommend for this purpose with a statement of the rank deemed proper and suitable for each person, in order that it may be submitted to the President— The points where we suppose the system would now be specially valuable are at Charleston, Pensacola, and Columbus, and officers sufficient for those three points would be very desirable.[20]

On November 23, by joint resolution, the Florida Senate and House expressed the thanks of the people of the state to Captain Dickison and "his brave troops." The resolution also recommended Dickison for promotion to colonel "which he so gallantly won and richly merits." In offering the resolution, Thomas Y. Henry of Gadsden County pointed out Dickison's "high soldierly qualities and daring acts as a military leader," which "challenged the admiration of the people of Florida and won their confidence to the utmost."[21]

Dickison's reputation as "the Knight of the Silver Spurs" and "the Swamp Fox of the Confederacy" continued to grow. With nearly all of Florida in Federal hands, only Dickison and his band could penetrate and successfully strike within the perimeter between St. Augustine, Fernandina, St. Johns Bluff, Amelia Island and the territory between the St. Johns River and the coast. Only Dickison prevented all the plantations of Central Florida from being broken up by the Federals.[22]

He once pursued an enemy wagon train loaded with plunder almost to the suburbs of St. Augustine because he recognized the loot as belonging to someone he knew.

The daring deeds of this Confederate leader were memorable, and the strategies he implemented embellished his legendary.

In spite of Dickison's repulsion of enemy forces, however, the Federals could not be coerced out of Jacksonville, which they heavily fortified and controlled through war's end. Seven batteries protected twelve thousand hurried reinforcements at a chain of breastworks. Union gunboats maintained their stranglehold on the St. Johns with former Confederate earthworks at Yellow Bluff and St. Johns Bluff serving as signal stations.[23]

Many Florida troops had grown weary of war. Confederate Soldier Albert Chalker wrote his sweetheart from Baldwin on October 12, 1864: "I am very tired of living this way. I very often say hard things about our Confederacy and officers."[24]

By the end of the year, General William Tecumseh Sherman had sacked Atlanta, General Phil Sheridan had ravaged the Shenandoah Valley of Virginia, and Abraham Lincoln had won an overwhelming victory in the November elections. The writing was on the wall for the failing Confederacy, but Florida, with communications cut off northward, was not aware of it.[25]

Florida, by December 20, was still unaware of Sherman's "March to the Sea," and the citizens had no idea the Thirteenth Amendment abolishing slavery in the United States, would become law in another month. Floridians saw only the bright side: slaves were being enlisted and armed to fight for the Confederacy. But for Dickison, there would be no aid.

Notes

[1]Samuel Proctor, "Florida a Hundred Years Ago," September 22, 1864.

[2]Marjory Stoneman Douglas, *Florida the Long Frontier,* p. 192.

[3]Kathryn Trimmer Abbey, *Florida Land of Change,* p. 286.

[4]Robert Macomber, "The Patriot and the Widow James and Sophire Thompson and the Civil War on the Coast," *Civil War Interactive,* p. 1; *Official Records of the Union and Confederate Navies in the War of the Rebellion,* Series I, Volume 17, East Gulf Blockade Squadron, United States Navy, 1903.

[5]Mark F. Boyd, *Battle of Marianna,* pamphlet reprinted from the *Florida Historical Quarterly,* April 1951, Volume XXIX, Number 4, p. 228.

[6]Georgia Atkinson Bradfield, great-granddaughter of Florida Governor John Milton, interview with author, October 13, 1992, Ormond Beach, Florida.

[7]Mark F. Boyd, *Battle of Marianna,* pp. 226-227.

[8]Ibid., pp. 231-235; *The History of St. Luke's Episcopal Church,* Tallahassee, P.M. Publishing and Typographics, Inc., 1988, pp. 13-14, 221; Michael Gannon, *Florida: A Short History,* p. 43.

[9]Marjory Stoneman Douglas, *Florida*

the Long Frontier, p. 192.

[10]Mark F. Boyd, "The Battle of Marianna," *Florida Historical Quarterly,* Vol. XXIX, April 1951, p. 234.

[11]*West Florida News* Extra, October 3, 1864.

[12]Mark F. Boyd, *Battle of Marianna,* pp. 235-236.

[13]A plaque, erected in 1921, now reads: "Battle of Marianna, September 27, 1864, where overwhelming Federal forces were stubbornly resisted by a Home Guard of old men and boys and a few sick and wounded Confederates on furlough 1860-1865 Confederate Heroes."

[14]Samuel Proctor, "Florida a Hundred years Ago," September 28, 1864.

[15]Ibid.

[16]Ibid., October 23-24, 1864; Mary Elizabeth Dickison, *Dickison and His men,* pp. 107-110.

[17]John E. Johns, *Florida During the Civil War,* Jacksonville, University of Florida Press, 1963, p. 69.

[18]Mary Elizabeth Dickison, *Dickison and His Men,* pp. 110-112.

[19]Samuel Proctor, "Florida a Hundred years Ago," November 13, 1864.

[20]Judah P. Benjamin letter to Edward Porter Alexander dated November 10, 1864. Southern Historical Collection, Wilson Library, University of North Carolina—Chapel Hill.

[21]Ibid., November 23, 1864.

[22]Alfred Jackson Hanna and Kathryn Abbey Hanna, *Florida's Golden Sands,* Indianapolis & New York, The Bobbs Merrill Company, Inc., 1950, p. 149.

[23]Dave Page, *Ships Versus Shore, Civil War Engagements Along Southern Shores and Rivers,* Nashville, Rutledge Hill Press, 1994, pp. 203-204.

[24]Albert S. Chalker letter to Miss Bardin dated October 12, 1864. Myron C. Prevatt, Jr., Collection.

[25]Marjory Stoneman Douglas, *Florida the Long Frontier,* pp. 192-193.

Chapter 10

"God Bless You, Colonel"

Through February 1865, Dickison's outposts at Green Cove Springs, Palatka, and up the St. Johns River to Volusia County were continually under siege. When scouts informed him that troops from the Federal garrison at Picolata, some four hundred strong, were terrorizing local citizenry, Dickison telegraphed his commanding general asking permission to cross the river and attack. His request was granted, but the general warned him of very heavy Union gunboat traffic patrolling the river.[1]

Dickison immediately gathered his men. Consisting of three companies, Dickison's troops numbered 127 men—Cavalry from Company H, sixty-four men under Lieutenants McCardell and McEaddy; thirty-three from Company B of the same regiment; and twenty-eight from Company H of the Fifth Cavalry Battalion.

He ordered his men to take five days' rations, and in setting out, the destination was not revealed to the men until they reached the St. Johns. At sunset, on the second of February, they reached the deserted town of Palatka, and before crossing the river, Dickison explained the dangers that lay ahead, giving every man the option of returning with the wagons to Waldo instead of fighting. Not one soldier left him.

The river crossing took all night, followed by a long and circuitous march into the following evening. Within a mile of the fort, Dickison called a halt and sent a young soldier, whose father lived within the picket line, ahead with a message. The boy's father returned with his son and informed them the Federals had been reinforced earlier that day with about four hundred men and several pieces of artillery. To attack the fort without artillery would be suicide.

The informant passed on to Dickison information regarding a certain house on the road from Jacksonville to St. Augustine where the citizens (Union sympathizers) were holding a dance. Many attractive "Southern" belles were to be present, as well as several Federal officers and soldiers.

Dickison's men, who had been continually on the march, would rest whenever their captain called a halt. Dickison awakened them.

Only twelve miles from the house was a Federal station where several soldiers and their horses were posted.

Marching into the night, the Swamp Fox arrived with his men at the station and quickly captured a dozen Federal cavalrymen and horses.

Dickison then decided to go on to the dance. He placed a detachment on the road to St. Augustine and another on the road to Jacksonville. Riding quietly up to the house, where the banquet and dance were held, he discovered a major and his adjutant riding away. Intercepting them, Dickison demanded a surrender and took their arms.

With the music of the dance band covering the sound of their movements, Dickison and his men crept up on the dance. Two officers and several soldiers were captured by the Swamp Fox, and the twelve-piece band was appropriated by his men. Fleeing Federals were captured by Dickison men hiding along the roadside. All together, Dickison took about forty prisoners (four officers), eighteen horses, an ambulance, and a dance band.

Here, Dickison learned the Seventeenth Connecticut under Colonel Albert H. Wilcoxon, had just departed via the old Government Road in the direction of Volusia County. Leaving several of his men with the prisoners, Dickison and the others rode off in pursuit of Wilcoxon's troops, instructing the others to catch up with them at Braddock's farm, six miles east of the river.

Along the way, Lieutenant McEaddy, who was commanding the advance guard, encountered a detachment of Federal cavalry under Captain Staples and a skirmish erupted. Under fire, the Federals retreated into the swamps, but McEaddy took a prisoner and two horses. When they reached the main road, they found wagon ruts and knew the enemy was not far off.

About midnight, they came upon a small farmhouse, and Dickison was told two of the occupants were believed to be deserters from the Confederate army. Lieutenant McEaddy remained with the troops, while Dickison and ten men surrounded the house. The Swamp Fox disguised himself as a Union colonel, and his men masqueraded in blue coats.

Thinking them Union soldiers, an obese woman came out to greet them. Dickison addressed her as a rebel woman, but she assured him she was a loyal Union sympathizer. She went on to add her two sons had deserted from the Confederate army and were hiding in the swamp until Dickison's men, who had routed them the day before, recrossed the river.

Dickison informed her he was trying to locate Colonel Wilcoxon and had been ordered to protect him in the rear. The gullible woman related that she had dined with Wilcoxon the day before and he had rested there.

Just then, several Dickison men rode up for water, and since these others were not attired in blue, the deception was nearly discovered. Dickison covered up quickly, however, and told her they were some of Dickison's men whom they had captured. At the same time, he ordered his ten Union impostors to guard the prisoners well and not let them escape.

Throwing her arms around him, the woman shouted "God bless you, Colonel," and begged him to capture "that man Dickison." With a straight face, he replied, "I'll get him before he crosses the river."[2]

As they walked to the gate, the woman asked Dickison to protect her stores, and since some of his men were in the barn taking fodder, he agreed to stop them. Scolding his men, he told them the fodder belonged to a good Union woman. Further taken in, she replied, "Oh, if they need it, let them have it."[3] Dickison promised her payment for the fodder but soon realized he had only

Confederate money, which was worthless on that side of the river.

Assuring her of the goodness of his intentions, he promised he would have his quartermaster provide her with flour and coffee as payment. She embraced him again, and his men restrained their laughter at the sight of the two-hundred-pound woman squeezing him amid verbal blessings. Not long after the "bluecoats" vanished, she realized she had been taken and no money would be forthcoming.

After riding only a few miles, a halt was called, and the men rested for an hour. Continuing, they met several deserters on their way to St. Augustine, and since Dickison and ten others in front of the formation wore the bluecoats, the deserters admitted they had left the Confederate army and were loyal to the Union. These turncoats were taken prisoner.

On the third evening, Dickison came upon more deserters riding in carts on their way to St. Augustine. He learned from them news of Colonel Wilcoxon, who had established headquarters at Braddock's farmhouse only two miles away. Dickison was told Colonel Wilcoxon had asked if they had seen anything of "Dixie." They related they had heard he was still at Waldo.

After taking them prisoners, Dickison rode on closer to Braddock's farm, then called another halt. Gathering his men around him, he let them know they would be outnumbered two to one by a tough enemy, but nonetheless he had decided to attack. He asked his men for their support and was given it unanimously. He ordered Lieutenant McEaddy to prepare his men for a charge.

Dickison rode at the head of the advance as they moved out, and the men watched for a wave of his handkerchief, which would signal their charge. Riding slowly, they came upon a heavy train of Federal wagons moving down a hill. Since they had just left headquarters, there was, to the delight of Dickison, no advance guard.

One lady who lived nearby recalled,

> Moving on slowly, [Dickison's] surgeon [Dr. Williams] by his side, he saw the enemy at some distance moving down a long hill with a heavy train of wagons. He could see them marching along in no particular order by the side of the wagons, having no advance guard, as they had just left their headquarters. A branch being between the enemy and our men, he ordered our advance, consisting of ten men under Sergeant William Cox, to dismount and take positions at the branch and await orders. The enemy hailed not over 150 yards distant, and our advance under the excitement fired into them without orders.[4]

The Confederates positioned themselves beside a small stream, and when the Federals halted 150 yards away, Dickison ordered a charge.[5]

"The heart of any commander would have thrilled with proud delight at the splendid heroism they displayed," recalled Mrs. Padgett. "They fought as only brave men fight. Charging up to the long line of wagons under a heavy fire, they pressed on until the enemy gave way and fell back to the woods, pursued by our intrepid dragoons."[6]

The Confederates raced alongside the retreating wagons, which they pursued into the woods. Dickison demanded a surrender, and the enemy believing they were facing superior numbers threw down their weapons.[7]

The battle, however, was far from over. As Captain Dickison and his troops circled the wagons, the Swamp Fox directed Dr. Williams to remain with the wagons and hold any other Dickison men charging toward them. Lieutenant McEaddy and several of his men suddenly charged a pond where Colonel

Wilcoxon and about twenty men were preparing to meet them.[8]

Colonel Wilcoxon, his staff, and a detachment of twenty cavalry, charged down a hill and attacked the Confederates gathered around the prisoners. A heated exchange developed, resulting in the wounding or death of all the Federals except Wilcoxon.[9]

Mrs. Padgett recalled: "They charged down the hill upon our men, coming up near where the prisoners had surrendered. Our command then fired into the colonel's escort, which dashed off on the road toward the wagons, where a lively fight ensued, our surgeon and Sergeant Cox with [ten] men killing and capturing every one, except Colonel Wilcoxson [sic]. He fought fearlessly."[10]

After firing his last shot, Wilcoxon hurled his pistol at one of the Confederates, drew his sword, and galloped down the road toward the prisoners.[11]

Captain Dickison feared this act of bravery might incite the prisoners to recommence fighting and rode toward Wilcoxon demanding his surrender. The Federal officer raised his sword at Dickison and charged directly at him. Dickison fired his pistol, hitting the colonel in the left side.

The horsemen galloped past each other, the wounded Federal still flashing his sword against the sky. Dickison quickly turned, and the adversaries met again, saber versus pistol. Another shot hit Wilcoxon, who fell from his saddle.

When the battle ended, Dickison learned the wounded Wilcoxon was not among the prisoners. Looking in the direction where the two had fought, he saw his adversary supported by a guard and was told the Federal wished to speak with him.[12]

Dickison dismounted and asked the wounded Federal, "Colonel, why did you throw your life away?" Wilcoxon, gallant to the end, answered, "Don't blame yourself, you are only doing your duty as a soldier. I alone am to blame." Shortly after, he died of his wounds.[13]

Mrs. Wilcoxon, widow of the colonel, wrote Dickison on March 23rd from Union-held St. Augustine and inquired if it were possible to have her husband's sword returned to her. She went on to say the sword would be part of the centennial celebration of the St. Johns lodge of Norwalk the following May and ended her letter by saying:

"What would I not give to be able to place in their hands the sword which, though it passed from my husband's hands in such a manner, has never been dishonored."[14]

Dickison received the letter under a flag of truce. Writing from Camp Baker, at Waldo, on the 31st, he replied:

"Previous to the receipt of your letter, at the request of your husband, I had concluded to send you the sword which was worn by him at the time of his capture. It is unusual, in time of war, to return captures of this description, but, in this instance, I will deviate from that course, on account of the feelings I entertained for your husband as a brave officer. With this, I send you his sword, trusting that it may reach you safely."[15]

In addition to the death of Colonel Wilcoxon, Adjutant Chatfield was killed, and thirty-two men and two officers were captured. The survivors were taken to the prison at Andersonville, Georgia, but with the war nearly over, they had not long to despair.

The Battle of Braddock's Farm, generally considered the southernmost battle of the Civil War, was called by Dickison "a decided and brilliant one." In total, about seventy-five men were captured, and the ten wagons pulled by horses and mules, were all loaded with Sea Island Cotton, which had been stolen and stored at Braddock's Farm.

One of the Braddock family members concurred: "The victory was a decided and brilliant one. The entire command was captured, about seventy-five in number, except four killed, also their wagon train, with ten fine wagons, each with six mules and horses, with best equipments all loaded with sea island cotton that had been stored at Braddock's farm, and all of their fine cavalry horses. Not a man was hurt on our side."[16]

Following the Battle at Braddock's Farm, Dickison and his men rode to a location eight or ten miles from the St. Johns River. Lieutenant McCardell's detachment was to meet them here, the command having divided three days earlier. McCardell did not arrive, and the Dickison soldiers were afraid their comrades had met with trouble.[17]

Riding another three miles, they halted, and Dickison sent four scouts to Horse Landing, the site of their capture of the Union gunboat *Columbine*. In the morning, the scouts met Dickison with a flatboat and the army crossed the river. He left a company of reserves behind at the damaged *Columbine*, instructing them to remove more weaponry, in case he needed help covering his return.

Dickison was certain the enemy was following him with a large force, attempting to pin him in between an impassable swamp and the St. Johns River. For that purpose, he dispatched a scout eight miles in his rear to spy on the Federal movements.

Dickison had to wait for McCardell, and he knew he was vulnerable. Should McCardell rendezvous with them, they would have two hundred fifty men, over two hundred horses, ten heavy wagons, and two ambulances to cross the river, perhaps under fire. Most frightening of all, Dickison had but one flatboat to get them all safely to "Dixieland," the western shore of the river, and its capacity was one wagon, or twelve men and horses.

Seventy of his infantry waited on the opposite shore, and he counted on them to assist with the arduous crossing. Dickison sent his prisoners across the St. Johns first, followed by the captured wagons and horses. The continued process of loading, crossing, and unloading, took not only all day, but all night.

While the undertaking was well under way, a courier came upon them with a message stating McCardell was safe and would soon join them. Twenty-five hours after the crossing commenced, Dickison came across on the last boat, amid repeated cheers. He immediately dispatched a courier to Waldo with a report of their operation, to be telegraphed to Tallahassee.

Honoring his men, his report read: "Brother officers and soldiers—again you have won fresh laurels. In your expedition across the St. Johns River and your engagement with the Federals, under Colonel Wilcoxon, you have achieved a brilliant victory. Receive, my brave men, the grateful thanks of your commander for your vigilance and undaunted courage you have exhibited, having undergone the fatigues of the campaign with patience and determination without a murmur."[18]

That same month, Confederate President Jefferson Davis appealed to the Southern people after General Sherman burned and destroyed Columbia, South Carolina: "There remains for us no choice but to continue the contest to a final issue." Floridians still clung to their faith in a victory.[19]

Like Davis, Governor Milton, in accepting two regimental standards, refused to give up the fight. He praised the "patriotism and invincible courage of Florida troops" in a "contest for the maintenance of their right to self govern-

General William T. Sherman. (National Archives)

ment-patriotism and courage which have exhibited their fixed determination to secure at all hazards, to themselves and their offspring the enjoyment of civil liberty, unrestrained save by the constitution of their own choice, and by laws imposed in accordance with the spirit and provisions of that constitution."[20]

Like both Davis and Milton, Dickison also refused to relinquish the fight. For him and his trusty band of guerrillas, there wasn't time to think about it.

Notes

[1]Mark F. Boyd, *The Battle of Natural Bridge,* Tallahassee, Reprinted from *The Florida Historical Quarterly,* October 1950, Volume XXIX, Number 2, pp. 95-96.

[2]Ibid.

[3]Ibid.

[4]Mrs. James (Braddock) Padgett, "Civil War Stories," Putnam County Clerk of Court; "Battle of Braddock's Farm," Putnam County Archives and History.

[5]Mark F. Boyd, *The Battle of Natural Bridge.*

[6]Mrs. James (Braddock) Padgett, "Civil War Stories," Putnam County Clerk of Court; "The Battle of Braddock's Farm," Putnam County Archives and History.

[7]Mark F. Boyd, *The Battle of Natural Bridge.*

[8]Mrs. James (Braddock) Padgett, "Civil War Stories," Putnam County Clerk of Court; "The Battle of Braddock's Farm," Putnam County Archives and History.

[9]Mark F. Boyd, *The Battle of Natural Bridge.*

[10]Mrs. James (Braddock) Padgett, "Civil War Stories," Putnam County Clerk of Court; "The Battle of Braddock's Farm," Putnam County Archives and History.

[11]Mark F. Boyd, *The Battle of Natural Bridge.*

[12]Zonira Hunter Tolles, *Shadows on the Sand,* pp. 165-167.

[13]Ibid.

[14]Ibid.

[15]Ibid.

[16]Mrs. James (Braddock) Padgett, "The Battle of Braddock's Farm," Putnam County Archives and History.

[17]Merlin G. Cox and J. E. Dovell, *Florida from Secession to Space Age,* St. Petersburg, Great Outdoors Publishing Company, 1974, p. 21.

[18]Samuel Proctor, "Florida a Hundred Years Ago," February 10, 1865.

[19]Marjory Stoneman Douglas, *Florida: The Long Frontier,* p. 193.

[20]*Pensacola News-Journal,* November 4, 1962.

Chapter 11

Station Four

On February 21, 1865, Major William Footman and two hundred seventy-five men of the Confederate "Cow Cavalry," attacked the Union garrison at Fort Myers. Although the attack was unsuccessful, the steamer *Alliance* pulled out before the engagement was finished, and brought news of the struggle to Brigadier-General John Newton, commander of the District of Key West and Tortugas.[1]

Newton decided to teach the pesky Confederates a lesson, and because of major Federal victories in South Carolina that month, he was certain the Floridians would give into any aggressive Federal operation. He began organizing a force to attack the Florida interior from the west coast, and many of the soldiers he chose were Union sympathizers from Taylor County, all of whom knew the land well.

The very evening Captain Dickison returned from his victory at Braddock's Farm, he received word from Captain E. J. Lutterlob, at the outpost near Cedar Key, reporting the landing of a large Federal force there supported by gunboats. The column, consisting of four hundred Negro troops and native "Union" cavalry, moved quickly out of Cedar Key up the east bank of the Suwannee River toward Levyville and Lake City. Along the way, the force collected Negro slaves and set fire to Confederate and state commissary stores. Horses, cattle, and cotton were also appropriated by the attackers.[2]

The Negro soldiers, or colored troops, as they were commonly called, wore a full blue uniform like their white counterparts and were composed of former slaves from Florida and other Confederate states. The Confederates were about to induct the slaves into their own army, but the war ended before this became a reality. Many slaves, however, were employed by the Confederacy for manual labor.[3]

Union troops, especially Negro troops, were ordered into the Florida interior to conduct raids resulting in the freedom of more slaves. These former slaves would be given the opportunity to join the growing Union force. Dickison's objective was to stop this escalation.

He telegraphed headquarters in Tallahassee and requested permission to move out against attacking Federals, who were under the leadership of Major

Edmund C. Weeks of the Second (Union) Florida Cavalry.[4] Weeks had organized a raiding force of about 400 men and marched his troops from Cedar Key into Levy County. Half of these Federal raiders were members of the Second Florida Cavalry directly under Major Weeks, while the others were from the Second United States Colored Infantry under Major Lincoln.[5]

Orders followed for him to move on with all the forces that he could muster and to harass the rear of the Federals until General Miller and his brigade coming from Lake City could meet the blues head on. Brigadier General Miller had been dispatched by Major-General Sam Jones to Newmansville to oppose Weeks.[6]

Meanwhile, troops of the Second United States Colored Infantry were already skirmishing Confederate pickets in the area. "I have been silent for some time, but once more I take opportunity offered to pen you the news from this vicinity," wrote Sergeant H. C. Jones of the Second. "Our battalion (the Second) was ordered to move with knapsacks, haversacks, canteens and eight days' rations. After marching some 40 or 50 miles, we were attacked by the Rebels at a place called Day Landing. In this engagement we lost but one. We were then ordered to a place called Sodom, where we had one wounded, and from which place we camped for the night, being very tired."[7]

With very little rest from their ten-day march at Braddock's Farm, Dickison, with only ninety men, set out to engage the Federals. After passing near Levyville, Dickison learned the enemy had been there and already vacated the town. When he was within four miles of the bluecoats, although he was aware he could not possibly cut them off, he pressed on. Just before sundown, Dickison arrived at Station Number Four near Cedar Key.[8]

More men reported to Dickison during the night, and by daylight the following morning, his force consisted of 160 men, including some artillery. A scout arrived bearing news that General Miller was now fifty miles to the rear and moving at a fast pace. Dickison was confident the enemy would fall back to the island under cover of their gunboats. He called immediately for a council of war, and it was quickly decided to attack the enemy at once.

Dickison knew he was up against overwhelming odds with the enemy occupying the high embankment above the railroad. The enemy reportedly consisted of two regiments of white and black troops— some 600 to 700 men.

"The sun rose clear and beautiful, and many who saw it rise never witnessed its setting, for we were called again into battle," recalled the Union Army's Sergeant H. C. Jones. "Our men stood up bravely, although the thing was managed poorly by those in command, and we had twice [sic] our number to contend with. We had only three companies."[9]

Leaving strong pickets on his right to prevent his being outflanked, Dickison moved slowly forward under fire from Federal pickets. Dickison called for a charge, and as he and his men dashed toward the enemy, volleys were discharged from both sides. The Federals in the stronghold finally gave way, and the Confederates took the road. Still, the Federals continued to rally and renewed the attack several times amid the heavy artillery shells.[10]

According to Sergeant Jones of the Union troops: "They opened on us again with their artillery, and we replied with our small arms. We called for no quarter. We had no time for fun either."[11]

Major Edmund C. Weeks said in his report on his return from Levyville that he "found his men flying in all directions" and "he left an officer to halt them and bring them up."[12]

Union reinforcements crossed a railroad trestle and began flanking Dickison's right. With the Confederate center barely able to hold its position, ten Confederate gunners moved to the trestle, which crossed over to the island, and fired their artillery. The Federals made several attempts to traverse three hundred yards toward their objective, but were repelled by volley after volley of Confederate shells.[13]

Lieutenant Bruton wheeled his artillery piece back and forth at advancing, then retreating, Federals to hit other enemies engaged with his own men. With only four shells remaining, Dickison ordered him to the center, leaving only Lieutenant McEaddy, his second in command, and ten men, to hold the trestle as long as they could. McEaddy had been with Dickison nearly from the time of the regiment's formation, and the captain trusted him more than any other.

Bruton, now in the center, held his grapeshot until the enemy was nearly upon him. When he did fire, heavy damage was inflicted on the opposing force, which fell back in confusion. When he had fired his final round, Bruton looked at Dickison and very calmly asked, "Captain, I have fired my last shell. What shall I do?" Dickison's reply was simply, "Remove your gun."[14]

Many of the Dickison men had fired their last shell, and no man had over three rounds left. With two hundred cartridges left in his satchel, Dickison rode along the line in the thick of the fight and distributed what he had to the men. When all these cartridges had been fired, Dickison ordered, in full view of the enemy, a retreat of some six hundred yards. The Federals did not pursue them.

At that bleak moment, a courier rode up with news of a Confederate wagon train coming, with ammunition for artillery and small arms, six to eight miles away. The wagons arrived some time after dark, and the men reloaded, ready to renew hostilities in the morning.

When the Confederates advanced in the early hours of morning, they found the Federals gone, having conducted a hasty and disorderly retreat during the night. Many of the Union dead had not been removed from the battlefield, and with many of the living cut off from the trestle, they retreated to the island. Some of these drowned as they attempted to swim the bay, while others were seen wading up to their necks.

When the Federal raiders returned to Cedar Key, they did so minus cattle, horses, and wagons. Their effort to move inland along the railroad had failed. According to Captain Dickison, "The slaves, horses, and several hundred head of cattle, with other valuable property, were captured, and returned to the owners. The enemy's loss was seventy killed and taken prisoner. We had six severely wounded."[15] Weeks, on the other hand, claimed only five killed, eighteen wounded, and three captured.

The victory was a typical Dickison rout. With a small force of one hundred sixty men, he had defeated an army of six hundred Federals. The Confederate soldiers and State Militia had fought side by side in grim determination.

In a running fight, Dickison and his men had chased Weeks all the way back to the Gulf. By the time Weeks reached his base, Brigadier-General John Newton's push on Tallahassee had already failed.[16]

Samuel Swann, Confederate commissariat at Gainesville described the Station Four battle in a letter to a friend:

> You will have heard by telegraph of the attack made on yesterday by Capt. Dickison at No. 4. Having to divide his ammunition with Lutterloh's and Williams' Companies, and the fight last-

> ing three hours, his powder and ball gave out, just as he was successfully driving the enemy into the water, and he was compelled to withdraw and await supplies. The engagement occurred directly at No. 4—the mainland terminus of this road. Capt D [Dickison] came upon them early yesterday morning while they were in the act of conveying to the island, the cattle, poultry & c they had stolen. He officially reports having killed about 50 or 60 and took 3 prisoners. We lost one man missing (supposed to have been captured) and 4 wounded. The enemy's force (about 600 strong) was composed principally of the deserters and negro garrison of Cedar Keys.[17]

The (Confederate) First Florida Reserves had also been summoned to fight the Union invaders, but after being told that Dickison and 145 men had already defeated the enemy, they turned back, disappointed at having failed to meet the enemy. One of these spunky soldiers, James Jaqueline Daniel, later wrote:

"The expedition made the long weeks of training worthwhile if only for the change our fruitless march worked on the men. I pray there will be no need, but should they be put to a test, I am confident they will bear their part well . . . I was pleased to see that many of the men shared this feeling, and, I confess, so did I."[18]

While returning to his headquarters at Waldo, Dickison met General Miller and his command at Gainesville. Major Weeks later reported to his superior that General Miller had arrived at the recent fight with 500 infantry and four pieces of artillery, forcing him to command a retreat. Weeks, of course, was in error because Miller and his brigade were met at Gainesville by Dickison, following his return from Station Four.[19]

The raid by Weeks alerted top-ranking Confederates in Tallahassee that the city might soon be under attack and provided General Miller with an opportunity to prepare for a more direct threat. Weeks provided Newton with an erroneous picture of Southern deployment in stressing that Confederate strength was concentrated further south than it really was.

The ladies of the town gave Dickison and his crew a dinner celebration, but despite the victories of the Swamp Fox, the war was lost. Savannah had surrendered on December 21st, a few months earlier, Fort Fisher on January 15, and Charleston was evacuated February 17, 1865, after a 167-day siege. Wilmington had surrendered on February 22nd, and Florida soldiers were making a last-ditch effort to save Columbia, South Carolina.[20]

As Weeks withdrew to Cedar Key, news of the defeat was again brought to Key West by the Alliance. General Newton reacted at once, asking Acting Rear Admiral C. R. Stribling, Commander of the East Gulf Blockading Squadron, to provide transports to carry reinforcements to Cedar Key.[21]

The initial destination of the steamer *Honduras* with its reinforcement troops, was Punta Rassa, where the men were expected to guard the Federal depot. On February 22, the steamer *Magnolia*, carrying the Ninety-ninth United States Colored Infantry, left for that same destination. Meanwhile, the *Honduras* returned with news that the Cow Cavalry had retreated from Fort Myers, and the ship readied itself to transport more troops the following day.

The commanders of the army and navy held a joint conference and decided to land a large force of troops at Tampa or Cedar Key to intercept a Confederate force believed to be on the lower peninsula. If no Confederate force was located, the Federal landing force would proceed to the area around St. Marks, the navy providing all ships it could spare from the blockade between St. George and Tampa.

On the 24th, the *Honduras* and *Magnolia*, with General Newton aboard

Major General John Newton. (National Archives)

the former, met at Punta Rassa, and, with Newton concluding there was no way of engaging the Confederates on the lower peninsula, the ships headed for Cedar Key. Recalling Major Weeks, a large Federal force embarked for St. Marks to put an end to Confederate resistance in Florida once and for all. Once St. Marks was taken and bridges and the railroad destroyed, Federals assumed Tallahassee would follow.

In a letter to Admiral C. K. Stribling, commander of the East Gulf Blockading Squadron, Newton wrote:

"As to proceeding to St. Marks, you are well aware Admiral, how fully I have been the [blank] to get there. We fully understand each other upon that point—that neighborhood is the one in which under present circumstances we ought to operate."[22]

Admiral Stribling pledged full naval support and ordered Lieutenant Commander William Gibson, the senior officer on the blockade at St. George's Sound, to ready all ships for an invasion against St. Marks.

Newton and three ships started for Apalachee Bay, arriving on February 28 in a dense fog. Other ships of the East Gulf Blockading Squadron joined him within a few days: the steamers *Stars and Stripes, Mahaska, Spirea, Fort Henry, Hibiscus*, and *Britannia*; the schooners *O. H. Lee, Mattew Vessor*, and *Two Sisters*; and a late arrival of the steamers *Proteus, Isonomia*, and *Hendrick Hudson*.[23]

Confederate victories in Florida such as at Olustee, Braddock's Farm, and Cedar Key mattered, perhaps, little in early 1865. The lower South was as isolated as the trans-Mississippi. Between the Confederacy's blockaded and garrisoned coast on one side and its sixty-mile path of devastation through the heart of Georgia on the other, Florida was like a shipless island.[24]

While Dickison and others in Florida kept winning, the South had collapsed all about them. The North had nearly a million men on land and sea while the South had but two hundred thousand. The North could call upon a million reserves, while the South had no reserves at all.

As early as June 1864, Southerners in Florida knew they were fighting a war they could not win. Under the title, "Depredations in Florida," the *Richmond* (Virginia) *Daily Dispatch* ran the following article:

> A letter from Florida, speaking of the Yankees, says:
>
> They are now scattered along the river from Jacksonville to Port Harney in bands from sixty to five hundred, occupying the east bank of the river, with a large train of wagons, busily

employed robbing every plantation they visit of everything they want, and burning or destroying what they do not want, insulting helpless women and children and driving them from their homes without even a change of clothing. The Yankees are very materially assisted by a large number of deserters of our army, who are well acquainted with the country, and act as guides. They are more infamous than the Yankees. Thousands of cattle have been run off by the Yankees, and several loyal citizens murdered.

The seaboard counties east of the river St. Johns, have suffered terribly from the depredations of the Yankees and deserters, the largest number of whom are in Volusia County. They have sixty men at Smyrna, sixty opposite Fort Gates, and others as far down as Fort Harney. St. Augustine is the base of their thieving and marauding operations. They had one negro regiment with them, but have from time to time detailed them as stock drovers, and now have only white troops—The Yankees say they do not intend to leave the country until the last horse, cow, and pig has been driven off, and from present indications they will accomplish the threat.[25]

Notes

[1]Mark F. Boyd, *The Battle of Natural Bridge,* pp. 95-96.

[2]Samuel Proctor, "Florida a Hundred Years Ago," February 8-10, 1865.

[3]Merlin G. Cox and J. E. Dovell, *Florida from Secession to Space Age,* p. 21.

[4]Charlton W. Tebeau, *A History of Florida,* Coral Gables, University of Miami Press, 1971, p. 217; Samuel Proctor, "Florida a Hundred Years Ago," February 1865; Mary Elizabeth Dickison, *Dickison and His men,* p. 136.

[5]Robert Bruce Graetz, "Triumph Amid Defeat: The Confederate Victory at Natural Bridge, Florida March 1865," An Honors Thesis submitted to the Florida State University Department of History, August 1986, p. 25.

[6]Mark F. Boyd, *The Battle of Natural Bridge,* p. 96.

[7]*Weekly Anglo-African,* February 13, 1865.

[8]Mary Elizabeth Dickison, *Dickison and His Men,* pp. 136-144.

[9]*Weekly Anglo-African,* February 13, 1865.

[10]Mary Elizabeth Dickison, *Dickison and His Men,* pp. 136-144.

[11]*Weekly Anglo-African,* February 13, 1865.

[12]Vince Murray, "Captain J. J. Dickison, Marion County's Civil War Hero," *Ocala Star-Banner.*

[13]Mary Elizabeth Dickison, *Dickison and His Men,* pp. 136-144.

[14]Ibid.

[15]Ibid.

[16]Dave Page, *Ships Versus Shore Civil War Engagements along Southern Shores and Rivers,* pp. 187-188.

[17]David James Coles, "Far from Fields of Glory: Military Operations in Florida During the Civil War, 1864-1865," pp. 237-238.

[18]Richard A. Martin, *The City Makers,* p. 68.

[19]Robert Bruce Graetz, "Triumph and Defeat: The Confederate Victory at Natural Bridge, Florida March 1865," p. 25.

[20]Merlin G. Cox and J. E. Dovell, *Florida from Secession to Space Age,* p. 24; Samuel Proctor, "Florida a Hundred Years Ago," February 1865.

[21]Mark F. Boyd, *The Battle of Natural Bridge,* pp. 96-97.

[22]Robert Bruce Graetz, "Triumph amid Defeat: The Confederate Victory at Natural Bridge, Florida March 1865," pp. 26-27.

[23]Ibid., pp. 27, 29.

[24]William Wood, *Captains of the Civil War,* New Haven, Yale University Press, 1921, pp. 379-380.

[25]*Richmond Daily Dispatch,* June 2, 1864.

Chapter 12

"Tallahassee or Hell"

The last major military battle in Florida occurred at Natural Bridge and ended in a Confederate victory. According to one Florida newspaper editor, "If the people of Georgia had turned out to oppose Sherman as the Floridians have in the battle fought at Natural Bridge he never could have reached Savannah."[1]

The two Confederate generals at Tallahassee were both experienced leaders. Major-General Samuel (Sam) Jones commanded the District of Florida. He had served as General Beauregard's chief of artillery at the Battle of First Manassas, and in 1862, was in command of the Department of Western Virginia. Relieved of command two years later for his "lackluster direction," Jones was assigned to command the Department of South Carolina, Georgia, and Florida before taking command of the District of Florida.[2]

Brigadier General William Miller, a veteran of the Mexican War, had led Florida troops at the Battle of Perryville, Kentucky, and was seriously wounded at the Battle of Murfreesboro. Commissioned a brigadier general in August 1864, he took command of Florida's reserve forces and soon after commanded the District of Florida. When replaced by General Sam Jones, Miller continued to lead reserve forces in Florida.

All Tallahassee rumbled with enthusiasm, when a courier arrived with word of a Federal landing at St. Marks by fourteen vessels. Intending to march on Tallahassee, the Federals were hindered by an intense fog and stopped by cannon fire while attempting to cross the St. Marks River at Newport. Unable to cross, the invaders slipped down the wooded east bank to a point eight miles from Tallahassee where the river sinks underground into a swampy region known as Natural Bridge.[3]

The Natural Bridge of the St. Marks River consists of a half-mile section of channels that flow above ground, then disappear underground at a sink. The final rise is in the basin, where the river continues above ground to its confluence with the Wakulla. A half mile below this basin, the river is dammed by a ledge of lime rock.[4]

Newton directed six men under pro-Union partisan leader William Strickland to land at the mouth of the Aucilla River. Strickland was to burn the railroad bridge over the river to prevent Confederate reinforcements from reaching Tallahassee from the east. Another landing party moved to Shell Point to burn the Ocklockonee River railroad bridge, preventing Confederate reinforcements from reaching the area from the west.[5]

As Strickland and his six-man force began burning the railroad bridge over the Aucilla River, eighteen-year-old Theodore Randell of the Second Florida Confederate Cavalry was on a train approaching the bridge. Randell later wrote:

> When we crossed the Aucilla River, we saw some lights under the Bridge, [and] thought they were campers, but they were Deserters (3) from Cedar Keys [and] Taylor Co, who had sawed the trestle and sit [sic] fire to the bridge—Track Dogs were used, and a Co of State troops, caught the deserters in Taylor Co. The 3 Deserters were Capt Strickland, who had a Deserter Co at Cedar Keys, [and] Brannan [and] Johnson when dogs came up, on the (3) Johnson shot one Dog, and the Confederates shot and kiled [sic] Johnson.[6]

Sylvanus Hankins of the First Florida Reserves was on the same train. Hankins later said the engineer tried to stop before reaching the burning bridge, but in finding he could not, "he put on all the Power his Engine had and [landed] us all OK acraust. . . . Some of the Bricks fell in as the last car got off of it."[7]

As Union troops approached, Confederate pickets waited at various defensive positions. Private David Shelton Sessions of Company I, Second Florida recalled:

> My command and I was [sic] at Natural Bridge when sixteen others and I were on outpost duty. Colonel McCormick and Lieutenant Ellis were in command of us; we were scouts. From two to four of the scouts were killed from ambush every week. Lieutenant Ellis was killed a short time before the surrender. He and a private by the name of Charley Bailey were killed at McGret's [McGirt's] Creek near Jacksonville, Fla., by a squad of Negro troops in an ambush in a thicket. They were not called upon to surrender till after being shot. Ellis clung to his horse for a hundred yards before he fell, and then pulled his pistol around to his front. He and Bailey took my place that day. Capt. Dickerson [Dickison] afterwards caught the squad of Negroes and hung them."[8]

Before abandoning the St. Marks River lighthouse, Confederates mined the structure, just before a thousand Federal troops came ashore. Meanwhile, some 300 Union seamen surprised Confederate pickets and seized the East River bridge, some four miles north of the lighthouse. Union warships, however, could not approach the old Spanish fort because of shallow water. After crossing the East River, Brigadier General John Newton sent his soldiers and sailors forth to find a place to cross the St. Marks River farther upstream.[9]

Newton later claimed that his objective had been to destroy valuable property in and around St. Marks and Newport but he had undoubtedly intended to capture the capital. The joint army-navy operation had originated at Key West and had not been planned overnight.[10]

Lieutenant Colonel John A. Wilder, second ranking officer in the Second United States Colored Infantry, wrote to his mother of Newton's designs on the capital. "The General has set foot on an expedition which is I suppose to attack Tallahassee but as it started while I was away I can not go," wrote Wilder. "I would give all my old [illegible] and more to go but can not."[11]

The Fifth Florida Cavalry defended the Newport Bridge. Newton, after leaving a small diversionary force there, continued up the east bank towards Natural

Bridge. But Confederate General William Miller wasn't fooled and sent forces, under Lieutenant Colonel George Washington Scott, to intercept them.[12]

While Scott and his men scrambled toward their objective, trains carrying Confederate militiamen neared the battle site. One young militiaman later recalled: "Companies of old men, and boys even smaller than ourselves came in and joined us during the evening; these we termed the 'Melish' and as to ourselves, why we became veterans of course, for the time at least.

"We left in the direction of St. Marks and the train stopped at a place called the 'oil still' where we unboarded and formed a line of march."[13]

Colonel J. J. Daniels and a guide walked in front of the young men. The colonel's horse followed as Daniels said he would rather march with his men than ride.

> The night was long and quite cool one of the boys said we had marched twenty-four hours that night and no sign of day. All the satisfaction we could get out of the guide was 'it is not much farther' this stereotyped phrase was repeated every time. Col[onel] Daniel [sic] when appealed to said he knew nothing his orders was to follow the guide, and the guide was right in not talking. At last just as we was about to enter a small clearing, I heard the guide tell Col. Daniels 'this is the place.'[14]

Colonel Scott and his men had reached Natural Bridge just as J. J. Daniels appeared with 380 reserves and militiamen with two pieces of artillery. Scott chose a defensive position but was already under attack before his men were aligned. Scott's cavalry defended the Confederate right, next to cadets lined up in the center. The Confederate line was arranged in a semi-circle, stretching from the river to the waterway. The "sloughs, ponds, marshes, and thickets" were great allies of the Confederate defense.[15]

For the citizens of Tallahassee, there was much excitement. Boys from the West Florida Seminary began digging earthworks at Fort Houston while awaiting hoped-for reinforcements from Confederate cavalry and state militia. Trains pulled out with rifle-clad young men; farmers armed with squirrel rifles trudged along on foot, and doctors raced their buggies in the direction of the impending battle.[16]

The cadets had been sent to Natural Bridge by Governor John Milton. Anxious to fight, they had assembled at the railroad station near the seminary for transport to the scene. A sister of one of the boys later recalled: "Mothers and sisters went to the station to say good-bye to them. The little fellows were full of patriotism and seemed to feel no fear. One little boy barefooted and wearing the cadets' uniform stood apart from the others, and was crying, because Captain Johnson refused to let him go, as he was the only son of a poor blind woman. Captain Johnson told him that good soldiers did not cry."[17]

The train brought the cadets to a point on the railroad opposite Newport. The boys marched the remaining six miles to town, linking up with Scott's Fifth Florida Cavalry. Scott's men had been skirmishing with the Federals for twenty-four hours and had slowly retreated from the East River Bridge towards Newport.

The cadets, arriving at Newport on March 5, marched through town to some breastworks running parallel to the river. Union troops fired at them from across the river as the young men ran, two at a time, into the trenches.

In the morning, the cadets left Newport to reinforce the lines at Natural Bridge. Marching along the old plank road, the boys could hear musket and cannon fire. As they approached the battlefield, they witnessed the tops of pine trees being blown away by Federal artillery.

Confederate troops arriving from Chattahoochie quickly unloaded their guns and equipment. Their three guns were placed to the right of Bruice's Light Artillery, two of these guns immediately in front of the opening of the Natural Bridge road. Hines' guns were placed to their right and supported by a company of dismounted cavalry.[18]

One of Daniels' young men recalled:

> When the skirmishers were formed in line in front of the main line, it had become light enough to take a view of the surroundings. The clearing proved to be an old abandoned field of not more than twenty acres. The hummock growth of hickory, oak, live oak, sweet gum and cypress grew quite thick right up to the edge of the clearing and probably two hundred yards in front of us. Some where near here the St. Marks River sinks in the ground, and emerges again a few hundred yards farther on. Hence the name of 'Natural Bridge.'[19]

Confederate troops were deployed in the timber and told to shoot anything that looked blue. "We beat around in the bush pretty much as we wished; I was investigating the effects of the firing on the bushes and timber when I came upon a dead Negro in U.S. uniform," recalled militiaman Joshua Hoyet Frier, II. "Some of the boys were more luckey [sic], and picked up some live ones, some were sent to the rear but it was said some of them never was."[20]

Federal troops, consisting of eight hundred Negro infantry with white officers, stormed the causeway, driving Confederate pickets from the bridge. Confederate cannon answered from the other side, and rifles cracked in the acrid smoke.[21]

One of the charging Negro troopers, Sergeant H. C. Jones, Second United States Colored Infantry, later wrote: "We have again been in action. We were ordered to move to Fort St. Marks at the Natural Bridge across the East River. There we captured one piece of artillery, and lost two men in the charge. We were repulsed for once and again made the charge and carried the breastworks. We lay 36 hours under fire. The 99th (U.S.C.T.) was too late."[22]

Some of the Negro troops had written "To Tallahassee or Hell" on their caps, and the ragged citizenry of Tallahassee that met their advance looked anything but like an army. Both sides charged and each pushed back. The Confederates lost a cannon.[23]

"About that time the Federals advanced their line, and we were called into action," recalled a Confederate soldier. "For a short time they made it hot for us with small-arm fire and a seacoast howitzer, a six-pounder with shells. At times I was ammunition carrier from limber to gun. If I had put my hat out (but I did not wear one) I could have caught a hatful of bullets, but I managed to escape every one, for which I was then and have been ever since very thankful."[24]

Local schoolboys, like those in the Battle of Marianna, fought to help defend the city. These Tallahassee schoolboys who took part in the Battle of Natural Bridge were known as the "Baby Corps."[25]

According to *The Tallahassee Floridian and Journal,* "Every man and boy capable of bearing arms was at his post. Never, since the commencement of the war, have the people exhibited a greater spirit."[26]

Although the young boys distinguished themselves well in battle, there were some amusing moments, according to one Confederate soldier: "The new issue boys were armed with old smooth, bore muskets, iron ramrod, shooting a ball and three buck shots. I was amused at four of these boys behind a small tree, the front one with one of these muskets along side of the tree, and the other three playing tag at his back. He fired the musket, which kicked him back, knocking those behind him down backward. All arose astonished; two of them ran off, and the other two stayed to reload the musket. They did not attempt to fire it again."[27]

Confederate militiaman Joshua Hoyet Frier, II, feared the worst when he discovered that his fellow defenders consisted of "old grey bearded men and boys almost too small to attend school." He did not feel the line could be held with such a force but was relieved to see "those undrilled little boys" holding their own.[28]

A spectator, Dr. Charles Hentz, later recalled: "I saw the flashing of the guns in the dark; immediately a cannon that was in position began throwing shell into the advancing Yankees; one after another some half dozen were thrown, and exploded down in the darkness about the bridge; when suddenly volleys of musketry were poured from the companies supporting the cannon; and replied to by the Yankees—sheets of flame illuminated the darkness, and minnie balls were whistling and shrieking all about us."[29]

Having been witness to an exaggerated report that a force of 5,000 Federals were attacking, Dr. Hentz wrote in his journal, "I could not see how, in our depleted condition, we could contend successfully with 5,000 troops; and with part of my family in Monticello, and part in Quincy, we would be in a most dreadful and deplorable condition if over run with negro soldiers."[30]

During the Federals' second charge, J. J. Daniels was thrown from his horse and severely injured. Scott took command, only to relinquish it when General Miller arrived. Miller commanded Scott "to combine a supervision of the line under his direction."[31]

General Newton, meanwhile, realized he could not take Natural Bridge by storming it. He then began to assess the Confederate flanks. But Colonel Scott, anticipating a flanking move from his adversary, quickly ordered Captain D. W. Gwynn to move further downriver to halt an attempted crossing. In the afternoon, Colonel Carraway Smith's cavalry arrived, extending Scott's right even further.

The Confederates began an artillery bombardment of Yankees positioned in the pine barrens. The Southerners followed with a bold charge over the Natural bridge but were driven back.

General Miller later stated that during the heavy fighting, Colonel John Joe Williams rode up with an order for him from General Sam Jones "to push your men into the hummocks and drive the enemy out." Miller was furious because he was certain such action would have slaughtered his men. He informed Williams to "Go back and tell General Jones if he wishes to murder his soldiers he must come on the ground and do it himself. I will not."[32]

After a temporary lull in the firing, the sound of hoofbeats, shouts, and rifle-fire announced the arrival of Florida cavalry and other Confederate reserves. Commanding the horse soldiers was Major William Henry Milton, son of Florida's governor, John Milton. Major Milton, had been adjutant-general of Florida in 1861, but he quit to form a cavalry unit that year and had been promoted from captain to major in 1863.[33]

Major Milton had a much younger half-brother, John, by his side in the battle that day. John, had joined the Confederate army in time for the Battle of Marianna and had followed his older half-brother throughout the course of the war. A descendant reflects:

"My whole family talked about how Governor Milton's son went to war at twelve. This nearly killed my great-grandfather [Governor Milton] to see this young boy of twelve with a gun on his shoulder. My grandmother didn't like to talk about it, and I don't blame her. They had to put it all behind them to live."[34]

The newly arrived Florida Cavalry dismounted and charged the Federal troops. One Confederate soldier later said the "shooting and shouting" reminded him "more of some kind of frolic then [sic] the serious work of battle." He added, "but the timber in front of us was a sight to me. Many trees of considerable size was cut down at various heights, the limbs and trunks of most of them seemed to have the [bark] stript from them as by lightning."[35]

Among the newly arrived Southern troops was Willie Bryant, who later recalled, "our Battn [did] all of the fighting after we got there, the Reserves having been there some hours [and] tired; It was a regular Indian swamp fight, being at close range, our men being behind trees mostly, [and] the Enemy behind entrenchments [and] logs."[36]

The Federals, upon the arrival of Floridian cavalry, hastily picked up their twenty-one dead and eighty-nine wounded, and retreated to their ships. The Confederate infantry pursued their enemy but were hindered by felled trees. Scott, however, managed to follow them with a small number of cavalry, inflicting casualties at every opportunity. The Confederate pursuers captured thirty-five prisoners.[37]

Despite their retreat, the Federals prepared several lines of earthworks to slow the Confederate advance. Confederate Colonel Carraway Smith asked for volunteer skirmishers to determine whether the enemy was in full retreat. One of the volunteers, young Willie Bryant, later recalled:

> As soon as the skirmishers crossed, the Enemy opened a terrible fire upon us, as far as noise was concerned, [and] then fell back—random shooting [and] an irregular fight was kept up until we brought up standing by another small stream, the bridge torn [and] burning [and] another line of entrenchments just where the pine woods joined the swamp confronting us—It was impossible to get the men to charge in a body, I tried in vain with those around me, then dashed into the road [and] on the Bridge myself to try example, a volley opened at once [and] no man came to me; I fired my gun, then stepped behind a tree [and] loaded again, [and] my blood being up to fighting . . . I took my hat in my hand, [and] cheering made another start, just then the word was given that we were being reinforced, when a few followed me, I being the first to cross the Burning Bridge [and] in the face of the Enemy, almost the whole Battallion being witness.[38]

Reaching the second Federal line, Bryant discovered that the enemy had "abandoned that line also [and] scampered across the open woods like black sheep, only a part of them going to their main works still further back. There was fun, as the black devils, with only white men as officers among them, we scampering for dear life, while the 5 or 6 of us in advance who reached the open woods first had nothing to do but shoot and yell at them."[39]

Three Confederate dead and twenty-two wounded were put on a train, and the town celebrated victory over a superior army. Tallahassee, at the end of the war, remained the only Confederate capital east of the Mississippi River, in Confederate hands.[40]

One Union sharpshooter, who had not retreated, fired three shots at the victorious Confederates from a tall cypress tree. Two of these shots struck a piece of artillery, the third shattered the left arm of Confederate gunner, George Griffin. The rebel gun sergeant spotted the sniper through his glass and fired back. Searching the cypress following the Federal retreat, the men found the sharpshooter's body had been cut nearly in half.

"Some of our soldiers, native, knew of a foot-log below the Natural Bridge," recounted a Confederate soldier. "The Federals had fallen back to the outside of the swamp on the road and had begun to throw up breastworks. About one hundred men were detailed under command of officers to dislodge the enemy. It was getting late in the afternoon when we heard an insistent roar of small arms across the swamp. We knew that our men had successfully crossed, but of the result of the firing we did not know. We had not long to wait, a courier from the commander came in and notified us that our men had come up in the rear of the Federal breastwork and after emptying their guns the Federal troops had fled in disorder, leaving their dead in our hands."[41]

The West Florida Seminary cadets were ordered back to Newport to guard against any Federal attempt to cross there. They were issued rations of corn pone, which they used as "ammunition" in a bread battle among themselves.[42]

Enthusiastic civilians met the cadets. The young, somewhat embarrassed heroes were crowned with wreaths of wild olives and young ladies serenaded them with new stanzas, composed for the occasion by Miss Mag Brown, of the song "Dixie.":

"The Young Cadets were the first to go
To meet and drive away the foe . . .
Look away! Look away! Look away for the land of Dixie!
They met the foe down at New Port.
Look away! &c.
They threw up breastworks with their hands.
Breastworks of logs, pine knots and sand;
Look away! Etc.
And fought against the combined powers
Of Yanks and Blacks and shrapnell [sic] showers
Look away! &c."xliii

As souvenir hunters raped the battlefield at Natural Bridge, the ladies of Tallahassee prepared a picnic banquet of whatever food they could forage for the troops. William Strickland and another man from the Taylor County Rangers (Southerners who were fighting for the Union) had been captured while trying to burn the Aucilla River bridge, and were both court-martialed as deserters and shot.[44]

General Newton and his defeated Federal army limped back to the safety of their ships. Newton returned to his command post at Key West, and the "invading" army was distributed to posts at Cedar Key, Punta Rassa, and Key West. The detachment at Fort Myers was broken up.[45]

Newton blamed the rout on his not being supported, but it was not only the grounded Federal warships that had cost him a victory. Almost 400 Federal soldiers at Cedar Key had also been ordered to reinforce Newton's attack on Tallahassee, and they, too, had failed in their mission.[46]

Quick to blame the navy for his failure, Newton played down the scope of his invasion, stating:

"The naval force, which exaggerated the importance of the expedition in the public eye, being unable to perform the part assigned, was, to say the least, of no benefit to our operations. The expedition was not undertaken to go to Thomasville, capture Tallahassee, or occupy any part of the country, unless it should afterward appear that St. Marks possessed great advantages for the latter purpose."[47]

Newton also stated that the Confederates had the advantage because of geography and "would not have stood before my troops in any other position, were impregnable at Natural Bridge, which could have been defended by 200 resolute men, with a few pieces of artillery, against five times their number."[48]

General Miller, the Confederate commander, credited the Natural Bridge for his victory as well. Referring to the battle, Miller later stated:

"Had the Federal General been a man of ability, had he studied all the routes through which to assail Tallahassee, instead of trying to force an almost impregnable pass, it would have taxed the powers of the ablest commander backed by all the forces of the State, besides the regular forces of the Confederate Commander. The proud capital of a proud people would have seen their country wasted by Federal troops, and their streets thronged by negro regiments."[49]

In his postwar memoirs, Miller criticized his own leader, Sam Jones, for remaining too far to the rear during the battle. "I never saw General Jones either at Newport or at the Natural Bridge until after our victory was complete," wrote Miller. In another account of the incident, Miller penned that when Jones finally did appear on the battlefield, "I write it with reluctance and humiliation—he was intoxicated and it was evident to men and officers."[50]

Although Confederates expected another all-out attack on the capital, the Federals did not bother to mount another effort. The war had been won, but a handful of loyal Floridians refused to believe it. Among those was Captain Dickison.[51]

Despite his country's inevitable demise, Dickison continued his operations through Federal-held territory along the St. Johns River. He knew the eccentric course of the river like no other, and his knowledge of its uniqueness enabled him to appear and vanish at will.

Still, in March 1865, one side of the river, "Dixieland," still belonged to Dickison, and he refused to relinquish it. On March 10, he received information at one of his river outposts from Colonel Samuel Owens of Marion County, reporting that the enemy had again advanced twelve miles into the interior, crossing and then burning the Marshall Bridge.[52]

Many of these black Union soldiers had left Jacksonville, traveled down "Dickison's" St. Johns River, stopped at Fort Gates, then crossed the Oklawaha River at Sharpes Ferry. These Union troops attacked the plantation of the widow of Colonel J. Foster Marshall, burning sugar, syrup, machinery, and plantation buildings. They appropriated slaves, horses, and wagons.[53]

A slave fled by horseback into Ocala and spread word of the disaster. The Home Guard, as well as Dickison, were alerted. Within two hours, Dickison and his men were on their way to meet the enemy. At Silver Springs, a courier intervened with news that the enemy had burned the Oklawaha Bridge and were heading toward the St. Johns River. Dickison then directed his men back in the direction of Palatka, and, after a bad wind delayed his crossing the river by ten hours, Dickison and fifty troops crossed by flatboat. The remainder of his troops and a single piece of artillery were positioned in several sites along the St. Johns to guard the river.[54]

Upon arriving in Palatka, Dickison learned that the Federals had gone up river on barges. Ordering an all-night march, often at half-speed, Dickison reached Fort Peaton, capturing four Negroes. Only seven miles from St. Augustine, he stepped up the march and captured twenty-four pickets, a wagon, and six ponies along the way.

The Federals, by now aware they were being pursued by Dickison, hastily abandoned wagons, mules, and provisions at the river where they crossed near Fort Gates. With the Federals safely reaching St. Augustine, Dickison and his men had little to show for their efforts. The four-day march with little or no provisions, however, did once again keep the Federals out of "Dixieland."

The Quincy [Florida] *Dispatch* of March 22nd reported: "Captain Dickison recrossed the river St. Johns a few days since with twenty-four Negroes, several deserters, wagons, mules, etc., which he had recaptured from the enemy within a mile of St. Augustine." After describing Dickison's latest valorous deed, it added: "The [Federal] cavalry, discovering themselves so closely pursued, put spurs to their horses and galloped into town, leaving their colored brethren' to fall a prey to the War Eagle of Florida. He made them right-about, and marched them back to the old plantation home."[55]

Moments of glory such as this were waning for the Confederacy, and the war was all but over in Florida as well as in the rest of the nation. With the outcome clear, it brought little comfort to Governor Milton that his was the only Confederate capitol east of the Mississippi River not in Union hands.[56]

Milton had done his best, and, still knowing he was dedicated to a lost cause, persevered. The governor openly expressed his belief: "Death would be preferable to reunion." He firmly believed in what he said "is the sentiment of all true Southern men."[57]

The majority of Floridians did not share his idea of death over surrender. A few Floridians had escaped to Latin America but most soldiers said "thank God it is over; one way or another."[58]

On April 1, 1865, Milton and his family arrived at Sylvania, their plantation near Marianna, following a long, tedious journey from Tallahassee. The governor, feeling tired, retired to his main floor bedroom to rest before dinner while his daughter helped with meal preparation in the kitchen. His son, Major William Henry Milton, was resting on the piazza.[59]

The house was suddenly disturbed by a shot, and when Milton's son raced into his father's bedroom, he found the senior Milton lying on the floor with blood rushing from his head. Across one of the governor's feet, he found an old muzzle-loading shotgun. Preferring death to dishonor, the governor had taken his own life with a single shot.

To him, death was preferable to the bonds and "loathsome embrace" he felt would follow.[60] Regarding his suicide, a descendant felt, "The family was always upset over that, but it was either that or go to prison or worse."[61] Milton had rendered every possible aid in the Civil War, besieging the United States Arsenal at Apalachicola, Forts Marion and Augustine, and the navy yard at Pensacola. Throughout the war, he had made repeated calls for more men.[62]

Even with the Governor gone, Dickison refused to abandon his cause, accepting neither death nor dishonor. On April 3, two of his pickets on the St. Johns River intercepted the courier line between St. Augustine and Jacksonville. Four Federals killed, one captured. In addition, Dickison took two horses and disappeared into "Dixieland" with the Federal mails from St. Augustine and Jacksonville.[63]

On behalf of all the ladies of Florida, a group of women from Madison presented Dickison with a sword as "a tribute to the invaluable service which you have rendered the Southern Confederacy, in her struggle for independence, and more

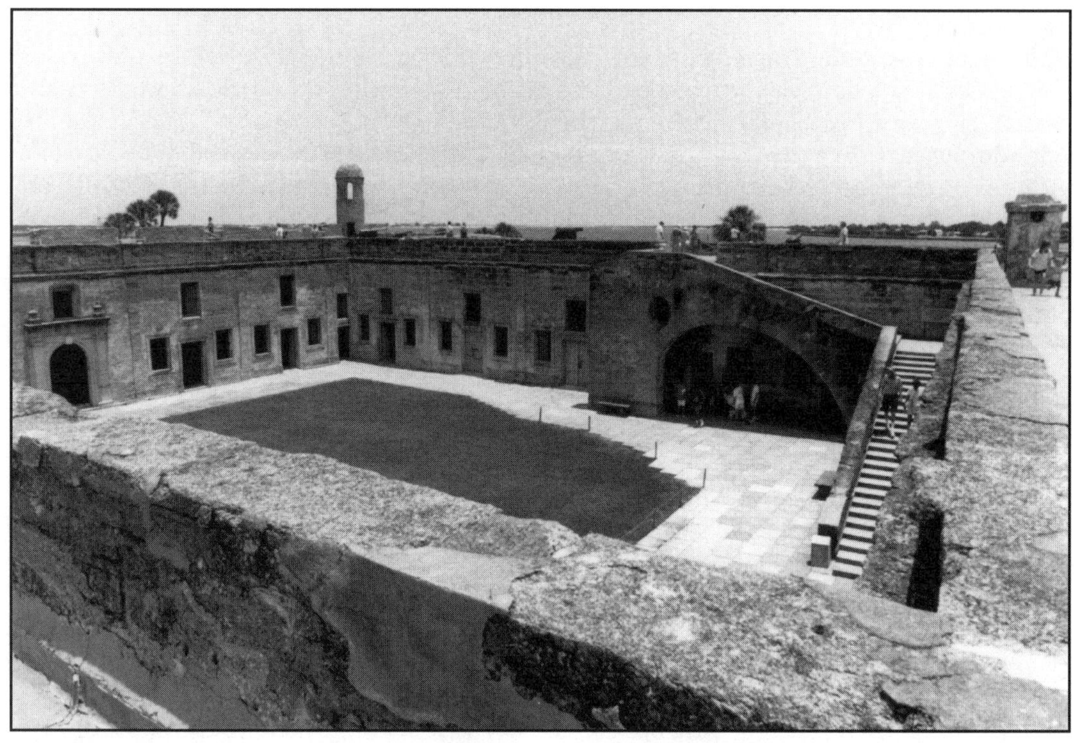

Fort Marion (Castillo de San Marcos), St. Augustine. In November 1961, General Robert E. Lee declared: "The small post posted at St. Augustine serves only as an invitation to attack." (Photo by Dave Page)

particularly, those which you have rendered the state of Florida, entitle you to the sincere thanks and warmest expression of gratitude from all your countrymen."[64]

The same day the *Gainesville Cotton States* reported Lieutenant A. A. Johnson of the Florida Militia had presented Dickison with a fine pair of spurs as a slight token of appreciation. "Spurs," the newspaper reported, "are indispensable to 'the War Eagle of the East.'" Another admirer presented him with a horse.[65]

But the big news came from Confederate Secretary of War John C. Breckinridge, writing from Greensboro, North Carolina: "You J. J. Dickison are informed that the President has appointed you a Colonel of Cavalry in the Provisional Army, in the service of the Confederate States. Should the Senate in the next session consent there to, you will be commissioned accordingly. Should you accept, you would report for duty to Major-General Sam Jones, commanding District of Florida."[66]

Dickison was elated over his promotion, but it came so late that little authority went with it. Over the final two months of the war, President Jefferson Davis had appointed General Robert E. Lee Commander-in-Chief of the Confederate Army. Lee and Joseph E. Johnston did their best to hold off Grant and Sherman, but each was facing an army that was alone a match for both.[67]

The Confederacy's sole chance of prolonging anything more than a small guerrilla war was for Lee and Johnston to join forces in southwestern Virginia. Here the only line of rails was safe from Union attack for the moment. But Grant

Residence of Jefferson Davis, 1201 East Clay Street (top), Richmond, Virginia. The Jefferson Davis home in Montgomery, Alabama. (National Archives)

General Joseph E. Johnston. (National Archives)

Portrait of Major General Ulysses S. Grant, Brady National Photographic Art Gallery, Washington, D.C. (National Archives)

and Sherman kept the two Southern generals apart, and then the Federal navy closed in from every direction applying the death grip.

Robert E. Lee surrendered on April 9, and Confederate troops in Florida laid down their arms under the terms of Joseph E. Johnston to William T. Sherman on April 26. On May 10, General E. M. McCook reached Tallahassee and accepted the surrender of the capitol and 8,000 troops in Florida.[68]

On May 20, the Stars and Stripes flew once more over the capitol in Tallahassee. Although 15,000 Floridians served in the Confederate army, 2,200 had served in the Union forces. Over a thousand of these had died on various battlefields and another 5,000 were wounded. One Confederate regiment of 1,276 men suffered the worst with only sixty-six surviving.

Most Floridians experienced relief when the war ended, despite its outcome, as evidenced by Davis Bryant at Camp Baker: "The majority of this command—and nearly all in our company—seem rejoiced and do not hesitate to express themselves to that effect. After the surrender orders were read yesterday when the ranks were broken a majority of our company set up a hearty yell, much to my annoyance and their disgrace, and it was remarked upon by some of the other camps."[69]

Colonel John J. Dickison's unit surrendered and was paroled at Waldo, Florida on May 20, 1865. Unlike Bryant's men, the Dickison men did not share the same enthusiasm over surrender and would have gladly continued their operations along the St. Johns.

While awaiting the formal surrender, Dickison addressed his troops and related, that "in taking leave of his fellow soldiers," he "felt a deep sympathy for them." He said, "It is, however, our duty to be cheerful and hopeful with the consolation and satisfaction of feeling that we are not whipped, but overpowered by the vastly superior force. You will go home, my brave men, with unconquered hearts and honorable names. May the blessing of God protect you forever is the farewell wish of your commander."[70]

Still, Dickison's men did not want to quit and asked why they had to surrender having never been defeated. They wanted Dickison to continue the fight, join the Trans-Mississippi army under General John Magruder and Florida's own General Kirby Smith or follow Jo Shelby to Mexico. Dickison may have considered such a connection except for the uncertainty as to the status of the Trans-Mississippi army. If Smith's men were about to surrender, the results might have been disastrous for Dickison's own troops.[71]

General Edmund Kirby Smith. (National Archives)

Jo Shelby. (Courtesy Armand DeGregoris)

Dickison's men accepted his judgment and laid down their arms. For the Swamp Fox of the Confederacy, War Eagle of the East, Knight of the Silver Spurs, Francis Marion of Florida, there would be no more all-night rides to capture an unsuspecting Federal force. The war for Dickison and the South was over, but for the Swamp Fox, there would be one more adventure.

Notes

[1]Samuel Proctor, "Florida a Hundred Years Ago," March 1865.

[2]Robert Bruce Graetz, "Triumph amid Defeat: The Confederate Victory at Natural Bridge, Florida March 1865," An Honors Thesis Submitted to the Florida State University Department of History, August 1986, pp. 8-9.

[3]Marjory Stoneman Douglas, *Florida: The Long Frontier,* p. 193.

[4]Mark F. Boyd, *The Battle of Natural Bridge,* p. 102.

[5]Robert Bruce Graetz, "Triumph amid Defeat: The Confederate Victory at Natural Bridge, Florida March 1865, p. 34.

[6]David James Coles, "Far from Fields of Glory: Military Operations in Florida During the Civil War, 1864-1865," p. 325.

[7]Ibid., pp. 325-326.

[8]Mamie Yeary, compiler, *Reminiscences of the Boys in Gray, 1861-1865,* Dayton, Ohio, Morningside Press, 1986,p. 677.

[9]Dave Page, *Ships Versus Shore Civil War Engagements along Southern Shores and Rivers,* p. 187.

[10]David Coles and Robert Bruce Graetz, "The Garnet and Gray West Florida Seminary in the Civil War," *Florida State, The Magazine of the Florida State University Alumni Association,* April 1986, p. 3.

[11]Robert Bruce Graetz, "Triumph amid Defeat: The Confederate Victory at Natural Bridge, Florida March 1865," pp. 33-34.

[12]Dave Page, *Ships Versus Shore Civil War Engagements along Southern Shores and Rivers,* p. 187.

[13]Joshua Hoyet Frier, II, "Reminiscences of the War Between the States by a Boy in the Far South at Home and in the Ranks of the Confederate Militia," unpublished manuscript transcribed by J. W. Hart, Florida State Archives, pp. 149-150.

[14]Ibid.

[15]Marion B. Lucas, "Civil War Career of George Washington Scott," pp. 145-146.

[16]Marjory Stoneman Douglas, *Florida: The Long Frontier,* p. 194.

[17]David Coles and Robert Bruce Graetz, "The Garnet and Gray West Florida Seminary in the Civil War," p. 3; David J. Coles, "Florida's Seed Corn: The History of the West Florida Seminary During the Civil War," *Florida Historical Quarterly,* Vol. LXXVII, No. 3, Winter 1999, p. 296.

[18]Mark F. Boyd, "The Joint Operations of the Federal Army and Navy Near St. Marks, Florida, March 1865," *Florida Historical Quarterly,* 1950, XXIX, pp. 96-124.

[19]Joshua Hoyet Frier, II, "Reminiscences of the War Between the States by a Boy in the Far South at Home and in the Ranks of the Confederate Militia," p. 156.

[20]Ibid., p. 157.

[21]Marjory Stoneman Douglas, *Florida: The Long Frontier,* p. 194.

[22]*Weekly Anglo-African,* April 1, 1865.

[23]Marjory Stoneman Douglas, *Florida: The Long Frontier,* p. 194.

[24]James M. Dancy, "Reminiscences of the Civil War," *Florida Historical Quarterly,* p. 82.

[25]Dennis Brindell-Fradin, *From Sea to Shining Sea Florida,* Chicago, Childrens Press, 1992, pp. 22-23.

[26]Richard A. Martin, *The City Makers,* p. 68.

[27]James M. Dancy, "Reminiscences of the Civil War," *Florida Historical Qaurterly,* 82.

[28]Joshua Hoyet Frier, II, "Reminiscences of the War Between the States by a Boy in the Far South at Home and in the Ranks of the Confederate Militia," pp. 160-162.

[29]Robert Bruce Graetz, "Triumph amid Defeat: The Confederate Victory at Natural Bridge, Florida March 1865," p. 51.

[30]Ibid., p. 40.

[31]Marion B. Lucas, "Civil War Career of Colonel George Washington Scott," pp.

145-146.

[32]Robert Bruce Graetz, "Triumph Amid Defeat: The Confederate Victory at Natural Bridge, Florida March 1865," pp. 58-59.

[33]*Pensacola News-Journal,* November 4, 1962; *Florida Edition: Makers of America,* Advance Sheets from Volume 1, Atlanta and Tallahassee, A.B. Caldwell Publishing, No date given, p. 6.

[34]Georgia Atkinson Bradfield interviews with author October 13 and October 21, 1992, Ormond Beach, Florida.

[35]Joshua Hoyet Frier, II, "Reminiscences of the War Between the States by a Boy in the Far South at Home and in the Ranks of the Confederate Militia," pp. 161-162.

[36]David James Coles, "Far from Fields of Glory: Military Operations in Florida During the Civil War, 1864-1865," p. 347.

[37]Marjory Stoneman Douglas, *Florida: The Long Frontier,* p. 194; Marion B. Lucas, "Civil War Career of Colonel George Washington Scott," pp. 145-146.

[38]David James Coles, "Far from Fields of Glory: Military Operations in Florida During the Civil War, 1864-1865," p. 348.

[39]Ibid., p. 349.

[40]Marjory Stoneman Douglas, *Florida: The Long Frontier,* p. 194.

[41]James M. Dancy, "Reminiscences of the Civil War," *Florida Historical Quarterly,* p. 83.

[42]David Coles & Robert Bruce Graetz, "The Garnet and Gray West Florida Seminary in the Civil War," p. 4.

[43]David J. Coles, "Florida's Seed Corn: The History of the West Florida Seminary During the Civil War," *Florida Historical Quarterly,* p. 301.

[44]Marjory Stoneman Douglas, *Florida: The Long Frontier,* p. 194.

[45]Mark F. Boyd, *The Battle of Natural Bridge,* pp. 113-114.

[46]Dave Page, *Ships Versus Shore Civil War Engagements along Southern Shores and Rivers,* p. 187.

[47]Robert Bruce Graetz, "Triumph Amid Defeat: The Confederate Victory at Natural Bridge, Florida March 1865, p. 70.

[48]Ibid., p. 60.

[49]Ibid.

[50]David James Coles, "Far from Fields of Glory: Military Operations in Florida During the Civil War, 1864-1865," pp. 359-360.

[51]Mark F. Boyd, *The Battle of Natural Bridge,* pp. 113-114.

[52]Samuel Proctor, "Florida a Hundred Years Ago," March 1865.

[53]Lucy B. Tobias, "River Raids," Internet.

[54]Samuel Proctor, "Florida a Hundred Years Ago," March 1865.

[55]*Quincy Dispatch,* March 22, 1865.

[56]Charlton W. Tebeau, *A History of Florida,* p. 217.

[57]Merlin G. Cox and J. E. Dovell, *Florida: From Secession to Space Age,* pp. 25-26.

[58]Ibid.

[59]Samuel Proctor, "Florida a Hundred Years Ago," April 1-2, 1865.

[60]*Pensacola News-Journal,* November 4, 1862.

[61]Georgia Atkinson Bradfield interviews with author October 13 and October 21, 1992.

[62]*Florida Edition: Makers of America,* p. 6.

[63]Samuel Proctor, "Florida a Hundred Years Ago," April 5, 1864.

[64]Ibid.

[65]Ibid.

[66]Ibid.

[67]William Wood, *Captains of the Civil War,* p. 381.

[68]David J. Coles, "Volusia County: The Land Warfare 1861-1865," *Civil War in Volusia County A Symposium,* p. 50; Samuel Proctor, "Florida a Hundred Years Ago," May 1865.

[69]Ibid.

[70]Ibid.

[71]Mary Elizabeth Dickison, *Dickison and His Men,* p. 229.

Jefferson Davis. (Courtesy Armand DeGregoris)

Chapter 13

Underground Passages

On May 10, 1865, President Jefferson Davis was captured near Irwinville, Georgia, during an attempt to flee the country. Several Confederate officials had accompanied Davis on this flight, including Secretary of State Judah P. Benjamin, Secretary of War John C. Breckinridge, Attorney General George Davis, and several other loyal cabinet members. Most, however, had parted company with the president before his capture; Judah Benjamin reaching Cuba via Florida's nearly uninhabited west coast, and Attorney General Davis passing through Lake City and Gainesville to live under an alias in Ocala.[1]

Jefferson Davis monument at capture site near Irwinville, Georgia. (National Archives)

Gamble Plantation near Tampa, Florida. In May 1865, Confederate Secretary of State Judah P. Benjamin hid in this house following his escape from Richmond. (Photo by Dave Page)

Also missing was the Confederate Baggage and Treasure Train with half a million dollars from the treasury in Richmond. The money on the treasure train was to be used for starting a new Confederacy west of the Mississippi, and for expenses paid to persons aiding and abetting the fleeing cabinet members.[2]

On May 15, 1865, the Treasure Train entered Florida through "underground passages" created by friends and fellow Confederates. Crossing a tributary of the Suwannee River, the cavalcade consisted of an ambulance and heavy wagon, both drawn by mules, and guarded by nine trusted Confederate cavalry men.

The convoy passed safely to the Yulee plantation near Gainesville, on May 22, only to learn from Mrs. Yulee that Jefferson Davis had been captured. Convinced all hope was gone for the "new" Confederacy, the treasury, now only $25,000, was apportioned and the trek of the "train" was over.[3]

Confederate Vice President Alexander Stephens. (National Archives)

When President Jefferson Davis was captured, the *New York Herald* regretted General Breckinridge, the rebel War

Secretary was not brought to justice with him. It did offer assurance, however, that "such disposition of the national cavalry had been made as, it is believed, will completely cut off the escape of Breckinridge . . . and other Cabinet officials and fellow criminals."[4]

Born in Lexington, Kentucky, January 16, 1821, Breckinridge had practiced law, and as a staunch, moderate Democrat, had risen from state representative in Frankfort, to the House of Representatives in Washington, and to vice-president of the United States under James Buchanan.[5]

After losing the presidential election to Abraham Lincoln in 1860, Breckinridge served as United States senator from Kentucky and endorsed a campaign of secession for his state. As a champion for the South, he was suspected of treason. When a warrant was issued for his arrest in September 1861, Breckinridge fled south and joined the Confederate Army.

In January 1865, Jefferson Davis appointed him Secretary of War, and as the war drew to a close, he advocated an honorable surrender for the Confederacy. Considered a traitor by the North, he, like President Davis and other mem-

Richmond, Virginia, street in the burned district. (National Archives)

bers of his cabinet, had to flee the country with Davis upon the South's defeat.

Breckinridge, however, had eluded the Federal cavalry, parting company with President Davis in Washington, Georgia, on May 4th. Moving with a small escort through Valdosta, Georgia, he spent several days in Madison, Florida, hiding in the home of General Joseph Finegan, the hero of Olustee.[6]

In Finegan's home, he met Captain John Taylor Wood, commander of the commerce raider *C.S.S. Tallahassee*. Wood was also in flight after having been captured with Davis at Irwinville only to escape his Yankee captors. Wood and Breckinridge decided to join forces in fleeing the country.

Wood was certain that the Federals in Florida were watching any possible escape routes for fleeing Confederates. Union Admiral Cornelius R. Stribling, commanding Key West, had already issued orders for his men to guard the southern coast of Florida. Stribling also had assumed that, since the Confederates could not travel to Key West, they would attempt to reach nearby islands. Wood decided to sail to the Bahamas from the east coast, eventually reaching the Trans-Mississippi Department.[7]

Wood traded his tired horse to Finegan, giving him fifty dollars to boot. After gathering supplies, the men rode eastward to the home of Lewis M. Moseley, who operated a ferry across the Suwannee River.

On May 16, the men crossed the limestone-banked Suwannee via Moseley's Ferry and continued riding through an isolated area along the St. Augustine Road. Plagued by mosquitoes, the men rode across a natural bridge over the underground Santa Fe River. They found water—bad water—at Double Sinks, the only available drinking water on their trek.

The two men traveled on horseback to Gainesville. Former Confederate Congressman James B. Dawkins was waiting for them. Since his house had other guests that night, Dawkins had them sleep in safety on the floor of a nearby tavern. Wood later referred to the accommodations as a "filthy hole."[8]

At Waldo, ten miles away, Captain Dickison was preparing to parole his men in two days. About ten o'clock in the evening, a courier handed him a mysterious note asking him to come to Gainesville at once, and signed simply "Confederate officer." Dickison left immediately, taking a small escort with him.[9]

Upon reaching Gainesville, he was met by Judge Dawkins and brought to his house. Waiting for him at the Dawkins house was General J. C. Breckinridge, Secretary of War, Confederate States of America. With the general were Captain John Taylor Wood, Chief-of-Staff Colonel J. H. Wilson, and Breckinridge's loyal black servant, Thomas Ferguson.

Breckinridge informed Dickison he was trying to reach the Trans-Mississippi department, west of the Mississippi River, to join Generals Kirby Smith and Magruder before they surrendered. The general felt that if he could find a way to Cuba, he could then make his way by boat to "Kirby-Smithdom." He asked for Dickison's assistance in preparing an escape route and providing a boat.

The Swamp Fox agreed with Wood's plan for heading towards the east coast, for, although there were several Federal blockade camps situated there, the coast could not be closely guarded because of inland waterways and keys. Dickison reminded the men that they must move quickly, for there were Federal patrols in the area and others were soon returning.[10]

Dickison told the general he would do all he could. The only boat at his disposal was a lifeboat from the *Columbine*, which he had captured on the St. Johns River. Dickison had hidden the lifeboat by sinking it in a lake, and he offered to raise it and give it to the general for his "heroic plan." John Taylor Wood referred to Dickison as "a most valuable friend."[11]

After the preliminary arrangements were worked out, Dickison returned to Waldo and paroled his men the next day. He had arranged, meanwhile, as escort, one of his sons to take the general and his party to Millwood Plantation, the home of Colonel Samuel Owens, that night, twenty miles away. Dickison rode to join them in the evening after getting the small boat ready.

Other sources state that Dickison and Breckinridge also stayed at the home of Confederate General Robert Bullock.[12]

Wood, meanwhile, rode southwest in search of Judah P. Benjamin who had passed Moseley's Ferry only two days ahead of them. Wood was hoping that the former Secretary of State wanted to join their group. Armed with a revolver given him by Dickison, Wood followed the Cedar Keys and Fernandina Railroad tracks to Archer. Here, he was welcomed by the wife of former United States and Confederacy Senator David L. Yulee at their Cottonwood Plantation.[13]

While Wood was unable to locate Benjamin, he did learn considerably about the Yankees in the area. Yulee returned from Jacksonville that evening where he had been discussing the situation of the postwar South with United States Supreme Court Chief Justice Salmon P. Chase. Wood learned that several Southerners might be charged with treason and that Jefferson Davis was a prisoner on a ship off the South Carolina coast bound for Federal prison.

Wood returned to Millwood Plantation on May 20, unaware that Confederate Secretary of the Navy Stephen R. Mallory had been arrested late that night at the home of former Confederate Senator Benjamin H. Hill in LaGrange, Georgia. Mallory was indicted for treason, and five days later, Yulee was arrested and also charged with treason.

Jefferson Davis. (Courtesy Armand DeGregoris)

The Swamp Fox knew the St. Johns River better than anyone, and laid out a plan for them to escape by Florida's eastern coast, thus avoiding the western route taken by Secretary of State, Judah P. Benjamin. In addition to providing a lifeboat, he gave them the services of the ever-faithful Lieutenant William H. McCardell as a guide.[15]

While Dickison was busy arranging for the escape, the fleeing Confederates visited the home of Owens' brother, Captain William A. Owens, at Rutland Plantation. While Breckinridge and the others stayed overnight at Rutland, Wood and McCardell traveled to Silver Springs, six miles northwest of Ocala, to be guests of wartime Florida legislator Hiram T. Mann, McCardell's father-in-law. Wood called the springs "the most beautiful submarine view I have ever seen."[15]

Wood and McCardell then rode south and rejoined Breckinridge at Wauchula Plantation, home of the former Confederate Quartermaster General of Florida Colonel A. G. Summer. The Florida heat and invading mosquitoes became unbearable, but still the men went hunting and remained at the plantation until the 23rd.

The following day, the horsemen camped at beautiful Lake Weir. On the 25th, they rode along the south shore of Lake Weir. Then McCardell swung eastward and stopped at the plantation of Major Thomas Stark, only a day's ride from the St. Johns River. The men were well-supplied with salt, meat, grits, and sweet potatoes, since procuring food to the south would be next to impossible. Breckinridge kept with him a pocket compass and a map of Florida.

The last leg of the ride consisted of thirty-two miles of heavy sand, dwarf pine, and scrub oak.

On May 26, Breckinridge and Wood reached the St. Johns River near the present town of Astor, and three of Dickison's men—Sergeant Joseph O'Toole, Corporal Richard R. Russell, and Private P. Murphy—all paroled soldiers from Dickison's unit—were waiting with the lifeboat. With little wind for the tiny sail, the men rowed furiously up the St. Johns, which Breckinridge regarded as a baffling stream.

Wood later referred to the three men as "most valuable and trustworthy comrades they proved to be, either in camp or in the boat, as hunters or fishermen."[16]

"The boat's head," Breckinridge recorded, "pointed to every point of the compass, and we were often puzzled and led astray by false channels that ended in nothing . . . [The river] abounds in cranes, pelicans, and other water fowl, and great numbers of crocodiles . . . I shot one with my pistol, and after we got him ashore, it required three more balls through the place where his brains should have been, to finish him . . . We caught some fish in the river, and found some sour oranges in a deserted orchard."[17]

Dickison's men could not remember when the mosquitoes on the St. Johns had been so terrible, and with nightfall, they anchored the boat in the middle of the river to sleep. This procedure repeated itself for four days when they finally reached Lake Harney. Near the mouth of the lake, George Sauls and his ox team were waiting to take them to the Atlantic.[18]

Before parting company with Lieutenant McCardell, Breckinridge wished to thank him for his courage.

Stating he had "but a few more hours of authority," as Secretary of War, Breckinridge penned a major's commission for McCardell.

Lieutenant General Richard Taylor, CSA. (Courtesy National Archives)

However, the Lieutenant had a request, "Well, you see, general, thar's a feller in our regiment what hain't done nothin' and he is a major and a quartermaster, and if it's all the same to you, I would just like to rank him onst."[19]

The Secretary of War was amused by the strange request of the Dickison man but, nonetheless, altered the commission to read Lieutenant-Colonel. Author William Davis summarizes the event:

> It was the last official act of the Confederate War Department, and of the Confederate States of America. The secretary did not know it, but General Richard Taylor had surrendered back on May 4, and most of the Trans-Mississippi was being turned over to the Federals just as Breckinridge wrote out the commission. . . . Curiously enough, then, the Confederate government was terminated here on the swampy banks of the St. Johns by a secretary of war who in times past had done his best to prevent the birth of that Confederacy, his final act a promotion given half in jest to a man who had already taken his parole from the enemy. The "magnificent epic" as Breckinridge termed it, could not have suffered a less dramatic demise.[20]

When the boat was loaded on the oxcart, Private Murphy, who claimed the lifeboat was his, left the party after receiving one hundred dollars from Breckinridge. Sergeant O'Toole and Corporal Russell, the other Dickison guides, continued on with the Breckinridge party overland.[21]

Leaving at sunrise on May 30, the men began their twenty-eight-mile overland trek through sandy palmetto barrens and grassy swamps. The men had to walk, the boat balanced on the wagon. Wood despised their two bulls, referring to them as "a compound of Caucasian, African and Indian."[22]

On May 31, they finally reached the Atlantic Ocean, fifty miles south of present day Daytona Beach and launched the lifeboat at Carlisle's Landing, three miles north of the present city of Titusville. Staying on the Indian River, they were plagued by mosquitoes from the swamps and marshes, and once slipped by a Federal camp in the middle of the night.

The men camped on the west bank of the river. Discovering the water too brackish to drink, they were able to dig in the sand and provide themselves with water slightly better. With little breeze, the mosquitoes were ferocious.

Wood wrote that "when sleeping on shore, the best protection was to bury ourselves in the sand, with cap drawn over the head, if in the boat to wrap the sail or tarpaulin around us."[23]

They entered the Atlantic Ocean near Jupiter Inlet, and, afraid of the blockading and patrol camps along the Florida coast, they decided to head for the Bahama Islands, only sixty miles distant. On June 5, a strong wind forced them back to the Florida coast.

Their good luck had apparently left them when they saw a large Federal steamer coming down the coast directly at them. Rowing to shore, Breckinridge and the Dickison men hid themselves and their boat. Thinking it safe, they stepped out, only to be sighted by the transport steamer, which turned around and came at them.

Three hundred yards from the shore, a boatload of Federals armed with cutlasses and pistols was lowered, and the first impulse of the escaping Confederates was to flee into the swamps. But John Taylor Wood and the two Dickison men rowed out to meet them, leaving Breckinridge and his two aides on shore.

"To the usual hail I paid no attention except to stop rowing," Wood wrote later. "A ten-oared cutter with a smart-looking crew dashed alongside. The sheen was not yet off the lace and buttons of the youngster in charge. With revolver in hand he asked us who we were, where we came from, and where we were going. 'Cap'n,' said I, 'please put away that-ar pistol; I don't like the looks of it, and I'll tell you all about us. We've been rebs, and there ain't no use saying we weren't; but it's all up now, and we got home too late to put in a crop, so we just made up our minds to come down shore and see if we couldn't find something.'"[24]

Acting foolish, Wood, O'Toole, and Russell pretended to be hunting, fishing and "wrecking" along the coast, and offered to sell the Federals turtle eggs. The ruse worked, but the escaping company entered the sea a little less comfortably.[25]

On the morning of June 6, they landed at a Seminole Indian village and obtained some *koonti*, which resembled a pancake but was "ten times as tough."

Reaching the southern extreme of Lake Worth, they found a boat coming directly at them. They considered jumping overboard, thinking the boat was another Federal patrol, but when it turned abruptly, Wood realized its crew probably consisted of deserters or escaped prisoners from the Dry Tortugas.

Pretending to be a Federal officer, Wood demanded their surrender. He then ordered them to trade boats with their party or be shot or taken to prison. When the trade was carried out, the terrified newcomers hurried off. By a simple act of piracy, the Breckinridge men sailed away in a much more seaworthy sloop.

On June 9, they put the coast of Florida behind them and entered the storm-ridden Gulf Stream to Cuba. After riding out a storm which nearly destroyed their craft, they entered the Cuban harbor of Cardenas on June 11.[26] Breckinridge was given asylum by the Cuban government.[27]

Breckinridge had considered linking up with Florida's General Kirby Smith, who had not surrendered at the time Breckinridge began his flight. Dickison probably contemplated the same idea. But, by the time Breckinridge reached Cuba, Smith had given up. Breckinridge decided to follow through and head for England.[28]

Before leaving for England, Breckinridge said goodbye to the two Dickison faithfuls, O'Toole and Russell, who returned to their homes in Florida.[29] After sentiment against him subsided, Breckinridge left Europe to reside in Niagara Falls, Ontario. Receiving amnesty from United States President Andrew Johnson in 1869, Breckinridge returned home and pursued his law practice while promoting a railroad business. He died on May 17, 1875, and was buried in Lexington.[30]

The Swamp Fox had certainly played a pivotal role in prolonging the Secretary of War's life, and it was not forgotten by the politician. On June 26, 1865, only two weeks after his escape to Cuba, Breckinridge penned a letter to J. J. Dickison, thanking him for helping mastermind his escape and for the aid of his two men. The men, he said, would provide him with an "account of our adventures, which may be termed both singular and perilous."[31]

One of Breckinridge's last official acts was to approve J. J. Dickison's appointment as colonel.[32]

Notes

[1]David J. Coles, "Volusia County: The Land Warfare 1861-1865," *Civil War in Volusia County: A Symposium,* pp. 51-52; Branch Cabell and A. J. Hanna, *The St. Johns, a Parade of Diversities,* pp. 218-220.

[2]A. J. Hanna, "The Confederate Baggage and Treasure Train Ends Its Flight in

Florida, A Diary of Tench Francis Tilghman," Reprinted from *Florida Historical Quarterly,* January 1939, pamphlet, no page numbers.

[3]Kathryn Trimmer Abbey, *Florida Land of Change,* pp. 291-292.

[4]David J. Coles, "Volusia County: The Land Warfare 1861-1865," *Civil War in Volusia County: A Symposium,* pp. 51-52; Branch Cabell and A.J. Hanna, *The St. Johns, a Parade of Diversities,* pp. 218-220.

[5]J. Erik Landrum, "John C. Breckinridge," unpublished manuscript.

[6]Mary Elizabeth Dickison, *Dickison and His Men,* pp. 224-226; A.J. Hanna, *Flight into Oblivion,* Richmond, Johnson Publishing Company, 1938, pp. 230-231.

[7]Royce Gordon Shingleton, *John Taylor Wood Sea Ghost of the Confederacy,* Athens, The University of Georgia Press, 1979, pp. 167-168.

[8]Ibid.

[9]A. J. Hanna, *Flight into Oblivion,* pp. 230-231.

[10]Royce Gordon Shingleton, *John Taylor Wood Sea Ghost of the Confederacy,* pp. 167-168.

[11]Ibid.

[12]Vince Murray, "Captain J. J. Dickison Marion County's Civil War Hero," *Ocala Star-Banner.*

[13]Royce Gordon Shingleton, *John Taylor Wood Sea Ghost of the Confederacy,* pp. 169-170.

[14]A. J. Hanna, *Flight into Oblivion,* pp. 230-231.

[15]Royce Gordon Shingleton, *John Taylor Wood Sea Ghost of the Confederacy,* pp. 171-173.

[16]John Taylor Wood, "Escape of the Confederate Secretary of War," *The Century Magazine,* 47, 1893-1894, p. 111; William C. Davis, *Statesman, Soldier, Symbol,* Baton Rouge, Louisiana State University Press, 1974, pp. 530-532.

[17]A. J. Hanna, *Flight into Oblivion,* pp. 230-231.

[18]Ibid. pp. 146-147.

[19]David J. Coles, "Volusia County: The Land Warfare 1861-1865, *Civil War in Volusia County A Symposium,* pp. 51-52.

[20]William Davis, *Breckinridge: Statesman, Soldier, Symbol,* Baton Rouge, Louisiana State University Press, 1974, pp. 525-540.

[21]A. J. Hanna, *Flight into Oblivion,* pp. 14-30, 185-190.

[22]Royce Gordon Shingleton, *John Taylor Wood Sea Ghost of the Confederacy, pp. 175-176.*

[23]Ibid., pp. 176-177.

[24]*Philadelphia Evening Bulletin,* June 22, 1865.

[25]Royce Gordon Shingleton, *John Taylor Wood Sea Ghost of the Confederacy,* pp. 182-183.

[26]A. J. Hanna, *Flight into Oblivion,* 170-190.

[27]J. Erik Landrum, "John C. Breckinridge."

[28]Vince Murray, "Captain J. J. Dickison Marion County's Civil War Hero, *Ocala Star-Banner.*

[29]Mary Elizabeth Dickison, *Dickison and His Men,* p. 227.

[30]J. Erik Landrum, "John C. Breckinridge."

[31]Mary Elizabeth Dickison, *Dickison and His Men,* p. 227.

[32]Vince Murray, "Captain J. J. Dickison Marion County's Civil War Hero," *Ocala Star-Banner.*

A Reb 'n' Proud

Keep your constitution of the United States,
With a passion that bloody paper I hate.
Keep your starred and striped flag
Whose black shadow makes me rage and gag.
For I fought in six burned 'n' ravaged states
For the love of Lee and the Confederacy's fate.
We fought those Yanks for four desperate year,
So don't ask me to ever an blue-belly endear
'N' if I could I'd fight 'em some more
I'd show 'em reconstruction out a this Reb's smokin' bore.
With shot, sabre, and bombs incendiary
We wrote three hundred thousand Northern obituary,
'N' still I'd like to kill some more
Till the Missi'sip' ran red with Northern gore.
Their ports would clog heavy with corpses decaying
For Sherman's march to the sea, a sweet repaying.
In my heart Dixie ever calls,
Through blood and tears to a South that will never fall.

- George Diezel II

Epilogue

Dickison's own official last act had been to aid in the escape of Secretary of War Breckinridge. With the war formally over, he went home to Ocala.[1] Still, his career was not over as a Southern leader, for, during the Johnsonian era of reconstruction, the government of Florida continued under ex-Confederates. Among the state senators were General Joseph Finegan, Colonel Theodore W. Brevard, and John L. Crawford. In the lower house were Colonel George Troup Maxwell, John A. Henderson, and, of course, Captain J. J. Dickison.[2]

In spite of his continued leadership, the war left Dickison, like most Southerners, a ruined man. Sunnyside, his plantation at Orange Lake was a shambles, his wealth was gone, and he could not get over the death of his son Charlie who, while serving under him, had died at Palatka on August 2, 1864.[3]

During the violent gubernatorial elections of 1868, Dickison was alleged to have taken part in certain acts of secret organizations of white conservatives. On November 5th of that year, sixty boxes of arms, including 1,200 muskets purchased in New York, were thrown from a train on its way to Tallahassee from Jacksonville. Thomas Gregory, later Woodrow Wilson's United States Attorney General, was informed by a member of the group that all the men operating the train—telegraphers, brakemen, conductors, and engineers—were members of the Ku Klux Klan.[4]

These desperate men, one of whom was believed to have been the Swamp Fox, had boarded the train between Madison and Lake City, disposed of the ammunition and arms, and departed the train at the next stop. There they returned to the scene of the dumping and destroyed the shipment. Soldiers who were guarding the munitions were stationed in two cars. None of them, however, were aware of the raid until the train pulled into Tallahassee. The supply car door had not, in fact, been broken, but unlocked, and half the shipment was missing.

The guns were being shipped to state units sanctioned under the militia law. Regulators and the Ku Klux Klan, however, had made up their minds that the guns would not be used to arm Black troops. A local militia officer charged that Dickison had been the leader of the group of raiders. He said Dickison was known for his "cruelties and atrocities" against Unionists during and following the Civil War.

In 1877, Dickison was appointed adjutant-general by Governor George B. Drew, thus becoming a member of the first Democratic state cabinet after Reconstruction. When the Florida Division of the United Confederate Veterans was organized in 1888, Dickison was elected commander, and he served six consecutive terms, holding the state military title of Major-General.[5]

The flag of the Marion Light Artillery, Florida Battery, was given to the Museum of the Confederacy in Richmond, as part of its Flag Conservation Program by Mr. and Mrs. Dickison in 1893. Made from a crimson shawl that was part of Mrs. Dickison's bridal gown, it had been presented to Dickison and his unit by the Ladies of Orange Lake Soldiers Association at Camp Langford on April 8, 1862.[6]

Lieutenant J. A. Neal had carried the flag through July 1864 when he sent it home to his mother and sisters in Zebulon, Georgia. Lieutenant Neal was killed in action the following month. In April 1865, a large body of Federal cavalry passed through Zebulon, and his sister, Miss Ella Neal, concealed the Marion Light's flag under her overskirt to prevent it from being captured.

In 1899, Dickison wrote *Military History of Florida*, considered yet today as one of the best books ever written on Florida's Civil War era. The Dickison book was one part of a multi-volume history published by the Confederate Publishing Company of Atlanta, Georgia.[7]

Throughout this latter period, Dickison had been in failing health and a near invalid. He died in his home in Ocala on August 23, 1902 at the age of eighty-eight.

According to his wishes, he was dressed in his full Confederate uniform, transported by train to Jacksonville, and buried in the Evergreen Cemetery August 26.

The service was conducted by Reverend E. G. Weed, Bishop of Florida. Following the service, the walk to the grave was headed by a detachment of police and infantry companies, the hearse and pallbearers, several Confederate veterans, and the Martha Reid Chapter of the Daughters of the Confederacy. Dickison's sword rested on the gray casket with the Confederate flag and beautiful flowers.[8]

Stores and offices throughout the city closed in honor of the fallen hero, and thousands of people lined the sidewalks to glimpse the black-draped, horse-drawn caisson move slowly down Main Street to the cemetery.

The *Ocala Banner* paid tribute by calling him "the most conspicuous soldier Florida contributed to the Civil War."[9]

General E. M. Law, in a *Florida Times Union and Citizen* article, wrote,

> He was the hope and defense of the state in the dark days of the Civil War, the only safeguard of the people against a foe that swarmed on every side. He swept from place to place with such rapidity and secrecy that his name struck terror to the hearts of the enemy and made them fearful of every rumor.
>
> He was grand in war, grander in peace. In the darkest days of adversity and personal suffering, he was always the same gentle, loving man, fearless in his advocacy of right, and daring in his defense of his friends.[10]

Richard P. Weinert, Office of the Chief of Military History historian, added, "Dickison was one of the ablest guerrilla commanders produced not only during the Civil War, but probably in all military history of America."[11]

An account of Dickison's exploits, recorded in the Putnam County Archives, states:

Grave of Captain J. J. Dickison, Evergreen Cemetery, Jacksonville, Florida. (Photo by J. Walker Fischer)

> Although Captain Dickison never attained the historical importance of General Francis Marion of Revolutionary War fame, his military tactics and exploits were similar. The British troops named General Marion, the "Swamp Fox." To Dickison the Union troops were a little more generous—they called him "DIXIE." Often in their dispatches Dixie was reported to be in a trap. Somehow the trap never closed fast enough, and Captain Dickison would be heard from several miles away from the purported trap, harassing the enemy's flank.[12]

Another account in the Putnam County Archives, from an August 28, 1902 obituary, states: "Many of Dickison's movements during the time he kept the enemy from overrunning the State calls to mind the career of Marion, the South Carolina partisan ranger of the Revolutionary War. The same shrewdness, daring and military mother wit belonged to both of these heroes."[13]

A memorial to Captain Dickison still stands in Hemming Park in downtown Jacksonville. At the base of the Confederate Monument is a bronze plaque of the Swamp Fox. Inscribed at the top are the words, "Tried and True."[14]

Like the Confederacy he loved, John J. Dickison, the Swamp Fox of the Confederacy, the Knight of the Silver Spurs, passed into history.

Notes

[1]Hal Bamford, *Florida History,* St. Petersburg, Great Outdoors Publishing Company, 1976, pp. 49-50.

[2]Merlin G. Cox and J. E. Dovell, *Florida: From Secession to Space Age,* pp. 35-36.

[3]Samuel Proctor Introduction to Mary Elizabeth Dickison, *Dickison and His Men,* p. XIX-XX; Hal Bamford, *Florida History,* p. 50.

[4]Vince Murray, "Captain J. J. Dickison Marion County's Civil War Hero," *Ocala Star-Banner.*

[5]Samuel Proctor Introduction to Mary Elizabeth Dickison, *Dickison and His Men,* pp. XIX-XX; Hal Bamford, *Florida History,* p. 50.

[6]The Museum of the Confederacy, Richmond Virginia, Flag Conservation Program brochure; Laura Mohammad, "Women Left at Home Forced to Fend for Themselves," *Ocala Star-Banner,* 1997, Internet.

[7]Samuel Proctor's Introduction to Mary Elizabeth Dickison, *Dickison and His Men,* XIX-XX; Hal Bamford, *Florida History,* p. 50.

[8]"Rebels of Palatka," pp. 8-9.

[9]Samuel Proctor's Introduction to Mary Elizabeth Dickison, *Dickison and His Men,* XIX-XX; Hal Bamford, *Florida History,* p.50.

[10]Vince Murray, "Captain J. J. Dickison Marion County's Civil War Hero," *Ocala Star-Banner.*

[11]Ibid.

[12]"John Jackson Dickison Biography," Putnam County Archives and History, Palatka, Florida.

[13]"Death of John Jackson Dickison reported on August 28, 1902, Florida's Hero Solider Passes Away at Ocala," Putnam County Archives and History under Dickison 1.

[14]Untitled manuscript in Putnam County Archives and History, Palatka, Florida.

Bibliography

Books

Abbey, Kathryn Trimmer, *Florida Land of Change,* Chapel Hill, University of North Carolina Press, 1949.

Akerman, Jr., Joe A., *Florida Cowman, A History of Florida Cattle Raising,* Kissimmee, Florida, Florida Cattlemen's Association, 1976.

Bamford, Hal, *Florida History,* St. Petersburg, Great Outdoors Publishing Company, 1976.

Bockelman, Charles, *Six Columns and Fort New Smyrna,* DeLeon Springs, Florida, E.O. Painter Printing Company for the Halifax Historical Society, 1985.

Boggess, Francis C.M., *A Veteran of Four Wars, the Autobiography of F.C.M. Boggess,* Arcadia, Champion Job Rooms, 1900.

Brindell-Fradin, Dennis, *From Sea to Shining Sea Florida,* Chicago, Childrens Press, 1992.

Brown, Jr., Canter, *Florida's Peace River Frontier,* Orlando, University of Central Florida Press, 1991.

Cabell, Branch and Hanna, A.J., *The St. Johns, A Parade of Diversities,* New York & Toronto, Rinehart & Company, Inc., 1943.

Catton, Bruce, narrator, McPherson, James M., editor, *The American Heritage New History of the Civil War,* New York, Penguin Books, 1996.

Chaitin, Peter M., *The Coastal War Chesapeake Bay to the Rio Grande,* Alexandria, Virginia, Time-Life Books, 1984.

Chandler, David Leon, *Henry Flagler, the Astonishing Life and Times of the Visionary Robber Baron Who Founded Florida,* New York, Macmillan Publishing Company, 1986.

Covington, James W., *The Story of Southwestern Florida,* Volume I, New York, Lewis Historical Publishing Company, 1957.

Cox, Merlin G. and Dovell, J.E., *Florida from Secession to Space Age,* St. Petersburg, Great Outdoors Publishing Company, 1974.

Crowninshield, Benjamin W., *A History of the First Regiment of Massachusetts Cavalry Volunteers,* written for the First Massachusetts Cavalry Association, Cambridge, Massachusetts, Houghton, Mifflin and Company—The Riverside Press, 1981.

Davis, William C., *Breckinridge: Statesman, Soldier, Symbol,* Baton Rouge, Louisiana State University Press, 1974.

Dickison, J.J., *Military History of Florida Volume X* of Clement A. Evans, *Confederate Military History,* Atlanta, Confederate Publishing Company, 1899.

Dickison, J.J., *Florida Confederate Military History, Volume XI,* Atlanta, Confederate Publishing Company, 1894 Reprint Edition, New York, 1962.

Dickison, Mary Elizabeth, *Dickison and His Men,* Gainesville, Florida, University of Florida Press, Facsimile of 1890 Edition, 1962.

Douglas, Marjorie Stoneman, *Florida The Long Frontier,* New York, Evanston & London, Harper & Row Publishers, 1967.

Dupuy, Ernest R. and Dupuy, Trevor N., *The Compact History of the Civil War,* New York, Hawthorn Books, Inc., 1960.

Emilio, Luis F., *A Brave Black Regiment,* New York, Bantam Books, Reprinted from the 1894 Boston Book Company Edition, 1991.

Eppes, Susan Bradford, *Through Some Eventful Years,* Gainesville, Florida, University of Florida Press, Facsimile of 1926 Edition, 1968.

Faust, Patricia L., editor, *Historical Times Illustrated Encyclopedia of the Civil War,* New York, Harper & Row, 1986.

Florida Edition: Makers of America, Advance Sheets from Volume 1, Atlanta and Tallahassee, A.B. Caldwell Publishing, no date given.

Foote, Shelby, *The Civil War A Narrative, Fredericksburg to Meridian,* New York, Random House, 1963.

Freeman, Douglas Southall, *Lee's Lieutenants, Gettysburg to Appomattox,* Volume 3, New York, Charles Scribner's Sons, 1972.

Gallagher, Gary W., editor, *Fighting For the Confederacy, The Personal Recollections of General Edward Porter Alexander,* Chapel Hill, North Carolina, London, England, The University of North Carolina Press, 1989.

Gannon, Michael, *Florida, A Short History,* Gainesville, Florida, University Press of Florida, 1993.

Glatthaar, Joseph T., *Forged in Battle, The Civil War Alliance of Black Soldiers and White Officers,* New York, The Free Press, 1990.

Gooding, Corporal James Henry (edited by Virginia M. Adams), *On the Altar of Freedom, A Black Soldier's Civil War Letters from the Front,* Amherst, The University of Massachusetts Press, 1991.

Graff, Mary B., *Mandarin on the St. Johns,* Gainesville, University of Florida Press, 1963.

Grismer, Karl H., *The Story of Fort Myers,* St. Petersburg, St. Petersburg Printing Company Inc., 1949.

Halifax Historical Society, Inc., *Civil War in Volusia County A Symposium,* Daytona Beach, Florida, 1987.

Hanna, A.J., *The Confederate Baggage and Treasure Train Ends Its Flight in Florida, A Diary of Tench Francis Tilghman,* Reprinted from *Florida Historical Quarterly,* January 1939.

Hanna, A.J., *Flight into Oblivion,* Richmond, Johnson Publishing Company, 1938.

Hanna, Alfred Jackson and Hanna, Kathryn Abbey, *Florida's Golden Sands,* Indianapolis & New York, the Bobbs-Merrill Company, Inc., 1950.

Hanna, Alfred Jackson and Hanna, Kathryn Abbey, *Lake Okeechobee, Wellspring of the Everglades,* Indianapolis, Bobbs-Merrill Company, 1948.

Hawk, Robert, *Florida's Army,* Englewood, Florida, Pineapple Press, Inc., 1986.

Hillhouse, Don, *Heavy Artillery & Light Infantry, A History of the 1st Florida Special Battalion & 10th Infantry Regiment, C.S.A.,* Jacksonville, Florida, privately printed, 1992.

The History of St. Luke's Episcopal Church, Tallahassee, P.M. Publishing and Typographics, Inc., 1988.

Holland, Keith V., Manley, Lee B., and Towart, James W., eds., *The Maple Leaf: An Extraordinary American Civil War Shipwreck,* Jacksonville, St. Johns Archaeological Expeditions, Inc., 1993.

Horner, Dave, *The Blockade-Runners,* New York, Dodd, Mead & Company, 1968.

Johns, John E., *Florida During the Civil War,* Jacksonville, University of Florida Press, 1963.

Loderhose, Gary, *Far, Far from Home,* Carmel, Indiana, Guild Press, 1999.

Long, E.B. with Long, Barbara, *The Civil War Day By Day, An Almanac 1861-1865,* New York, Da Capo Press, Inc., 1971.

MacDonald, John, *Great Battles of the Civil War,* New York, Collier Books—Macmillan Publishing Company, 1988.

Marcus, Edward, editor, *A New Canaan Private in the Civil War: Letters of Justis Silliman, 17th Connecticut Volunteers,* New Canaan, Connecticut, New Canaan Historical Society, 1984.

Martin, Richard A., *The City Makers,* Jacksonville, Florida, Convention Press, Inc., 1972.

Morris, Allen, *The Florida Handbook 1961-1962,* Tallahassee, Peninsular Publishing Company, 1961.

Musicant, Ivan, *Divided Waters, The Naval History of the Civil War,* New York, Harper Collins Publishers, 1995.

Page, Dave, *Ships Versus Shore, Civil War Engagements Along Southern Shores and Rivers,* Nashville, Rutledge Hill Press, 1994

Patrick, Rembert W., *Florida Under Five Flags,* Gainesville, University of Florida Press, 1955.

Panagopoulos, E.P., *New Smyrna, An Eighteenth Century Greek Odyssey,* Brookline, Massachusetts, Holy Cross Orthodox Press, 1978.

Pratt, Fletcher, *The Navy, A History,* Garden City, New York, Garden City Publishing Company, 1938.

Rasico, Philip D., *The Minorcans of Florida, Their History, Language and Culture,* New Smyrna Beach, Florida, Luthers, 1990.

Reeder, MatiBelle, *History of Welaka 1853-1935,* Welaka, no publication date given.

Shingleton, Royce Gordon, *John Taylor Wood Sea Ghost of the Confederacy,* Athens, The University of Georgia Press, 1979.

Simmons, Henry E., *A Concise Encyclopedia of the Civil War,* New York, Bonanza Books, 1964.

Tebeau, Charlton W., *A History of Florida,* Coral Gables, Florida, University of Miami Press, 1971.

Time-Life Books, *The Civil War, The Blockade,* Alexandria, Virginia, 1983.

Tolles, Zonira Hunter, *Shadows on the Sand,* Gainesville, Storter Printing Company, 1976.

Vandiver, Frank E., *Their Tattered Flags, The Epic of the Confederacy,* New York & Evanston, Harper & Row, 1970.

Warner, Ezra J., *Generals in Gray, Lives of the Confederate Commanders,* Baton Rouge, Louisiana State University Press, 1959.
Williams, Joy, *The Florida Keys,* New York, Random House, 1996.

Wood, William, *Captains of the Civil War,* New Haven, Yale University Press, 1921.

Yeary, Mamie, compiler, *Reminiscences of the Boys in Gray, 1861-1865,* Dayton, Ohio, Morningside Press, 1986.

Magazines, Articles, Pamphlets, and Presentations

Bearss, Edwin L., "Asboth's Expedition up the Alabama and Florida Railroad," *Florida Historical Quarterly,* Volume XXIX, October 1960.

Boyd, Mark F., *Battle of Marianna,* pamphlet reprinted from the *Florida Historical Quarterly,* April 1951, Volume XXIX, Number 4.

Boyd, Mark F., *The Battle of Natural Bridge,* Tallahassee, Reprinted from *Florida Historical Quarterly,* October 1950, Volume XXIX, Number 2.

Boyd, Mark F., "The Joint Operations of the Federal Army and Navy Near St. Marks, Florida, March 1865," *Florida Historical Quarterly,* 1950, XXIX.

Bradley, Paul F., "Rebel Raider of the High Seas," *America's Civil War,* March 1999.

Cardwell, Sr., Harold D., "Civil War in Volusia," *The Civil War in Volusia County A Symposium,* Daytona Beach, Florida, Halifax Historical Society, Inc., 1987.

Cardwell, Sr., Harold D., "New Smyrna" Confederacy's Keyhole Through the Union Blockade," *The Civil War in Volusia County,* Daytona Beach, Florida, Halifax Historical Society, Inc., 1987.

Cardwell, Sr., Harold D., "Salt Making at Flagler," *The Civil War in Volusia County A Symposium,* Daytona Beach, Florida, Halifax Historical Society, Inc., 1987.

Christensen, Celia Langford, "Richard Cabal (Cab) Langford, printed internet January 10, 1999.

Coles, David J., "Florida's Seed Corn: The History of the West Florida Seminary During the Civil War," *Florida Historical Quarterly,* Volume LXXVII, Number 3, Winter 1999.

Coles, David J., "Volusia County: The Land Warfare 1861-1865," *Civil War in Volusia County A Symposium,* Daytona Beach, Florida, Halifax Historical Society, Inc., 1987.

Coles, David & Graetz, Robert Bruce, "The Garnet and Gray West Florida Seminary in the Civil War," *Florida State, The Magazine of the Florida State University Alumni Association,* April 1986.

Coles, David J. and Waters, Zack C., "Indian Fighter, Confederate Soldier, Blockade Runner, and Scout: The Life and Letters of Jacob E. Mickler," *El Escribano: The St. Augustine Journal of History,* Volume 34, 1997.

Dancy, James M., "Reminiscences of the Civil War," *Florida Historical Quarterly,* Volume 37.

Dillon, Jr., Rodney E., "The Battle of Fort Myers," *Tampa Bay History,* Date unknown.

Dodd, Dorothy, "Florida in the War, 1861-1865," in Allen Morris, comp., *The Florida Handbook, 1961-1962.*

Fort Clinch, "Fort Clinch State Park."

Gallant, Gene, "The Gray Fox of the Confederacy," Putnam County Archives and History, Palatka, Florida.

The General's Orders, "135 Years Ago," The Newsletter for the Joseph E. Johnston Camp, #28, February 1999.

Graham, Thomas, "Naval Activities at Mosquito Inlet," *The Civil War in Volusia County A Symposium,* Daytona Beach, Florida, Halifax Historical Society, Inc., 1987.

Hazel, Ianthe Bond, "A Unique Battle," *Civil War in Volusia County A Symposium.*

Hillhouse, Don, "From Olustee to Appomattox: The 1st Florida Special Battalion," *Civil War Regiments: A Journal of the American Civil War,* Volume 3, Number 1, 1993.

"History of Florida's Oldest Remaining House of Worship 'The Orange Springs Community Church,'" Putnam County Archives & History.

Langford, Glenn, "Action at Cedar Keys," internet.

Lucas, Marion R., "Civil War Career of George Washington Scott," *Florida Historical Quarterly,* Volume 58, 1979.

Luther, Gary, *History of New Smyrna East Florida,* New Smyrna, Florida, Privately printed, 1976.

Macomber, Robert, "The Patriot and the Widow James and Sophire Thompson and the Civil War on the Coast," *Civil War Interactive.*

Moore, Dorothy L., "Old Stone Wharf," *Musqueto (Mosquitoes) Newsletter,* Southeast Volusia Historical Society, Inc., April 11, 1991.

The Museum of the Confederacy, Richmond, Virginia, Flag Conservation Program brochure.

Proctor, Samuel, Introduction to Mary Elizabeth Dickison, *Dickison and His Men.*

Proctor, Samuel, "Florida A Hundred Years Ago," Coral Gables, Florida, published monthly by the Florida Library and Historical Commission and the Florida Civil War Centennial Commission during the One Hundredth Anniversary of the Civil War and Reconstruction Era, 1960-1965.

"Rebels of Palatka," internet.

Rodgers, Thomas G., "Florida's War of Nerves," *Civil War Times Illustrated,* June 1999.

Rye, Scott, "Burn the Rebel Pirate!" *Civil War Times Illustrated,* June 1999.

"Second Florida Cavalry Horse Artillery."

Shofner, Jerrell H., "Florida in the Civil War," *Civil War in Volusia County A Symposium,* Daytona Beach, Florida, Halifax Historical Society, Inc., 1987.

Strickland, Alice, *Blockade Runners,* pamphlet published by *Florida Historical Quarterly,* no publication date.

Sweett, Zelia Wilson, *New Smyrna, Florida in the Civil War,* New Smyrna, Florida, A Volusia County Historical Commission Publication, 1962.

Tobias, Lucy B., "River Raids," internet.

Waters, Zack C., "Florida's Confederate Guerrillas: John W. Pearson and the Oklawaha Rangers," The Florida Historical Society, Volume LXX, Number 2, October 1991.

Waters, Zack C., "Tampa's Forgotten Defenders, The Confederate Commanders of Fort Brooke," *Sunland Tribune: Journal of the Tampa Historical Society,* Volume XVII, November 1991.

Weinert, Richard P., "The Confederate Swamp Fox," Putnam County Archives and History, Palatka, Florida.

Williams, Frederick, "The Columbine—Legends, Facts and Artifacts," October 1979, Putnam County Archives & History.

Williams, Frederick, "The Action at Horse Landing," talk delivered to Kirby-Smith Camp, Sons of Confederate veterans at Jacksonville, Florida, on October 6, 1979. Transcript Putnam County Archives & History.

Wood, John Taylor, "Escape of the Confederate Secretary of War," *The Century Magazine,* 47, 1893-1894.

Manuscripts, Letters and Theses

Benjamin, Judah P. letter to Edward Porter Alexander dated November 10, 1864. Southern Historical Collection, Wilson Library, University of North Carolina Press—Chapel Hill.

Chalker, Albert S. letter to Miss Bardin dated October 12, 1864. Myron C. Prevatt, Jr., Collection.

Coles, David James, "Far From Fields of Glory: Military Operations in Florida During the Civil War, 1864-1865," a dissertation submitted to the Florida State University Department of History, 1996.

DeGroff, Lieutenant Nicholas letter dated February 20, 1864. Thomas Hayes Collection.

Dickison 1 File, "Death of John Jackson Dickison reported on August 28, 1902, Florida's Hero Soldier Passes Away at Ocala," Putnam County Archives & History, Palatka, Florida.

Ellis, T.B., "Short Record of T.B. Ellis, Sr."

Flynn, James, 7th New Hampshire, letter to his wife Susannah dated March 30, 1864. Gerard Flynn Collection.

Flynn, Thomas, Army of West Virginia, letter to his mother dated September 23, 1864. Gerard Flynn Collection.

Frier II, Joshua Hoyet, "Reminiscences of the War Between the States by a Boy in the Far South at Home and in the Ranks of the Confederate Militia," unpublished manuscript transcribed by J.W. Hart, Florida State Archives.

Graetz, Robert Bruce, "Triumph Amid Defeat: The Confederate Victory at Natural Bridge, Florida March 1865," Honors Thesis submitted to the Florida State University Department of History, August 1986.

"John Jackson Dickison Biography," Putnam County Archives & History, Palatka, Florida.

Jordan, Private James Matt letter, Volume 2 of *Letters From Confederate Soldiers,* United Daughters of the Confederacy Collection, Georgia State Archives.

Landrum, J. Erik, "John C. Breckinridge," unpublished manuscript.

McCrea, Lieutenant Tully, letter to his sweetheart dated February 7, 1864, Thomas Hayes Collection.

Stephens, Lieutenant Winston, letter to his wife dated February 21, 1864. Thomas Hayes "Letters from Olustee" Collection.

Stephens, Lieutenant Winston, letter to his wife dated February 27, 1864. Thomas Hayes "Letters from Olustee" Collection.

Suarez, Frank, Memoir at Pensacola Historical Society.

Untitled manuscript in Putnam County Archives & History re: Dickison and Florida.

Richard Watson, "Diary of Richard Watson of Key West."

Newspapers

Athens (Georgia) Southern Banner, March 9, 1864. Letter from "H.W.B." to editor.

Atlanta Intelligencer, March 2, 1864, letter from Cpl. Henry Shackelford to his mother dated February 20, 1864.

Augusta (Georgia) Chronicle & Sentinel, March 1, 1864.

Boston Herald, February 22, 1864, March 1, 1864, March 2, 1864, March 9, 1864, March 18, 1864, February 22, 1864, February 24, 1864.

Boston Journal, February 29, 1864. A letter of Charles Remick of the 40th Massachusetts Mounted Infantry to the newspaper's editor dated February 18, 1864.

Boston Journal, March 1, 1864, March 2, 1864, March 4, 1864, March 10, 1864.

Chelsea (Massachusetts) *Telegraph & Pioneer,* March 5, 1864, March 12, 1864, March 26, 1864.

Fernandina East Floridian, November 14, 1860.

Florida Times Union, Harper, Jack, "He Drove Yankees from St. Johns River," February 6, 1984.

Lake City (Florida) *Columbian,* September 1, 1864.

Lowell (Massachusetts) *Daily Courier,* May 9, 1861.

New Bedford (Massachusetts) *Evening Standard,* April 27, 1861.

New Bedford (Massachusetts) *Mercury,* March 9, 1864, Letter from Captain James W. Grace to editor dated February 25, 1864.

Ocala (Florida) *Star-Banner,* William Henry McConn interview with Frances Sheppard DeVore, Sunday, June 3, 1951.

Ocala Star-Banner, Vince Murray, "Captain J.J. Dickison, Marion County's Civil War Hero," Date Unknown, 1997.

Ocala Star-Banner, Laura Mohammad, "Women Left at Home Forced to Fend for Themselves," April 22, 1999.

Ocala Star-Banner, Darrell G. Riley, "The Civil War Years," Date Unknown, 1997.

Palatka (Florida) *Daily News,* Tuesday Morning, May 24, 1887.

Panama City (Florida) *News-Herald,* article by Marlene Womack, Sunday, March 8, 1987.

Panama City (Florida) *News-Herald,* article by Marlene Womack, Sunday, June 2, 1996.

Pensacola News-Journal, article by Earle Bowden, November 4, 1962.

Philadelphia Evening Bulletin, June 22, 1865.

Quincy (Massachusetts) *Dispatch,* March 22, 1865.

Richmond (Virginia) *Daily Dispatch,* June 2, 1864.

Tampa Tribune, Sunday, August 28, 1960.

Tampa Tribune, article by Leland Hawes, Sunday, May 3, 1992.

Taunton (Massachusetts) *Daily Gazette,* April 24, 1861.

Weekly Anglo-African, April 23, 1864, February 13, 1865, April 1, 1865.

West Florida News Extra, October 3, 1864.

Worcester (Massachusetts) *Aegis & Transcript,* December 7, 1861.

Interviews

Bradfield, Georgia Atkinson, great-granddaughter of Florida Governor John Milton, with author October 13, 1992, Ormond Beach, Florida.

Bradfield, Georgia Atkinson with author October 21, 1992, Ormond Beach, Florida.

Cardwell, Sr., Harold D., with author October 18, 1992, Ormond Beach, Florida.

Strickland, Alice with author October 15, 1992, Ormond Beach, Florida.

Public Documents and Records

Adams, Captain Richard Joseph, "Civil War Stories," Putnam County Clerk of Court, Palatka, Florida.

Albert Peck Papers, Florida State Archives, Bureau of Archives and Records Management, Tallahassee, Florida.

Anderson, General James Patton, "Civil War Stories," Putnam County Clerk of Court.

Army and Navy Journal, July 24, 1875, Volume 12, p. 798.

"Battle of Braddock's Farm," Putnam County Archives & History, Palatka, Florida.

Boyd, Mary Emily, "Civil War Stories," Putnam County Clerk of Court.

Brigadier General Jno. P. Hatch, Commanding Officer, U.S. Forces, District of Florida: Report on the engagement at Olustee concerning Union wounded and dead, September 25, 1864.

Brigadier General Joseph Finegan, commanding Confederate forces in Florida: Final report on the engagement at Olustee, February 26, 1864. Thomas Hayes Collection.

Confederate Army and Navy Records, Report of Col. W.S. Dilsworth, Commanding Forces of the Department of East and Middle Florida, April 4, 1862.

Federal Navy Records, A Letter from S. Dupont, Flag Officer Commanding South Atlantic Blockade Squadron to Hon. Gideon Welles, Secretary of the Navy, dated March 24, 1862.

Hazel, Ellen Firzpatrick McCallum, "Civil War Stories," Putnam County Clerk of Court.

Official Records of the Union and Confederate Armies in the War of the Rebellion, Series 1, Part II, XXXV.

Official Records of the Union and Confederate Armies in the War of the Rebellion, Series I, Volume 14.

Official Records of the Union and Confederate Navies in the War of the Rebellion, "Third Conference Report for Consideration of Measures for Effectually Blockading the South Atlantic Coast," July 26, 1861, Washington: GPO, 1894-1927, Series I, Volume 12.

Official Records of the Union and Confederate Navies in the War of the Rebellion, Series I, Volume 15.

Official Records of the Union and Confederate Navies in the War of the Rebellion, East Gulf Blockade Squadron, United States Navy, 1903, Series I, Volume 17.

Official Records of the Union and Confederate Navies in the War of the Rebellion, "Report of Lieutenant-Commander Earl English, U.S. Navy Commanding U.S.S. Sagamore," August 12, 1863, Series I, Volume 67.

Padgett, Mrs. James Braddock, "Civil War Stories," Putnam County Clerk of Court.

Seymour, Brigadier General Truman, Commanding Officer, U.S. Forces, District of Florida: Initial Report on the engagement at Olustee. Thomas Hayes Collection.

Wakulla County, Florida Civil War Collection.

Index

About the Author

John J. Koblas is the author and/or editor of six books on the lives of F. Scott Fitzgerald and Sinclair Lewis. His book, *F. Scott Fitzgerald in Minnesota: Toward the Summit*, published by North Star Press, was a 1996 Minnesota Book Award nominee. Other works include: *F. Scott Fitzgerald in Minnesota: His Homes and Haunts* (Minnesota Historical Society Press, 1978), *Sinclair Lewis: Home at Last* (Voyageur Press, 1981), *Selected Letters of Sinclair Lewis, Sinclair Lewis & Mantrap: The Saskatchewan Trip,* and *Sinclair Lewis: Final Voyage* (1985).

Five years ago, Mr. Koblas' work was featured on a television segment of *Good Morning America.* In 1985, he was a guest of Charles Kuralt on *CBS Sunday Morning* in New York for the Sinclair Lewis Centenary. That same year, Koblas was chosen by the Postmaster General in Washington to present the Sinclair Lewis Stamp at its First Day of Issue Ceremony. The following year, he received an award from the governor of Minnesota for his Fitzgerald work at the Minnesota Walk of Fame dedication.

In addition to biographical endeavors, Koblas has been a visiting instructor of writing at Brevard College in North Carolina, feature writer for the Daytona Beach (Florida) News-Journal, and author of a sydicated column that was carried in 105 newspapers nationwide. He is the author of more than 500 short stories, articles, and verse published worldwide.

Recently, Mr. Koblas has taught courses on Fitzgerald and Lewis at the Elder Learning Center of the University of Minnesota and Elder Hostel sessions.

The Jesse James Northfield Raid: Confessions of the Ninth Man was published in 1999. This book is currently being filmed as a documentary by the Old West Society. Another book, *Willow River Almanac: A Father Copes with Divorce and Nature*, will be published in 2000 by North Star Press. *H. V. Jones, an Adventure* will be published in 2001.

Other Civil War and Minnesota History Titles
by
North Star Press

The Jesse James Northfield Raid: Confessions of the Ninth Man — **John Koblas**
Controversy has dogged the heels of Jesse James through history. Koblas, with superior researching skills, has sorted fact from folk legend and documented the lives of Jesse and his gang. He follows their lives after Northfield, giving a well-rounded picture of the men who made the famous Minnesota raid on the bank in Northfield.
ISBN: 0-87839-124-X Paper, illustrated $14.95; ISBN: 0-87839-125-8 Cloth $24.95

F. Scott Fitzgerald in Minnesota: Toward the Summit — **David Page and Jack Koblas**
America's premiere fiction writer F. Scott Fitzgerald had roots in Minnesota. Born in St. Paul, Fitzgerald spend much time in the state, and his experiences here greatly influenced his fiction. Fitzgerald's close connections with his hometown and the state of Minnesota worked their way into his fiction. **ISBN: 0-87839-107-X Paper, illustrated $14.95**

The Story of a Regiment — Judson W. Bishop, Ed. by Newell Chester
Published in 1890, this is a reprint of the account of Col. Biship's service with the Minnesota Second in the Civil War with additional chapters by Chester.
ISBN: 0-87839-114-2 Paper $14.95; ISBN: 0-87839-126-6 Cloth $24.95

Drummer-Boy's Diary — **Newell Chester, editor**
Minnesotan William Bircher joined the Minnesota volunteers to fight in the Civil War. At his age, he could only be a drummer boy, but that proved to be almost as dangerous as the front lines.
ISBN: 0-87839-094-4 Cloth, illustrated $24.95; ISBN: 0-87839-095-2 Paper, $14.95

Behind Barbed Wire: German Prisoners of War in Minnesota — **Anita A. Buck**
More than fifteen POW camps housing German captives existed in Minnesota during World War II. This is the history of those camps, where they were, how they worked, how the POWs contributed to Minnesota economy, and how and when they ended. ISBN: 0-87839-113-4 Paper, illustrated $14.95

From the Ashes: The Story of the Hinckley Fire of 1894 — **Grace Stageberg Swenson**
This is the complete account of the 1894 Hinckley Fire, one of our nation's most devastating forest fires. Over 400 lives were lost and thousands of square miles burned, including Hinckley and other towns. Centennial edition. **ISBN: 0-87839-047-2 Paper, illustrated $14.95**